CW01337645

WARTIME with SHELL

The Autobiography of

CAPT. R. S. (Bob) ALLEN

Edited by Norman L. Middlemiss

SHIELD PUBLICATIONS LTD.
NEWCASTLE-UPON-TYNE
GREAT BRITAIN

ISBN   1 871128 13 7

British Library Cataloguing-in-Publication Data.
A Catalogue Record is available from the British Library

Celia & Bob Allen on their Wedding Day of 21st July,1941

Published by   SHIELD PUBLICATIONS LTD.
               7, Verne Road,
               NORTH SHIELDS.
               TYNE & WEAR. NE29 7LP.
Printed by   Smith, Settle
               Ilkley Road,
               OTLEY.
               W. YORKS. LS21 3JP.

CONTENTS

FOREWORD

I dedicate my memoirs primarily to my wife, Celia, for her encouragement; putting up with endless scraps of paper littering the house; numerous telephone calls and cries for Help when the typewriter would no do my bidding (all this over a period of six years); and to my daughter, Lesley, and her daughters, Annabel and Kate, who always evinced a lively interest in my earlier days. Thanks must go to Ian Freer who 'lifted the latch off the door' and encouraged me; to Gaye Brand who carried out the bulk of the task of putting it all together despite her normal workload; to Judy McGrath and Doreen Beadle who did a lot of the initial spadework; Bryan Kelly for his enthusiastic responses to my early efforts; the Stonnington Library staff who made encouraging 'noises' from the sidelines, and to the Shell company, the wisest and prettiest of the 'seven sisters' who employed me for thirty-three years.

Last but not least, I dedicate this book to all Merchant Navy crews who served during World War II.

Captain R. S. Allen

INTRODUCTION

I am delighted to publish this autobiography of Bob Allen giving a detailed insight into what it was like to sail and survive six years in tankers on convoys during World War II, it is by far the best autobiography I have received for possible publication in over eight years of maritime publishing. Robert Stephenson Allen went to sea for the first time in 1930 at the age of 16 years on Headlam of Whitby tramps at the start of a four year apprenticeship. He first sailed away on a tanker on New Year's Day, 1939 bound for Aruba in the service of what was then the Anglo-American Oil Co. Ltd (now Esso or Exxon to be exact), and joined Shell as Second Officer in May, 1939. He obtained his Certificate of Competency as a Master Mariner, Foreign Going on 12th October, 1940 in Newcastle and subsequently served with distinction and was recommended for a bravery award while serving on the Shell tankers *Cymbula, Opalia* and *Cardium*. He joined the Macship *Adula* in April, 1944 - one of those strange but highly effective wartime conversions of tanker to Merchant Aircraft Carriers (MAC) which gave such splendid air cover to North Atlantic convoys during the last two years of the war. It is this section of the book which I think is particularly valuable in terms of maritime history.

In October, 1942 after merchant shipping losses had reached alarming proportions, the Admiralty decided to convert nine Shell tankers and six grain-carrying tramps into Merchant Aircraft Carriers (MACs). The Shell tankers *Rapana, Amastra* and *Gadila* were converted at Smith's Dock Co. Ltd, North Shields; *Ancylus, Miralda* and *Macoma* at Palmers Hebburn Co. Ltd, Hebburn; *Acavus* and *Adula* at Silley, Cox & Co. Ltd, Falmouth and *Alexia* by T. W. Greenwell & Co. Ltd, Sunderland. *Gadila* and *Macoma* were Dutch-flag Shell tankers, all of the remainder were British-flag Shell tankers. All nine were 'Triple Twelves', so called because they carried 12,000 tons of oil at 12 knots on 12 tons/day oil consumption, which simplified the planning of the work and issuing of blueprints and speeded up the conversions of subsequent ships. The technical department of Anglo-Saxon took the outline proposals several stages further but the final detail plans for all nine were prepared by Smith's Dock Co. Ltd and Palmers, Hebburn in association. The primary difference between the freighter conversions and the tanker conversions was that the latter had no hangar and this presented some problems.

Aircraft continuously parked in the open could not have the same servicing facilities as those available in a hangar, with only minor adjustments possible. The sections of the flight deck were arranged with an expansion joint between them and so did not have the strength of purpose-built 'flat-tops'. One joint was placed immediately fore and aft of the exising 'midships erection with a further joint forward of the poop section. The decks were thus made of prefabricated sections, the total weighing 957 tons. The tanker conversions were fitted with nine guns on large gun sponsons protruding out over the sides of the ship, above the former main deck, and this armament included two oerlikon guns more than the freighter conversions total complement of seven guns. The lifeboats with gravity type davits were rearranged into the well spaces, four in the aft well and two in the forward well just forward of the two-tiered bridge erection.

The tankers were to be under the overall command of a senior Shell tanker master, but were to carry men from the Fleet Air Arm to man and maintain the aircraft, swelling the complement to 122. The tanker conversions carried three Swordfish aircraft, whereas the grain-carrying tramp conversions fitted with a hangar could accomodate four of these aircraft, which had a crew of three in the pilot, navigator/observer, and rear gunner/radio operator.

Rapana was the first tanker conversion to commission in July,1943 and *Macoma* was the last to commission in May,1944. The Admiralty in addition gave orders for the completion of four new tankers on the stocks as MACs, all to be ready by the end of 1943 with 'Empire' names. Two came from the Wallsend yard of Swan, Hunter & Wigham Richardson Ltd, one from Cammell, Laird & Co. Ltd at Birkenhead and one from the Belfast yard of Harland & Wolff Ltd. Three of these were entrusted to the management of the British Tanker Co. Ltd (BP) and one to Shell. There were thus thirteen tanker version MACs and six grain-carrying versions to give a total of nineteen MACs, and all were converted back to commercial ships in the years after the end of the war and their subsequent careers are given in Appendix 2 of this book.

The shipyards involved on the Tyne, Wear and Fal had the difficult job of erecting a complete flight deck some fifteen feet above the weather deck of the tankers. The first step was to arrange several huge transverse girders welded to doubling plates on the weather deck and the side webs were connected to the deck stringers and sheerstrakes. More well-braced fore-and-aft girders completed the criss-cross support system, upon which the the flight deck sections were placed and joined together by three expansion joints. The addition of the flight deck and supports was equal to a 25% increase in weight on the original light displacement of the tanker, and also had to be achieved with minimum disturbance to the deck piping and valves.

All of the conversion work had to be done quickly, the average time for the conversion work on the existing tankers was six months, while the extra time taken to complete the new tankers, as compared with the normal constructional period had they been completed as ordinary tankers, was just under three months. A figure of 10% reduction in the dwt carrying capacity of the existing tankers was achieved due

"RAPANA" CLASS M.A.Cs
OUTLINE GENERAL ARRANGEMENT

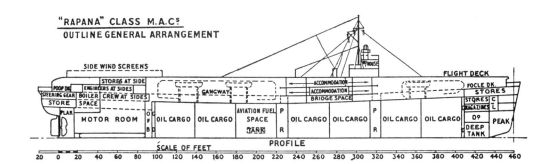

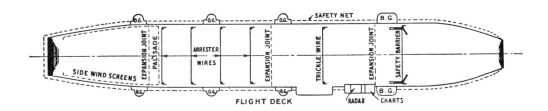

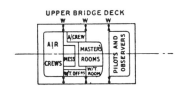

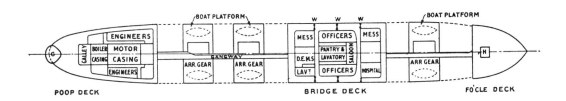

to the weight of the flight deck and supports and defensive armament. A reduction of this order was not too significant in view of the deterrent effect of the 'Swordfish' aircraft in keeping the U-boats under the surface. The Swordfish petrol tanks were refuelled from no. 4 centre tank (See MAC diagrams) and there were a number of advantages of choosing this particular tank. The proximity to the cargo pump room in order to install petrol pumps to service the aircraft, flooding valves for quickly surrounding the petrol tanks in the case of an emergency, and ease of ventilation of petrol vapours.

Care had to be taken, however, during the loading and ballasting of the conversion 'MAC's, as it would have been possible under normal procedures of filling cargo tanks to produce a condition approaching negative stability. To overcome this, instructions were issued to fill at least four tanks to about half their depth at the beginning of loading, after which the remaining tanks could be safely filled. The reverse order had to be carried out during unloading. Capt. Allen in his chapter in this book accurately and clearly describes the balancing arrangements to be carried out to the port side tanks to allow for the weight of the bridge structure on the starboard side.

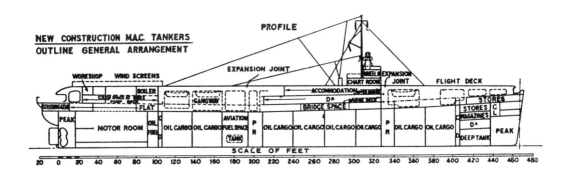

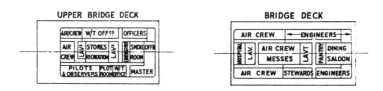

Flight deck and other arrangements generally similar to
existing tankers *Rapana* class

Capt. Allen was then appointed to the command of the Shell tanker *Newcombia* in November,1946 and her voyaging in world-wide trading particularly in the Far East for the next twenty months is covered in the final chapter. He was appointed pilot/ loading master for Shell at Miri in the Sarawak oilfield in 1949 and for the next four years, in addition to normal duties as pilot, he assisted in laying three sealines, each three miles long, and was in command of a construction barge engaged in the construction of offshore platforms. He was officially commended by the Managing Director for salvage services in September,1953. He was appointed Marine Superintendent for the Shell Company of Australia and S. W. Pacific Islands in February,1954. This function included all aspects of tanker turn-round, safety, cargo stowage/segregation and liaison with Port and Pilotage authorities.

He was responsible for the continuing survey of marine facilities covering 67 ports in Australia and S. W. Pacific islands including Papua/New Guinea, Fiji, New Caledonia, New Hebrides and Cook Islands. This included berth design, layout, depth of water, turning circles and all associated technical data. He was responsible for studying and recommending new port sites which included Trial Bay (N.S.W.), Anewa Bay (Bougainville), Honiara (Solomon Islands). These recommendations were approved and acted upon by Shell Australia with the approval of Shell International Marine in London and local authorities. He was Controller of the 'RIP survey' carried out at Port Phillip Heads in 1965, to determine under keel clearances in the main ship channel, and in charge of the successful salvage of motor vessel *Kuanua* in 1970 in Rabaul harbour.

He was a Member of the Oil Industry Marine Facilities sub-committee until his retirement from Shell in May,1972 after 33 years of service to the company. Similarly until retirement he was a member of the Victorian Steering Committee and Technical Committee of the Chamber of Shipping, and member of the Marine OIl Spillages Committee. During 18 years with Shell in Australia he was constantly in touch and in discussions with various Port and Pilotage authorities on all aspects of tanker berths and wharves from siting to orientation.

On retirement from Shell he formed the company of Capt. R. S. Allen and Associates, Marine Consultants and Cargo Surveyors, and was appointed Assessor to the Marine Board of Victoria from June,1972 until 1984. Since retirement, in addition to cargo surveying for various insurance companies, he has carried out various port site studies for C. R. A. Group, A. C. I. and Australian Gypsum. He has been in court as 'expert witness' in two salvage cases and also as Marine Adviser to Ampol before the Royal Commission on the Petroleum Industry. In October,1973 he made trips to study port facilities, dry-docks and tanker berths in the Republic of Singapore; and made a similar trip there in September,1974 during which port operations in general were covered.

He visited the U. K. in April/May, 1977 and had a series of discussions with various companies concerned with offshore supply work, marine construction and also insurance surveys and average adjusting. In 1979 he made 'follow up' visits to Singapore on port facilities studies and also visited Mombasa. In 1981 he supervised the drydocking and overhaul of a Japanese-built 'Freedom' class general cargo ship in Singapore, and in 1983 he was assisting the Marine Superintendent of the oil company Santos (South Australia & Northern Territory Oil Search Ltd) during tanker loading operations near Wyalla in South Australia. During 1982 to 1990 he was appointed as an examiner for the speedboat driver's licences granted by the Maritime Services Board of New South Wales. He has been a Member of the Honourable Company of Master Mariners in London since 1951, and is the author of ten articles for their Technical Journal.

It has been a great pleasure for me to edit and publish this autobiography of Capt. Bob Allen. The one great quality that comes shining through in the text is his irrepressible sense of humour often in very trying and dangerous circumstances. His home has been in Victoria in Australia for many years now after leaving South Shields, and he has been happily married to Celia for 54 years and they have one daughter Lesley, a teacher who works as a student counsellor at a local girls school, and two grand-daughters, Annabel and Kate, who have obtained or are studying for University degrees. Annabel now works as a research assistant to a Professor at Deakin University and is also studying for her Master's degree. I wish Capt. Bob Allen all the best for his future remaining years and heartily recommend his autobiography of life on tankers and tramps to all who should read it.

Norman L. Middlemiss

Newcastle-upon-Tyne

January, 1996

**Shell tanker putting to sea past
the Groyne at South Shields.
(South Shields Photographic Society)**

TRAMPING DAYS

I sailed on deep-sea tramps on world-wide voyaging for eight years from the start of my apprenticeship in 1930, and the following is the voyage pattern of the six ships I served in :-

27.11.1930 SNEATON Tyne (coal), Cape Verde Islands, New Orleans (timber), Laurenco Marques, Durban (dry-dock & coal), Marmagoa (manganese ore), Workington.
Cardiff (coal), Las Palmas, Gulfport (timber), Mobile (timber) Rosario, Santa Fe (grain), Manchester.
Cardiff (coal), Zarate (grain), Buenos Aires, Southampton.
Cardiff (coal), Las Palmas, Buenoa Aires, San Nicholas (grain), Gothenburg, Bornholm, Stockholm, Uleaborg (pitprops), Cardiff.
Cardiff (coal), Plate, Conception del Uruguay (linseed), Rotterdam.

11.3.1933 GOATHLAND Tyne (ballast), Plate, San Nicholas (grain), Santander, Bilbao, Cardiff.
Cardiff (coal), Rosario (grain), Rotterdam, Cardiff.
Cardiff (coal), Rosario (grain), Madeira, Cardiff.
Cardiff (coal), Zarate, Rosario (grain), St. Vincent, Birkenhead.
Barry (coal), Villa Constitucion, Rosario (grain), Belfast.
Barry (coal), Rosario (grain), Manchester.

1.7.1935 STREONSHALH Tyne (coal), Madeira, Barry.
Barry (coal), Rosario (grain), San Lorenzo (grain), Dublin.

29.11.1935 SANDSEND Cardiff(coal), Fray Bentos, Rosario(grain),Copenhagen, Falster, Stockholm, Swansea.
Swansea (coal), Montreal, Sorel (grain), Barry.
Swansea (coal), Montreal (grain), Sharpness.

26.8.1936 GLAISDALE Barry (coal), Rosario (grain), Londonderry.
Barry (coal), Fray Bentos, Rosario (grain), Amsterdam.
Cardiff(coal), Fray Bentos, Conception del Uruguay (linseed), Montreal (grain), London.

2.12.1937 THISTLEBRAE Tyne, Cardiff (coal), Villa Constitucion - five months waiting for grain cargo - Dakar, Oslo, Gothenburg, Stockholm, Tyne. Arrived 3.10.1938 and paid off.

As the steam tramp *Sneaton* managed by Headlam & Sons of Whitby left Dunston Staithes on a misty evening in November, 1930 she carried some 5,300 tons of Tyne coal, destined for ship's bunkers, to St. Vincent, Cape Verde Islands. She had a crew of 32, all of whom seemed to know what they were doing except me, a sixteen year-old covered in coal dust and shivering with mixed emotions. Excitement, apprehension, joy and a general feeling of 'This is it - I'm about to become a sailor at last !'. I had joined three days earlier, complete with straw mattress (known as a donkey's breakfast), seabag and resplendent in my brass-buttoned uniform, the company badge still gleaming in my cap. I was inspected by the First Mate, who didn't seem overly impressed, and sent to join the other five apprentices who lived in the port side of the fo'c'stle head. None of this 'Junior Officers living amidships' nonsense in Rowland & Marwood's Steamship Co. Ltd (Headlam & Sons, managers). Apprentices forward, sailors and firemen aft and often the 'twain shall meet in the course of their duties.

The accomodation for the apprentices occupied most of the port side of the fo'c'stle and comprised one single room with six bunks. Two of these were athwartships, one over the other and four bunks fore-and-aft. The room measured some eight feet across at the forward end, and fifteen feet at the after end with an overall length of about eighteen feet. There were two portholes on the ship's side and one on the after end. A chest containing six drawers ran across the after end and we kept all our good gear in these drawers. The rest, in seabags, was under the bunks. Inboard of the chest of drawers was a steel trunkway which was part of the ventilator into no. 1 hold, and all of our plates, cutlery, jam, butter, bread etc were kept in two lockers. A table ran fore and aft from the athwartships bunks to the door with a 'three-seater' bench fixed to the fore and aft bulkhead, and a similar moveable bench on the other side of the table. This 'five star' accomodation was completed by a portable, coal-fired, round, cast-iron stove known as a 'bogey' which took up most of the remaining space and provided heat in cold weather.

There was a small bathroom and toilet forward of the accomodation reached by a narrow passageway alongside the inboard fore and aft bulkhead. There was a cast iron bath but only a salt water supply, as fresh water had to be brought from amidships in a bucket. Two electric light globes provided light when the ship was at sea and two oil lamps were provided for use in port. The occupant of the top bunk at the forward end of the fore-and-aft bunks had to be extremely careful when getting out of bed, not to do himself a mischief on the bogey funnel which ran through the deckhead to a chimney on the fo'c'stle head. This 8' x 15' x 18' steel enclosed space was 'home' to six of us, and of course the bogey was inoperable in bad weather as seas would be pouring over the fo'c'stle head and down the bogey chimney.

My future shipmates were a reasonable bunch of lads, ranging from Leo, of my own age but already with two years seatime under his belt, to Ross (Rastus) Dunseath, 22 years old and almost finished his time. Rastus had started his apprenticeship as a Marine Engineer in a shipyard, but the Depression had forced the yard to close down and he had come to sea as an 18-year old deck apprentice. Tom, Alf and Ben were my other three shipmates and they soon gave me the 'form' -

in no time I was out of my eye-catching uniform into dungarees and on deck under the eagle eye of the Bosun.

The jobs I carried out were many and varied. Lifting wooden hatches on to the steel beams which ran transversely across the holds (already filled with coal) after shovelling all of the coal which had spilled on to the decks during the loading into the holds. The spreading of tarpaulins and helping Chippy (the Carpenter) to drive in the wedges which held the long steel battens between the cleats and the hatch coaming, and keeping the tarpaulins secure. By 4.00 p.m. I was somewhat weary but was then told to trim the lamps, a task for which my five years at a Yorkshire boarding school had left me ill-prepared. However with the help and advice of Tom Calvert, the next Junior Apprentice to me, I loaded up with kerosene, cotton waste, old newspapers and lamptrimmer's scissors. Thus armed I went round the ship and serviced some eighteen kerosene lamps. Cleaning the glass chimneys, trimming the burnt tops off the wicks and topping up the oil. The lamps consisted of those in the sailor's accomodation, Bosun's, Chippy's, the three Mates, Sparks (Radio Officer), galley, apprentices and the gangway lamp.

The ship had a dynamo but it was considered too expensive to run in port. After all, bunker coal was 7/6d a ton in November,1930 plus overtime at a shilling/hour for the donkey man to maintain steam on the donkey boiler. The donkey boiler was a small auxiliary boiler used to supply steam for the winches in port as the main boilers were shut down on arrival. The oil lamps were nicknamed 'paraffin dynamos' and there are still lots of old sailors, peering through pebble-lensed glasses at television who owe their myopia to those lamps. I was then dispatched to my other permanent post to lower, fold and stow the company houseflag, flown from the mainmast, and the Red Ensign from the poop. The raising and lowering of flags, known as colours in the Royal Navy, are traditionally done at 8.00 a.m. and sunset. The Merchant Navy in those days was a little less formal, but nonetheless carried out the tradition in most deep-sea ships. However as I lowered my first Red Ensign in November,1930 the sun had long disappeared in the coal dust and fog of Tyneside, it was also invisible when I hoisted the flags the next day.

The following two days passed swiftly and around 7.00 p.m. on 27th November *Sneaton* cast off her moorings and left in the stygian gloom. I was given the job of driving the poop winch as we hauled in the mooring ropes. The poop winch was a noisy piece of machinery with steam hissing out of every joint and it scared the life out of me at first. The noise, the steam, the darkness, the all-enveloping coal dust, the incomprehensible orders all conspired to fill me with terror. I had been given a one minute 'crash course' on how to operate this monstrous machine - steam on - steam off - stop - reverse - steam on again ! All very bewildering to a sixteen year old. However by the time the crew had recovered the fourth rope I felt I had mastered the machine and was drunk with power. Some of the crew were drunk too, but it wasn't with power - Newcastle Brown Ale is a very potent brew !

Down the Tyne we sailed, the triple expansion engine groaning and grunting whilst the ship felt alive and vibrating. Mooring ropes were stowed down below under the fo'c'stle and poop. The last of the derricks were lowered and secured, the runners hove tight and the guys lashed to the derricks. We followed the Bosun around the decks, making sure that nothing would go 'bump in the night' and generally secured the ship for sea. The dynamo had been aroused from its long sleep and there were a few dim lights around the decks. At 9.00 p.m. I was sent to stand by the pilot ladder and shook hands with old George Harrison, the pilot, as he left. He was one of the Tyne pilots who had known me all of my life. A last glimpse of my home on the Lawe Top overlooking the harbour entrance reminded me of my mother watching my departure from the upstairs window. Only briefly, as the dulcet tones of the Bosun reminded me to 'pull up that bloody ladder and stop looking around'.

Soon the lights of the Tyne Piers were behind us as we nosed round to the southerly course down the chilly, choppy waters of the North Sea. Securing half a bucket of water I managed to remove some of the coal dust from my torso, and thankfully crept on to my Donkey's Breakfast. It seemed like three minutes later that Alf, the second senior apprentice, woke me at 6.30 a.m. After a questionable cup of coffee I was out on deck at 7.00 a.m. with the deck gang, washing down the ship and removing several tons of ashes from the after well deck. These ashes were from the donkey boiler and had accumulated whilst the ship was in port. The common practice was to pile all of the ashes and any disposable garbage at the forward end of the well deck. At the first available opportunity after a ship left harbour, this was shovelled over the side. Environmental protection and anti-pollution was unknown in those days - in fact it was normal practice for oil tankers to steam up and down about three miles offshore and happily wash out fuel oil tanks, pumping all of the washings into the sea. Beaches were frequently covered with huge patches of black, sticky fuel oil. The advance of technology has minimised fuel oil patches but has replaced them with washed up plastic containers - nothing like progress !

The ship began to look a lot cleaner after the disposal of the ashes and I had time to look around. I bacame aware of the motion of the ship which reacted with the porridge and tough mutton chop and mashed potatoes of breakfast. My feet seemed to land where there wasn't any deck and I stumbled around the ship with my head in a whirl, bemused, bewildered and generally wondering what I had let myself in for - the feeling of great adventure had vanished !

The Bosun subscribed to the theory that fresh air and hard work were the sovereign remedies for sea-sickness and kept me at it until noon when we knocked off for dinner. I took one look at the watery cabbage, boiled potatoes and slice of stringy meat and decided a weak cup of coffee and short rest was needed. However soon after I crawled into my bunk, Rastus came in from a two hour stint at the wheel and promptly hauled me out 'Worst thing you can do - sea-sickness is worse when you're lying down. Get out on deck, admire the waves and if you're going to be sick, do it over the lee side !' He then proceeded to devour his dinner and mine with evident relish - he was right of course and usually was. The night before sailing my mother had taken Rastus and I out to tea at Fenwicks in Newcastle and he promised to keep an eye on me - for the next eight months he was true to his word.

Oddly enough, I was never actually sea-sick but just felt terrible and had visions of spending the rest of my life drinking dubious coffee, gazing at the sea and distant coastline, and longing to be on terra firma. My visions were disturbed at 1.00 p.m. by the Bosun dishing me out an empty herring tin, some colza oil, bathbrick, oil bunting and cotton waste. It was then sent to the bridge where I was instructed how to scrape the bathbrick into the herring tin, mix with colza oil and using the bunting, clean the compass binnacle and other brasswork on the bridge and monkey island above, which held the standard compass and was reached by a vertical ladder from the navigating bridge. To climb this ladder clutching a herring tin, colza oil, bathbrick, bunting and cotton waste with a cold North Sea wind whipping around your nether regions was freezing work but was a good cure for sea sickness. It seemed to me that the brass had not be cleaned for some years - an illusion I was assured. In the event I scrubbed and polished, knocking pieces of flesh off my frozen knuckles until a kindly second mate sent me for 'smoko' at 3.00 p.m. - common practice on tramp steamers although no morning smoking was ever contemplated.

We were never issued with dry tea, tea was brewed by the cook in a three gallon pan on the galley stove. A cigarette tin full of 'crew' tea was added with a pinch of washing soda to make it 'draw' and it was then dished out into our 'growler' - no such thing as tea or coffee pots. A 'growler' was made from an empty 7 lb butter tin and was carried by a piece of wire stretched across the top. However tea at 'smoko' was not catered for, but as apprentices we were allowed to have the 'boilings' from the Chief Steward. These were the tea leaves left over after he had made afternoon tea for the Captain, three Mates, Sparks, the cook and himself. With a bit of luck we would get some from the messroom steward after he had made the Engineer's tea, splash in a little boiling water from the galley and with a dash of condensed milk you had a drinkable tea. Fifteen minutes later back to the brasswork or whatever was in store.

The dayworkers knocked off at 5 p.m. and some ships allowed the men to knock off ten minutes early to clean up before tea, but this enlightened thinking had not reached Headlams. Fortunately, the weather though cold was not too rough and we were not shipping much water, despite the low freeboard of three or four feet between the main deck and sea. After a rather hurried tea of a meatball and a slice of bread, I spent the evening on the fo'c'stle head, chatting to whoever was on lookout, and by 10.00 p.m. I was so weary I was able to get into my bunk and not feel too queasy. The next two days were fine and I was told to accompany the First Mate down the forepeak under our accomodation and check all of the stores taken aboard at Dunston - eight months supply. Although the work was relatively easy, the atmosphere brought back my dizzy feeling. Crouched in the forepeak with only a hurricane lamp to see by, we counted what seemed like hundreds but was actually dozens of items. Drums of red lead, white lead, white enamel, boot topping, anti-fouling and various other paints. Coils of rope, wire and all of the impedimenta for an eight month voyage. The owners definitely did not intend to pay inflated prices in foreign parts. Bales of canvas, bundles of waste, drums of linseed oil, kerosene, scrapers, chipping hammers, brooms, paint brushes, seizing wire, spun yard, oakum - you name it we had it !

The weather across the Bay of Biscay was for once extremely tranquil, and as we forged steadily southwards the weather got warmer, the seas bluer and a new treat was in store for us. Down the holds and scraping the 'deck heads' as they were called - in fact the underside of the main decks and virtually the roof of the holds. These were only readily accessible when a dirty cargo such as coal was in the holds. Apart from a couple of corner hatches being lifted off, the only light was that of individual ducklamps - another invention to make a sailor's life unpleasant - which were cone-shaped cans filled with colza oil with a cotton wick emerging from a spout on one side and a handle on the other side. When lit they provided about a two candle power illumination accompanied by large volumes of foul black smoke. With steel scrapers and chipping hammers, we did our best to remove rust and scale from the deck head plates. Due to the irregular surface of the coal cargo, you were on your back in some places, face upwards, some six inches from the plates and covering yourself in rust flakes. In other places the scraper was lashed to a broom handle and you were reaching up some six feet to attack the rust. In any case, a faceful of rust was your constant lot - coal dust, rust, ducklamp and paint fumes were a steady diet. The smoke from the ducklamps was so thick that it was possible to write on the plates by holding the wick close, and some elegant graffiti was left on the plates of the deckheads of the final day, only to be revealed when the holds were empty.

As the weather grew better, *Sneaton* sailed southwards in a gentle swell, my stomach lost its disorientation and life assumed a regular pattern. Some ten days after leaving the Tyne we dropped anchor in the harbour of St. Vincent, Cape Verde Islands off the coast of West Africa. A Portuguese colony, St. Vincent was one of a group of four coaling stations serving ships on the run to South America. It was a fairly busy trade in those days for medium-sized tramps around five to seven thousand deadweight. The voyage pattern was to carry coal out to Argentina and then load grain for the U.K. / Continent. St. Vincent along with Madeira and the two main islands of the Canaries were busy bunkering points, enabling ships to lift as much cargo as possible from the Plate ports. At 6.00 a.m. the next day the ship was swarming with stevedores, barges were bumping alongside, hundreds of coal baskets were hauled aboard, derricks topped, hatches uncovered and all of the tarpaulins folded and stowed away under lock and key. Confusion seemed to reign supreme and anything not screwed down was securely locked away, as the locals had a great tendency to spirit them away. Ten days were spent in St. Vincent and we appreciated the warm tropical weather with no flies or mosquitoes due to the scarcity of water. Cargo was worked from 6.00 a.m. to 6.00 p.m. and the ship lay in a cloud of dust all day long. The deck gang were over the side on wooden stages, chipping, scraping and painting rusty patches on the ship's side most of the time. We had one Sunday free in St. Vincent, so we were allowed to take a lifeboat away with the Third Mate in charge and sailed round the harbour most of the day. Very exhilarating and good for our seamanship, with sacks of sand collected from the beaches for use in cleaning the decks. Holystoning was carried out on rainy days when chipping, scraping or painting was not possible. The wooden decks, fo'c'stle, amidships and poop were liberally sprinkled with sand then heavy 5lb stones were pushed up and down until the dirt and dead wood was removed. There is a great deal of satisfaction to be derived from seeing a freshly holystoned deck which has been hosed down and dried out.

William Cory & Son Ltd ran the bunkering station and only when the last basket of coal had been tipped into the last lighter, were we allowed to depart for our next loading port of New Orleans. It was a fair weather voyage of 3,850 miles, which took us seventeen days, most of which were occupied in cleaning holds, chipping and scraping rust off the deck and bulkheads - a never-ending task akin to painting the Sydney Harbour Bridge. We spent Christmas and New Year at sea, a whole egg with a rasher of bacon being allowed for breakfast on the former day. Normally Sunday was the only day for bacon and egg, but never a whole egg each for the apprentices and crew. It was a ratio of one egg for two men, liberally mixed with flour and water and laughingly called an omelette. Pancakes, when served were in the ratio of one egg to six men with molasses added to give a touch of gastronomic delight. The fresh (sic) meat from the ice box gave out whilst we were in St. Vincent so we were on salt beef, salt pork and tinned meat by this time, with a daily issue of lime juice as per Board of Trade regulations. Dried peas and beans with rather mouldy potatoes and an occasional onion formed our daily vegetable intake, but gave a rapid increase in general flatulence.

We arrived off our loading berth, Chalmette Slip, about seven miles down-river from New Orleans and dropped anchor to await quarantine and fumigation. Quarantine was a very serious business in America in 1931 with all of the ship's company examined for sexually transmitted diseases (known as V. D. in those days). We dutifully dropped our natty gents pants while the Port Health Doctor gave our 'private parts' the once-over. After having our privacy intruded upon, we were all bundled into a launch and dumped ashore until 5.00 p.m. with not a cent between us. Bitterly cold, we walked around the suburbs making rude remarks about the Captain, the ship and the American fumigation service. Returning to the ship at 6.00 p.m. we managed to wheedle some stew out of the cook and our little fo'c'stle never seemed better, after we got the bogey going to create a nice 'fug' and thawed out. We went alongside the next morning and were swamped with negro stevedores as we began to load huge baulks of timber destined for the mines of South Africa.

As loading progressed I became Chippy's assistant caulking the planks on the boat deck, and my job was to roll the oakum into suitable lengths while Chippy hammered the oakum in between the planks. Later we boiled the pitch and Chippy carefully ladled it on top of the oakum. In the morning at 7.00 a.m. it was bitterly cold with frost on the levees along the river bank and we were muffled up to our ears. By midday we had stripped down to singlets only, and were sweating under the hot sun, with the previous days pitch all soft and sticky. By 3.00 p.m. it was starting to cool off so we started to pour and the pitch set immediately. Old Chippy knew exactly how many yards of deck to caulk, so that by 4.00 p.m. the job was finished. I was off on my lamp trimming rounds and was becoming quite expert, managing to finish in time to pull the flags down by 5.00 p.m. The holds were filled with timber and then it had to be stacked on deck to a height of about ten feet. The last two days were spent lashing it down securely with what seemed several miles of wire then tightening the whole lot with bottlescrews or turnbuckles. This last job was Chippy's and under his guidance I learnt a lot about securing timber deck cargoes. Sixty years later I reckon I could still secure one.

New Orleans in the Depression years saw most local men on the street corners selling apples for five cents each, so we were often asked to 'spare a dime for a cup of coffee'. They made a song of it and it was a grim reality then, however New Orleans with the lights on Canal Street will always be associated, in my mind, with gaiety and movement. Some time early in February we slid down the broad Mississippi, passing lines of United Fruit and other American ships, laid-up at the buoys for want of work. United Fruit had virtually run the Central American republics for several decades and were feeling the pinch of the Depression.

St. Lucia in the West Indies was our next port of call, to top up our coal bunkers, and once bunkering was finished we set sail on our 8,300 mile journey to Lourenco Marques. The voyage took forty days, and by now I was a reasonably competent helmsman and joined the watchkeepers. In 1931 we worked under the old 'watch and watch' system - four hours on and four hours off which meant that the maximum sleeping time ever achieved was three and a half hours. Deck and Engineer Officers worked the 'four hours on and eight hours off' system as did the firemen and the trimmers. The watch usually consisted of two apprentices and one able seamen, leaving the balance as day workers. The two spare hands of the watchkeepers worked on deck during the day, but at night the four hours were spent with two hours at the wheel, one hour 'stand-by' and one hour as lookout on the fo'c'stle head. A very boring system and designed to send anyone 'round the bend'. It was to be another seven years before the four hours on, eight hours off system became the norm for the deck department. Mention of a 56 or 84 hour week to a union official today would probably bring on apoplexy !

We eventually reached our destination of Lourenco Marques and then to the area known as Portuguese East Africa. From my recollection of it, the Portuguese were probably glad to give the locals their independence. We lay at anchor discharging the timber into barges for three weeks. I was night watchman all that time from 6.00 p.m. to 6.00 a.m. every night, and sleep, if you could, was during the daytime with the constant rattle of the winches, shouts of the stevedores and heat and swarms and mosquitoes by day and night. We were all dosed with quinine every day but despite that several of us had touches of malaria. One apprentice, Tom Calvert, got a severe dose of malaria and was later hospitalised in Durban. In mid-April 1931 we hove up anchor and departed for Durban where we were due to dry-dock and then load coal for Marmagoa on the West coast of India, and still a Portuguese colony.

We moved into dry-dock where the bottom was duly scraped and painted then moved over to the coal loader at the Bluff over the Easter period, Durban being technically a British port with both Good Friday and Easter Monday as holidays. It rained heavily while we were loading cargo and bunkers, a fact which had serious consequences later on, as Durban coal was extremely susceptible to spontaneous combustion. I managed to grab another night ashore to sample the delights of civilisation as well as meeting an old school chum, Ross Lloyd. After forty days at sea and three weeks in Lourenco Marques I needed some reassurance that civilisation did indeed exist. After fond farewells to Ross, we left Durban and steamed out into the Indian Ocean for Marmagoa, some 3,700 miles to the North East. One ocean looks pretty much the same as another in the tropics, and we were back to the old routine of chipping, painting, washing paintwork, splicing ropes and cargo runners. Sixteen days later when we were 12 hours out of Marmagoa, the Chief Engineer and his men became aware that all was not well in the starboard bunker (known as the 'side pocket'). Spontaneous combustion had taken place and fire had broken out, apparently in the middle of the bunkers and smoke was seeping out of the hatch and the stokehold was even hotter than usual.

All hands turned out and started the task of shovelling coal out of the 'side pocket' and transferring it into the main cross bunker, forward of the stokehold. The hatch on deck could not be opened, as this would allow more air into the bunker and we would soon have had a full scale fire on our hands. Consequently, it had to be done from the stokehold through the small hatch which fed coal into the stokehold. All hands worked on this hot and arduous job, as it was impossible to work more than half an hour in that heat. All of the coal had to be shovelled through a hatch measuring about four feet square into the stokehold then transferred through a similar hatch into the main cross bunker using barrows at both ends.

We berthed in Marmagoa and in all it was nearly two days before it was under control. I can recall to this day, the line of coal-blackened men and boys including myself who lined up to receive a tot of rum after the job was finished - neat Demerara rum was something to be reckoned with and still is I've no doubt. We spent about two weeks there, discharging coal and loading manganese ore, and each weekend we were allowed to go swimming at a lovely beach near one of the old Portuguese forts. The paint on the ship's side near the side bunker was all blistered from the fire so we spent several days scraping and painting as well as touching up rust spots around the hull. The drydocking in Durban had only been to clean and paint the underwater parts of the hull. Among other ships in port was Clan Ross of the Clan Line of Glasgow - a cargo-liner on a regular trade between the U. K. and India. We became friendly with the apprentices on her, and as they were keen on football had arranged a match with the local team. They were a couple of men short from their European officers and Lascar crew so Leo and I were asked to play for them. We won but my contribution was extremely minor and we were asked to dinner, but as Leo was night watchman he couldn't accept. Suitably attired in my white uniform I repaired on board, and to say I was dazzled by the apparent luxury of the ship would be an understatement. Firstly they had electric light and fans in their cabins, then before dinner a Steward brought in a bottle of cold beer for each of us. Dinner in the saloon with the officers consisted of four courses and not a crumb was wasted. After dinner we had a good old natter before I returned to the hot mosquito-filled fo'c'stle, lit with two kerosene lamps and regaled my shipmates with stories of how the other half lived.

Peanuts were one of Marmagoa's exports, and the night before sailing we discovered one of the shallow, tarpaulin covered pits in which the peanuts were stored. It didn't take long to fill several sacks with peanuts and haul them on board. We ate masses of them that night with disastrous results as they are notorious for their bowel moving capabilities. So westward we steamed some 3,000 miles to Suez - hot, hard working and not terribly well fed. We were soon on to salt and tinned meat with dubious potatoes, haricot beans and dried peas. Salt fish every Friday and bacon that was so salty it made Lot's wife look like a sugar factory. June is not a good time to traverse the Red Sea westbound and living on the port side, and we discovered to our cost the meaning of 'Port Out - Starboard Home'. We arrived at Suez in early June and encountered a blinding sandstorm halfway through the Canal. Leo and I were on the 4 to 8 morning watch and we tied up to the bank just as we came off watch so it was 9.30 before we got to bed. Everything was screwed down to keep the sand out but it still crept in and the thermometer rose rapidly. We were called at seven bells (11.30) temperature 95 F, and the dinner was a hard lump of salt beef with a coating of fat, two potatoes with more eyes than the night has stars and haricot beans that rattled as they moved. A slice of suet pudding topped with a quarter teaspoonful of molasses was the sweet, and remembering the *Clan Ross* I could have cried. The final blow, when we went amidships for our ration of lime juice, was to find that the Arab boatmen had guzzled all the lime juice. The Steward, who's heart would have made Aberdeen granite look like marshmallow, refused to issue anymore and it would have been difficult to find a more fed up pair of apprentices in the world.

However once through the Canal and into the Mediterranean the change in climate brought a new lease of life - with the resilience of youth we were soon singing away as we holystoned the wooden decks, painted the bulkheads and generally smartened up the ship for arrival in the U. K. After passing through the Straits of Gibraltar we ran into heavy weather which reduced our speed and soon bunkers became low, and the Captain and Chief Engineer advised putting into Corcubian in North Spain to take extra bunkers from an old coaling hulk, once the proud sailing ship *Monkbarns*. It was sad to see such a fine ship in reduced circumstances. Our own *Polly Woodside* at the Maritime Museum in Melbourne is of a similar vintage but was rescued by far-sighted citizens and still brings pleasure to thousands of people as a reminder of what life was like on the great sailing ships. It was my first contact with sunny Spain - another boyhood illusion shattered as it was cold and windy with heavy rain. Bunkering finished, we cast off and headed for Workington to discharge our cargo of manganese ore to the steel works. We steamed up the Irish Sea in perfect late June weather with everyone having an attack of 'channel fever' - that strange feeling of euphoria which all British crews experience on returning home after a long absence.

After five days in Workington we sailed for Cardiff and payoff, but soon hit another gale from the Atlantic and as we were in ballast our propeller was only partly submerged and without full propulsion we were in danger of being blown on to the Skerries off North Wales. All hands turned out at 1.00 a.m. to lift all the dunnage, spars and bilge boards from the aft hold, which was then flooded to bring the propeller more underwater. This was successful and we cleared the Skerries at 5.00 a.m. with a mile or so to spare. The underwriters slept undisturbed and the Lutine bell at Lloyds remained silent, however the crew of *Sneaton* had to restow many tons of timber once we were safe in the Bristol Channel. We worked up to our waists in water keeping the bilges clear of coal and ore while the water was being pumped out. The Old Man opened his heart and issued a tot of rum to all hands.

We pulled into Roath Dock at Cardiff on 6th July, 1931 and moved under the coal loading tips. The crew paid off and went home to Whitby, paying their own fares to and from ship, signing on the dole when they got home to wait for another ship. However many stayed on the same ship for voyage after voyage but were off-pay between voyages. No paid leave for anyone in those days and little for the apprentices who stayed aboard ship to assist the riggers load the ship and do odd jobs around the ship. A total of forty pounds for four years hard work plus five pounds bonus on satisfactory completion of indentures was the lot of the apprentices. A few better companies paid sixty pounds for the four years but we were definitely 'down-market'. After six days the ship was loaded, stored, crew signed on, hatches battened down and away we sailed - this time to Las Palmas and another of William Cory & Sons Ltd bunkering stations. We had new deck officers and the Mate lived up to his name of 'chipping hammer Tommy' inherited from his father who was reputed to be even tougher than his son. Rastus Dunseath left to go for his Second Mate's certificate and was replaced by Tom Houghton, and Tom Calvert rejoined having come home from Durban on a Union-Castle Line ship which had thoroughly spoiled him for life on a tramp steamer. I was still junior apprentice.

After discharging our coal at Las Palmas we headed for Gulfport on the Mississippi, where we loaded a part cargo of timber then on to Mobile in Alabama to complete. This was dressed timber for housing construction in Rosario and Sante Fe in Argentina, and the deck cargo was four feet higher than our previous timber cargo, almost covering the forward cabin portholes amidships. The derricks could not be stowed in their normal positions fore and aft, parallel with the deck, but had to be topped until they were vertical and then lashed to the crosstrees. We were thus top heavy and very 'tender' i.e. liable to capsize but this improved after we picked up bunkers at Pensacola in Florida with more from St. Thomas in the Virgin Islands. The crew acquired some local rum which caused a certain amount of mayhem after we sailed, and cost some of them a day's pay and a ten shilling fine but no bones were broken. The 3,800 mile trip to Rosario passed without further incident, the weather remained good as the old girl rolled her stately way down the South American coast. The slightest alteration in course made her heel over alarmingly due to the deck cargo and caused some concern we we embarked the pilot at Recalada for the run to Rosario, some 300 miles up the Parana river. The original name given by the early Spanish settlers was Rio del Plata (river of silver) and generally known as the Plate. However the Plate is 50% pure mud and brown in colour and fast flowing with lots of twists and turns, so we had some breath-taking moments as we altered course and the ship heeled over, sometimes brushing the overhanging foliage on the river bank.

We arrived safely in Rosario on my first visit to that most entertaining and lovely city. At the end of September,1931 after discharge of most of the cargo we moved upriver to offload the balance at Santa Fe. This was as far as deep-sea ships could go and we spent two weeks there. It was fiesta time and the plaza was thronged with people, lots of lovely senoritas, and we found it all lighthearted and colourful, the town band played endless tangoes and everyone had a good time. After loading a few thousand tons of wheat we proceeded downriver to a place called San Pedro to complete cargo, where we anchored and the anchor cable promptly parted. The apprentices spent Saturday afternoon, evening and up to 1.30 a.m. on Sunday rowing up and down, dragging a grappling iron astern trying to locate 600 feet of anchor chain. According to their indentures they were required to work 'when and where required' - we found the chain and by using mooring wires and a great deal of ingenuity and gallons of sweat the end was brought aboard and reconnected. All hands except Leo and I got a tot of rum and went to bed and the attendant mosquitoes. As a reward for our labours we were allowed to use the lifeboat for a picnic and swimming party on Sunday.

Loading completed we sailed away with the usual 'Land's End for Orders' and back into the old routine. Homeward bound the ship was tidied up, decks scraped and oiled, bulkheads and masts painted, wooden decks holystoned plus the constant trimming of ventilators to reduce condensation in the holds. Grain cargoes can be easily damaged by water both fresh and salt so the officer of the watch had to keep a careful eye on wind and weather changes. We discharged at Manchester, pausing at Eastham at the Canal entrance to drop our topmasts, then on to Cardiff where we paid off on 7th December,1931. Three years still to go !

The ship laid-up for a month or so, and we got leave over the Christmas and New Year to our joy. On our return we loaded coal for Zarate up the Plate, where the Smithfield and Argentine Meat Company had a huge meat canning and freezing plant which required vast quantities of coal for steam generation. The Plate had many 'frigorificos' as they were called, run by such household names as Swifts, Armours, Vestey (Blue Star) and Leibigs, and each plant received a weekly coal cargo. After ten days discharge, all hands set to cleaning holds and bilges then erecting 'shifting boards' - temporary fore-and-aft wooden bulkheads running along the centre line of the ship to prevent the grain shifting. Backbreaking work and not our favourite pastime, however we were cheered by the news we were to load in Buenos Aires, one of the most exciting cities in South America. We spent eighteen days there along with two other Headlam tramps, thus over a dozen apprentices haunted the 'Flying Angel' Missions to Seamen, the British Sailor's Society and Stella Maris 'Fellowship of the Sea'. All of these missions were well supported by the local English community and put on very good concerts, dances and other functions. They were well patronised as the port was always full of British ships together with many European flag ships. The famous Canon Brady was in charge of the Flying Angel and all three missions provided a splendid service to sailors of all nationalities. We sailed and dropped the pilot at Recalada and thirty days later berthed at Southampton to discharge the grain in May,1932, taking the opportunity to look over the Cunard liner *Berengaria* while in port. From Southampton we went to Cardiff to load coal amid the rows of laid-up ships.

A further economy measure now came into force - all Third Mates and Fourth Engineers were paid off. I next saw Tony Jewell, the Third Mate, in Bermuda nine years later when he was, like myself, Chief Officer of an Anglo-Saxon tanker and we sailed in convoy together. The convoy scattered in extremely bad weather and his tanker, the *Clea*, was never seen again with the loss of all 59 crew. We discharged our coal in Las Palmas and then proceeded in ballast to the Plate. This gave us ample time to clean the holds and bilges then erect the shifting boards in all holds including the cross bunker between the bridge and engine room. Outward-bound the cross bunker carried coal but by the time we reached the Plate we had transferred the remaining coal to the side pocket bunkers, stowing any surplus on deck. Working bunkers was not a favourite pastime as the coal was hoisted up in baskets, port and starboard simultaneously, tipped into barrows and trundled to the side pockets. All hands were on this job. Some down the cross bunker, filling baskets, two men 'whipping' the baskets up with the 'midships winch, two more barrowing each side and balance of the manpower trimming the coal way from the side pocket hatches. The dust and noise had to be seen to be believed. Down below you had to be constantly on your guard as baskets were hoisted up, odd chunks of coal would fall out and clobber someone who happened to be underneath. We worked hard and fast to get it over with and it usually took two days.

On this particular voyage, we needn't have hurried as we finished up spending six weeks of June and July in Buenos Aires roads waiting for a cargo. No shore leave but you could barely see the shore it was so far away. We were hungry and worked bell to bell for six days a week and were just about ripe for mutiny ! It was bitterly cold being Southern hemisphere winter and every day we were over the sides on stages chipping, scraping and painting the hull, fingers blue and the Mate showed his face every ten minutes to check we weren't up the old 'double hammer game'. We always worked in pairs and if the hammers stopped for more than a minute, he would scream at us to get on with it. To get a spell, one of us would take two hammers and pound away at the plates whilst his mate rolled up a cigarette and had a couple of puffs - the cunning of the young !

However eventually we got orders to proceed upriver to San Nicholas where we loaded for Gothenburg, Ronne (Bornholm) and Stockholm. Duly loaded and battened down we steamed down river, changed pilots at Intersection in Buenos Aires roads and finally dropped the sea pilot at Recalada off the entrance to the Plate. All the way homeward we were kept at it - chipping, scraping, painting, overhauling cargo gear and generally getting the ship as smart as possible for arrival in Europe. All the deck houses were painted before we arrived in St. Vincent for bunkers, the reason being that coal dust washes easily off the surface of new paint. If the paint is old, the coal dust gets ingrained and has to be washed with soda solution (Suji Muji) then fresh water washed. Labour intensive and time consuming ! We always reckoned that the locals at St. Vincent and other bunkering stations saw the Plate traders at their best. Derricks and deck houses painted, the former with no gear draped around them and everything neat and tidy, not to mention being locked away, even to the brass caps on the sounding pipes. The locals had long and prehensile fingers and regarded all property as common.

I had consolidated my position as Chippy's assistant by this time and this had certain advantages. Our job was to overhaul all of the cargo gear after leaving port for long voyage. Each cargo derrick had four big steel hoisting and running blocks plus four wooden blocks for the guys which gave lateral control of the derricks. Some ninety blocks in all. These, together with the cargo runners and hoisting tackles were stripped from the derricks, coiled, lashed, labelled and carried under the fo'c'stle head or the poop. All hands took about two days to do this, then Chippy and I had to strip down every block, pack the bearings with grease, clean out the accumulated dirt, red lead the bare parts then put them all together again. At times it got a bit monotonous but at least you could knock off for a smoke plus the odd cup of tea scrounged from the cook due to Chippy being a Chief Petty Officer. Every inch of wire had been oiled before being stowed away and it was a really messy job but a drop of kerosene at 5.00 p.m. removed most of that. On fine days outside, on the nearest hatch and on wet days under the fo'c'stle or poop. We were lucky because the rest of the gang were out washing paintwork, or even worse, holystoning the wooden decks when it was raining.

In perfect weather in late August,1932 we sailed up the English Channel appreciatively sniffing the offshore breeze and watching with interest the passing traffic. Derricks were being rigged, brass polished and final coats of paint being applied. Everyone was happy and in the grip of Channel fever, that mysterious feeling that every Britisher seems to experience after months of absence. Arriving at Gothenburg in early September I was given the job of night watchman but managed a couple of mild daytime runs ashore and enjoyed the sights and sounds of that lovely city. Then on to Ronne on the Danish island of Bornholm where we discharged further cargo and enjoyed our first experience of Danish pastry and cream cakes. Cakes were so cheap, even the apprentices could afford them and we could fill the table for about three shillings. At the Tivoli Gardens, the girls were all willing to dance with us and everyone was extremely friendly so we carried away happy memories of Ronne, its cream cakes and friendly citizens.

The next stop was Stockholm, the Venice of the North, with the perfect weather still holding. We enjoyed our four days there, one reason being the free low alcohol beer for stevedores, presumably on account of the hot weather, and they happily shared this with us, much to our delight, It would have taken an enormous amount to get anyone into a state of euphoria, but it tasted well and the price was right. The Baltic in summer is a delight with so many islands and pleasure craft and is extremely interesting to observers like ourselves. Everything clean and sparkling bright, different shades of green and blue with patches of colour in small gardens at the water's edge. A huge improvement after endless weeks of blue sea and sky, and we loved it. From Stockholm we went up to the Northern end of the Baltic to load pitprops at Uleaborg and Oyjoroyta in Finland. It was the end of September and winter starts early up there, so out came the bogey and the cold weather gear. The Finns made a particularly tasty version of the Hot Dog and these figure largely in my memory but the cold weather, allied to being stoney broke, precluded much shore going activities. The ports were only tiny, so after the delights of Stockholm and Ronne these had little to offer.

With our holds full of pitprops and our decks piled up to the lower bridge level, we left Finland and proceeded gingerly down the Baltic, out of the Skagerrack and into the North Sea bound for Cardiff, the cargo being destined for the collieries of the Rhonda Valley. I say gingerly because we were extremely top heavy. Many a timber ship has been lost or become a salvage case through the deck cargo shifting due to a sudden alteration of course. It was not uncommon to see timber ships arrive with a 15 degree list or more. We safely passed down the North Sea encountering the four-masted barque *Pamir* under the Finnish flag, she was amongst the last of the 'square riggers'. She later sank in an Atlantic storm on 22nd September,1957 with only five surviving from a complement of 87. Down Channel and round the Longships we sailed and headed up the Bristol Channel and into Roath Dock, Cardiff. It was now early October and a nasty swell when a bit of a blow from the North West caught us just before Lundy Island. The ship developed a five degree list to starboard but fate was kind to us and soon we were warping into Roath Dock with sighs of relief all round.

As a further economy move Headlams decided to do away with the shore gang of riggers, who usually worked the ship until the crew signed on. This was not a popular move in the Bristol Channel area where unemployment was already at staggering levels but shipowners were not competing in popularity stakes. We however considered all shipowners to be rich, mean and hard-hearted but it is a fact that a number of them went broke in the 1930 - 1935 period and those left had a hard time surviving. As apprentices we were not into high economics and all we knew was that now we had to shift ship, take stores and generally do everything that six or eight riggers did. As the riggers and teemers were often family-related, the teemers expressed their disapproval by calling for the maximum number of moves or 'shift ship', often six or seven times during the night. So out would come the apprentices and the two Mates and warp the ship forty or fifty feet along the wharf. However the teemers soon realised the shipowners meant business and ceased taking it out on the poor apprentices. Unemployment was so bad that literally dozens of sailors, firemen and stewards would meet every ship arriving in a U.K. port hopeful of a berth. Most of our crews were recruited from the Whitby area, and it was falsely rumoured that the local Vicar would announce from the pulpit every Sunday the week's requirement for sailors and firemen. Unfortunately crew changes were not very common and the same faces were encountered from ship to ship. The only exception were the trimmers who were recruited from local youths often from the Rhonda Valley and they only did one trip. In those days a first trip trimmer was paid four pounds/month for the first three months, after which his pay went up automatically to eight pounds two shillings/month. As the average voyage to the Plate and back was three and a half months, the trimmers were always paid off and new first trippers engaged. The going rate for Able Seamen was eight pounds two shillings/month, and firemen got eight pounds twelve shillings/month. Overtime was sixpence/hour, but as most overtime was worked unpaid by the apprentices, the overtime bill was hardly a financial burden on the owners.

On completion of discharge of pitprops, we warped over to the coal tips and started to load coal for Colon in Argentina. Six apprentices and two Mates did it all, shifting our own ropes as required - no mean feat. In addition to the coal we took on some 300 tons of general cargo, mainly tin plate and machinery spares also destined for the Leibigs freezing and meat packing plant around which Colon was built. We sailed in November,1932 minus Chippy who was another economy victim, and I inherited his routine jobs of soundings, and looking after the windlass and similar chores. Two days out our first trip trimmers collapsed with seasickness and general debility, so Tom and I were seconded to the Second Engineer for trimming and firing. We were out of the cold and our job was easy as far as we were concerned. This lasted a few days then with the advent of fine weather, I went back to overhauling cargo gear with Bill Duck, one of our long serving Able Seamen who had been promoted to Bosun. The rest of the lads and the crew were down below scraping deckheads !

We picked up the sea pilot at Recalada in mid November, changed to the river pilot at Intersection then up the river Uruguay to Colon with its one huge frigorifico, mainly shut down for annual overhaul, and around three million mosquitoes. Summer up river in Argentina - what bliss ! All of the local casual labour had departed and we had to supply our own winch drivers, so the apprentices were about to acquire more skills. The summer working hours for Argentina were about 6.00 a.m. to 11.00 a.m. then a four hour siesta in the heat of the day and resume work from 3.00 p.m. to 6.00 p.m. We winch drivers worked these hours but the Mate was all for working us around the ship when the wharfies knocked off from 11.00 a.m. to 3.00 p.m. Mutiny was in the air but we were saved from industrial action by the Chief Engineer with whom we had a good rapport since our trimming and firing days. He told the Old Man of our outrageous hours and he decreed that the winch drivers worked the same hours as the wharfies. It was still an eight hour day, but better than a twelve hour one - the Mate never forgave us ! It was some years later that I discovered that the cargo receivers paid the ship for providing winch drivers. We certainly never received any money, and I like to think that it helped to pay off the mortgage of the Old Man's residence in Penarth. Following discharge we moved down-river to another small port, Conception del Uruguay, also in Argentina despite the name. We loaded a full bagged cargo of linseed there for Rotterdam and departed mid-January, 1933.

In Rotterdam we berthed at dolphins in the middle of Katendrecht Haven and huge elevators sucked out the linseed as the stevedores bled the sacks down the holds. We got rid of all of the cargo in about three days and then, to my joy, headed for my home port of South Shields and Brigham & Cowan's dry-dock - fifteen minutes walk from home. Headlams mostly traded out of the Bristol Channel - Cardiff, Barry and Swansea - and this was a break for me. We were supposed to dock for a month but after two weeks my luck ran out - another of the company tramps, *Goathland*, was in the Tyne for bunkers and stores before departing in ballast for the Plate. Two of the apprentices had gone sick so Jack Austin and I were told to pack our seabags, grab our things and head for Tyne Dock to join the ship. We were not particularly enamoured of losing two weeks of comparative idleness as we only worked a six hour day in dry-dock - but go we must !

Goathland steamed out between the Tyne piers on 11th March, 1933 and that was the last I saw of home, mother and the South Shields 'Brassie Snatchers' for over two years. Steaming down the North Sea I was able to take stock of my new ship and shipmates. She was about the same size as *Sneaton* but a different type of ship in so far as she had a 'short welldeck' forward and aft whereas *Sneaton* was the 'long welldeck' or 'three island' ship. In *Goathland* nos. 2 and 3 holds had 'tween decks therefore more steel beams, more wooden hatches and more cleaning after each cargo. Alan (Bing) Crosby was the senior apprentice, then Jimmie Scott, Henry Mullins, 'Poot' Braim and I were were level pegging with Jack Austin as junior. A very good bunch and we all lived in harmony with rarely a cross word. The Captain was both competent and kind-hearted up to a point, as were the First and Second Mates. The Second Mate was Fred 'Sugar' Wormald, and he and I sailed together later when I was Second Mate and our paths crossed frequently over the next thirty five years.

Once we were clear of coastal waters Bing Crosby took over the 8 to 12 watch which lightened the burden of the two Mates and life went on in a very uncomplicated pattern. We cleaned holds, erected shifting boards, over-hauled cargo gear, chipped, scraped, painted and holystoned all of the way to the Plate. It says something of the economics of the day that we made a round voyage of three months and 14 days for one cargo of 5,200 tons of grain at a freight rate of 15 shillings/ton. No doubt the owners lost money but at least their ship was being maintained and it was cheaper than laying her up. Headlam & Sons managed thirteen ships, eleven of them with a funnel emblem of a red cross on a white band. The other two, *Glaisdale* and *Dunsley*, were owned by the Headlam family and had a blue cross on a white band. The Geneva Convention of 1933 made a multilateral decision that the red cross was only to be used to indicate a 'life saving and humanitarian' situation, so our red crosses were painted over with a blue cross. Likewise our houseflags were changed over to a blue cross with the flag having a red border. We were then known as the 'Whitby Greeks' - blue being part of the Greek national flag and a favourite colour on the funnels of Greek ships on the Plate run. As 'lifesaving and humanitarian' feelings had never been a strong point with Headlams, we thought the change most appropriate.

We loaded a full cargo of assorted grains in San Nicholas, some 200 miles up river from Buenos Aires. The only event remaining in my mind of our time there was that Bing and I managed to capsize the punt from which we were painting the boot topping. The currents run very strongly under the cliff berths at San Nicholas and many sailors have drowned after falling in there. Bing and I were lucky and managed to hang on until help arrived. The Bosun was not amused at us losing a newly opened five gallon tin of paint plus four brushes. It's as well we were able to salvage the punt or he would probably have pushed us back in the river. As it was, we had barely time to change before he had us over the side on a stage, hoping no doubt we'd fall on the dock and break our necks !

So once more we sailed down the 'silver river' past the dreaded Martin Garcia Bar, where at least one ship a week went aground but fortunately refloated within a day or so. We then topped up our fresh water tanks at Banco Ingles and headed for the South Atlantic. Some 28 days later we arrived at Santander in northern Spain to discharge part cargo. This was a different Spain to that which I had visited two years earlier. Glorious weather, tied up alongside the Town Square with senoritas parading around every evening, the occasional band concert and vino at sixpence/bottle. Ten minutes walk to the nearest clean sandy beach and five minutes walk in the opposite direction to the bars, cantinas and cabarets. We enjoyed two weekends in this Northern Spain summer playground.

The punt had been repaired and caulked and Bing and I were over the side most days and found a post under the overhang of the counter stern where nobody could see us from on deck. We worked hard all one morning and completed the job before lunch. After lunch we returned to our hidey hole with a bottle of vino and spent a relaxing afternoon putting the world to rights and increasing the profitability of the local vintner's operations. The warmth and the vino lulled us to sleep and we didn't wake up until 5.15 p.m. - fifteen minutes after knocking off time. The Bosun did not believe our story of being keen to finish the job, and never let us out of his sight after that ! On to Bilbao with the balance of our cargo, then over to Cardiff to load coal for Rosario and resume our long running war with the teemers and trimmers. This time we loaded relatively 'clean' coal of small nuggets for the power station called Usina at the northern end of Rosario. Poot Braim left and a first tripper, Bill Laddle from Hull, joined in his place. So we sailed on another 'Plate' voyage with the usual thirty days or more at sea, duly arriving at Usina without incident. The berth was well out into the river and the coal, after being dropped into a huge hopper, came up a conveyor belt from the wharf and was dumped into storage bins at the power house. This had been built by and was owned by an Italian firm and some workers had stayed on to run the plant. As a result there was a big colony of Italian descent amongst the locals, plus a few English who worked for the railways. The Ferro Carril Central Argentina (FCCA) or Central Argentine Railways was British-owned with big workshops and marshalling yards at Rosario and Villa Constitucion, some forty miles down river from Rosario. The latter was a fine city with lots of parks and gardens and plenty of night life - bars, cabarets, movies and important to us a thriving Flying Angel Mission. At this time it was common to have a dozen or more ships loading grain in port, mostly British, and Rosario was the second largest grain loading port in the country after Buenos Aires. Horse racing and football every Saturday and plenty of Churches for anyone's spiritual needs, we attended the Mission on Sundays. I was lucky to have friends in the city from family connections and got about quite a lot. Often I was a guest at the English Club in the northern suburb of Sorrento and introduced them to the Palais Glide, a popular dance then in favour in England. After loading grain there we were off again, this time to Rotterdam where we had a three day turnround. Britain had just come off the Gold Standard so we got a rude shock at the cost of everything in Holland, but the Mission was helpful as always and we were able to get a free lift ashore in the Mission launch from our berth at the dolphins. Back to Cardiff for more coal for Usina at Rosario, we locked out in late October glad to leave the Depression and lines of idle, rusting ships behind us.

Having a short welldeck had certain disadvantages. In bad weather the seas shipped on board did not drain away so well as a long welldeck ship so we got a large amount of water into our accomodation, despite steel doors. Also the bogey could not be got going as the funnel would have been swept away so we were very wet and cold apprentices. Getting food, such as it was, from the galley amidships to the fo'c'stle was an obstacle race of some magnitude and losses were high. However we were soon into sunny weather and the discomfort was soon forgotten as life took on a familiar pattern of the constant battle against corrosion. Chipping, painting, scraping and holystoning during wet weather, and every Saturday afternoon boat drill known as 'Boat of Trade sports'. Now and again we were called upon to do the firing and trimming in the stokehold - everything in fact 'when and where required' - we got well trained in Headlams. All in all *Goathland* was a happy ship, the Able Seamen and firemen a cheerful and matey lot and we all got on extremely well with each other. After discharge at Usina we swam in the river Parana after work and at the weekend strolled ashore.

The holds were washed ready for the grain cargo as the weather was hot and this saved us a lot of extra work. Normally we would have had to climb up the cargo battens and sweep down from the top, collect and dump the sweepings, then do the whole thing again. It was easy with a hose and two men so we were done and dusted in two days instead of about six. After putting up the grain shifting boards we loaded at the grain berths for the usual 'Land's End for Orders'. It took about thirty days from the Plate to Europe and the cargo would change hands several times during the voyage, with the final destination only known as we entered the English Channel. We had the usual break, calling this time at Madeira for bunkers. We also took our own private bunkers in the form of fruit and local vino, the latter illegally and therefore more satisfying. A couple of the crew got drunk as usual and six hours later we were on our merry way. This time we ended up at Spillers Mill in Cardiff, which was virtually our home port by now. Mid-January, 1934 was cold, wet and windy and generally miserable but it didn't seem to bother us and we had a month there discharging then loading coal.

Mid-February,1934 and we pulled away from the coal spouts and out into the stormy Bristol Channel with a full cargo for Zarate, where I had been before in the *Sneaton*. At Zarate we had a pleasant time as the Old Man was very friendly with the English manager of the meat works where we discharged our coal, and 'persona grata' with the English and Anglo-Argentine colony in general. As a result we were asked out to several homes for dinner and one memorable Saturday actually played tennis, followed by an 'asado' or barbeque alongside the court. There were several attractive daughters but the chaperone system was strong then, even extending to the British, so we kept our hands to ourselves. Going ashore in our white uniforms through the all-pervading clouds of coal dust was a bit of a trauma but this was overcome by going ashore in ordinary gear with white jacket, trousers and cap all wrapped in a sheet under our arms - then we changed at the watchman's hut at the end of the jetty and reversed the procedure on our return. We used to slip Pedro the watchman some English marmalade - a great delicacy in Argentina and for a seven pound tin he would have given us the whole frigorifico, wharf and all !

We left Zarate waving a fond farewell to our friends and moved upriver to Rosario to load another grain cargo, washing holds and erecting shifting boards en route. We took about ten days to load as we had a mixed cargo of bags and bulk, and this gave us time for a few runs ashore to the English Club. In mid-April, 1934 we washed away the last of the grain and coal dust and headed for Europe. There was a slight hiatus en route when one of the thick bolts holding the medium pressure piston to the crankshaft broke, and a piece of the bolt shot up and fractured the collar of the cylinder where the piston enters. I can't describe it more accurately as I am not an Engineer but the whole engine came to a shuddering halt and a rather torrid time followed. These bolts were about four inches in diameter, three feet long and the spares were too big and had to be filed down to size by hand. A new collar had to be made by cutting it out of a solid steel plate also by hand. All hands worked for over 36 hours sharpening chisels, wielding the heavy hammers and taking turns at filing those huge bolts. We only had three Engineers that trip but had our Chippy back and he did wonders with the little portable forge, keeping the chisels up to scratch. We were right on the Equator in the doldrums and it was extremely hot, the butter was liquid the whole time and the ship rolled constantly in the swell. We fished during our off-duty time but caught nothing, and eventually the Engineers and firemen reassembled the engine and it worked to everyone's joy and relief. The Old Man and Chief Engineer were especially pleased as they would have had a lot to explain if we had become a salvage job. The Chief Engineer gave us apprentices a tot from his own private bottle as a reward for all of the blisters and work. Calling at St. Vincent for bunkers we finally made it to the Mersey and the West Float in Birkenhead to discharge.

I had relatives there and got well fed, with my cousins taking me out and about, although rather disappointed that I wasn't wearing my uniform. They were quite surprised to hear that it wasn't only 'nice girls' who loved sailors, and on Merseyside as at all ports there were lots of other girls not so nice. Five days later we were sailing to Barry Dock and under the coal tips once more. We had a few runs to Barry Island, which was a great holiday resort, had a few beers and heard some wonderful Welsh miners singing in the pubs. A few girls were chatted up with varying success and we generally enjoyed the late May sunshine as for once it wasn't raining in South Wales. The last day of May saw us pulling out of the locks at Barry Dock for the Plate once more - this time for Villa Constitution and the railway depot of the Central Argentine Railways. We were minus Chippy again so I was back to the old sounding rod and oil can for the steering chains. We steered the old 'rod and chain' gear via a quadrant on the poop and it was part of the Chippy's job to make sure the gear on the poop was oiled and greased every day. The steering gear was at the top of the engine room and was actuated when the helmsman turned the bridge wheel. A series of rods and sections of chains connected the whole thing to the quadrant at the stern and turned the rudder - one felt that Heath Robinson had quite an influence on this particular design !

So we rolled sedately down to Villa Constitution, a town I was to know intimately some four years later, and berthed there at the end of June. After discharge of our coal we anchored off Rosario and cleaned holds by hand for five days before loading various parcels of grain. This took another two weeks then it was off to sea once more, this time to Belfast, then a relatively peaceful place. We arrived there in August in time for two events which brought a little colour into our lives, the Apprentice Day parade and the Ulster T. T. motorcycle race. Another highlight of our stay in Belfast was a visit to the sailing ship *Herzogin Cecile* another of the few remaining 'square riggers'. We went back to Barry from Belfast and loaded coal again for Rosario. Bing Crosby left to go for his Second Mate's certificate and I became senior apprentice and eventually temporary, probationary, acting, unpaid Third Mate once we had cleared the Bristol Channel. I had the 8 to 12 watch morning and evening and instead of chipping and scraping I now sewed canvas on watch and also from 1 p.m. to 3 p.m. every afternoon. All of the Mates worked at least two hours over and above their watches and made all of the canvas covers for ventilators, lifeboats, wire reels, awnings etc. - even main hatch tarpaulins were made as often as possible. I got on well with the Mate and Second Mate, and must have sewn miles of canvas particularly with the Second Mate, Ron Bird. I talked the Old Man into letting me use the empty Third Mate's cabin whilst we were at sea so I could study more easily and, at last, had my own little 'pied a terre' as it were. Once we got to Recalada however it was back to the fo'c'stle with the rest of the apprentices and out with the paint-stained working gear. Nonetheless, I treasured those few weeks of privacy after four years of communal living, even though I had to take my meals in the fo'c'stle with the rest of the apprentices.

After discharge up-river we cleaned holds and then loaded a mixed cargo of grain including a lot of bagged stuff. This got me out of a lot of hard work painting over the side, as I was given the job of tallying the bags as they came on board at one of the holds. We were working three holds, so the Mate and Second Mate had their hands full - monotonous but pleasant in the early summer sunshine. As this was my tenth consecutive voyage to the Plate I had acquired a reasonable amount of Spanish and was able to practice it on the tally clerks who accompanied me. It was not yet hot enough to work the summer hours so we usually finished at 5.00 p.m. then off ashore to the Mission or if finances allowed to a bar. The local currency of the peso was very much in our favour and for our needs living was cheap. We used to buy small tins of Vienna sausages and pate de foie to supplement the ship's plain fare and these were only a few pence per item.

Just before leaving Rosario I completed my indentures and was duly signed on as an Able Seaman at the sum of eight pounds two shillings/month. A distinct advance on my salary of fifteen pounds/annum for my last year. The Old Man let me have a sub of one pound which paid for a good night ashore for all of us as we were to sail the next day. An uneventful voyage and we arrived off Point Lynas at the Mersey Bar and picked up the pilot who took us to Eastham locks. Down came the topmasts and next day we moved up to Manchester, where on 21st December,1934 I was paid off in the late afternoon. Cold, damp and foggy though it was outside, I had an enormous feeling of freedom and warmth in my heart as I joined my shipmates for a farewell party. Looking back on those four hard years, there seemed to be a certain amount of stability in our lives. Prices seemed to remain steady and I can recall commodities which never altered in price almost to the outbreak of World War II.

I then attended South Shields Marine School and in April,1935 obtained my Certificate of Competency as Second Mate of a foreign-going steamship. In June,1935 the British Government realised the plight of the British fleet and decided to grant certain shipowners a subsidy. To qualify, each ship had to be manned fully according to the National Maritime Board and meant taking three Deck and four Engineer officers and a Carpenter in the case of Headlam ships. This was a bit of an upsurge with full complements and brought some hope to the legion of the unemployed. The summer of 1935 remains a pleasant memory to me as I met and fell in love with my future wife in July, 1935 and within five days I was appointed to a Headlam ship as Third Mate. Meetings and partings seemed to dominate our lives for the next twenty years but that is normal for the maritime industry. I joined the *Streonshalh* at Dunston Staithes and my one stripe with diamond was already sewn on my best and only uniform and I had the shoulder boards ready for my 'patrol' jacket. This single breasted jacket was buttoned up to the throat and was the forerunner of the modern battledress jacket for working wear (unless loading coal).

Suitably equipped with my sextant (present from Uncle Tom), mattress, pillow, linen and packed seabag I reported on board *Streonshalh* at the same berth where I had joined *Sneaton* four years and eight months earlier. It wasn't the same coal dust but looked remarkably similar and enveloped the ship so I was hastily out of my shore gear and into a boiler suit. Loading was almost finished and there was an air of ordered confusion about the place. A new Second Mate Rem Gillman was taking over from the old Second Mate Fred Hodgson, and the Mate Ron Coultas was everywhere at once. The Bosun had been ashore imbibing Newcastle Brown

Ale and we hoisted him aboard in a coal basket - apart from that everything seemed normal. I knew five out of the six apprentices including Bill Laddle who had sailed with me in *Goathland* and they were a good bunch, nonetheless fraternisation was frowned upon. Later I met Captain George Readman and he didn't seem overjoyed at my presence but was civil in the extreme. During my five months with him we got on as well as possible in those formal days. I met him again many years later when I was Chief Officer of the 'MAC' ship *Adula* in Halifax (NS) and he was most affable.

Our cargo was for Funchal in Madeira, another of the North Atlantic bunkering stations and only nine days run from the Tyne. Madeira is a Portuguese colony but Spanish is widely used so I was able to further my grasp of the language. The Second Mate was studying Spanish in depth and we spent every evening from then on studying Spanish, with Sparks and the Fourth Engineer also keen to learn the language. I was now earning £10 / 12 /9d per month out of which I was leaving six pounds to my mother. Living costs in Madeira were high and we had to budget carefully, as a lot of upper class English favoured Madeira as a holiday resort for a variety of reasons and prices were geared accordingly. We discharged our coal into barges and lay at anchor the whole time but had several runs ashore. The U. S. Navy had two battleships in the harbour showing the flag, *Arkansas* and *Wyoming*, later the *Arkansas* was sunk at Pearl Harbour. After discharge instead of proceeding on to the Plate we were ordered back to Barry to load coal and then on to the Plate. I paid off 28 days after signing on, but signed on again the next day and under the coal tips we went, and left in early September with *Streonshalh* wallowing across the Bay of Biscay and on to Rosario where we discarged at Swift's frigorifico and went out on the town. By this time I had a fairly wide circle of friends in Rosario and it was almost a home port. We washed and cleaned holds after discharge, then moved up river to a port called San Lorenzo to load grain for Dublin.

Clearing Recalada after dropping the pilot we headed for Dublin and resumed what, by now, was a reasonably pleasant routine - mostly sewing canvas on watch and in the afternoon, keeping an eye on the weather and making sure the hold ventilators were properly trimmed. The Captain and the Mate both had the new short wave radios and were able to keep in touch with shore stations until we steamed up the Liffey in mid-November,1935 on a damp and misty morning all eager to sample a Guinness. Our agents were the Saorstat & Continental Steamship Co. Ltd and their annual staff dance took place whilst we were in port. We were invited and had a riotous evening with them with the prospect of more to follow. Unfortunately for me the Third Mate of the *Sandsend*, loading coal in Cardiff was taken to hospital and the ship was due to sail in two days time. *Streonshalh* had another seven days discharge time left so I was was sent off on the night ferry. I paid off on 28th November,1935 and joined *Sandsend* the next day feeling somewhat jaded after a farewell party and an all night crossing of the Irish Sea.

My reception was anything but cordial as the Old Man had been expecting a very experienced Third Mate of the same name. He had been my first Captain on *Sneaton* and time hadn't improved him. However the Second Mate was a cheery soul and the Mate wasn't too bad so I was soon into my boiler suit and out on deck. The fact that I had been travelling some seventeen hours and had little or no sleep carried very little weight. Two days later we locked out of Cardiff and were heading into a half gale for the next three days. *Sandsend* was a three island ship and sister to *Sneaton* and *Streonshalh* in most respects. They were mad on cribbage in that ship and a lot of our spare time, such as it was, was spent playing crib in the Engineer's messroom. A nice bunch of Engineers, Chief was Benny Winspear with whom I had sailed previously when he was Second Engineer and whose greeting was in direct contrast to the Old Man's and offset my initial dismay. Another pastime was deck tennis played with a rope quoit played on no. 2 hatch in good weather. It could be quite lethal in cold weather as the rope quoits were extremely hard and thrown to win by wounding if necessary !

Our destination this time was once more up the Plate to Fray Bentos in Uruguay where Lord Vestey of the Blue Star Line had one of his international chain of frigorificos. The employees club of Fray Bentos was called the 'Estrella Azul' or Blue Star in Spanish. At Fray Bentos the stevedores worked round the clock so there was a deck officer on duty all night. I didn't see much of the place as we were soon off to Rosario and Buenos Aires to load a variety of grains for Scandinavia. On our voyage we called in at Dartmouth in Devon for bunkers. Despite his obvious dislike for me for no reason that I could fathom, the Old Man had some faith in my abilities as a helmsman. He insisted I take the wheel when entering or leaving port in any tricky situation. Leaving Dartmouth at night the steering gear jammed and the combined efforts of the pilot, Old Man and myself failed to move it. Fortunately we were at dead slow ahead, so whilst the Old Man rang full astern I raced forward and let go the anchor. Both the Mate and Chippy had been at 'harbour stations' three minutes previously but had been told to stand down, so it was just as well I was a good runner. We didn't touch bottom but it was a very close thing.

We proceeded up Channel and across the North Sea to our first port of Copenhagen, with the traffic in the Channel and North Sea considerable and vessels of all shapes and sizes going in every direction. Visibility was mostly poor as it was February and after four hours of dodging around trawlers, drifters, Thames barges, ferries and tramps on converging courses, it was a relief to get off the bridge and relax. Often we had to go into double watches which meant four hours on and four off. Fortunately I was paired off with the Mate, known as Willie, with whom I was on good terms. Mac the Second Mate was paired off with the Old Man which suited me fine. We weaved our way through the Skagerack, Scaw and Kattegat dodging every conceivable kind of floating object and into Copenhagen Sound. I was at the wheel entering Copenhagen for nearly five hours, freezing cold and was never more relieved in my life to hear pilot say 'finished with engines'. I seem to recall that I almost sat on the galley stove for an hour to thaw out. We were in the Frihaven at Copenhagen and gave the Tuborg canteen a fair amount of attention. The beer was about twopence a bottle in this duty-free area so we laid in a fair stock before we sailed down to Nykoping on the island of Falster. We were really in the ice area down there and needed an icebreaker to get us in and out of port. It was possible to walk on the ice on the offshore side of the ship within an hour of berthing.

After two days at Falster we were off to our final destination of Stockholm, also icebound, but not so much as Falster. After some good runs ashore we sailed for Swansea and spent six more hectic days weaving our way through the Baltic,

Skaw, North Sea and the English Channel. Bad visibility and double watches all of the way so we were more than happy to get into Swansea locks and get a decent sleep. Our next cargo was anthracite for Montreal but we couldn't sail until the ice was clear on the St. Lawrence river in early April. Mac and I were paid off leaving The Mate and six apprentices to load the ship and take her to lay-up at the buoys. By this time we were using riggers again and the Mate had his wife and family on board so it was not a great hardship for him. Naturally we paid our own fares back home and were off pay until we signed on again at Swansea Shipping Office on 5th April, 1936.

All Headlam tramps on the Swansea to Montreal run were carrying twelve passengers each way, and this money-making innovation started in 1935 with the deck officer's messroom on *Sandsend* and the pilot's room converted into four berth cabins. The Third Mate and Fourth Engineer were required to double up with the Second Mate and Third Engineer and caused some unhappy feelings amongst the four gentlemen concerned. Jobs were still hard to come by so the time was not ripe for revolution. In the event there were only eight passengers on that trip so the Fourth Engineer and I retained our cabins. In point of fact neither of us had a cabin as the Board of Trade had tacked the cabin space on to the net tonnage. The usual statutory notice 'Certified to accomodate one seamen' had been erased and the owners were taxed on the extra tonnage. As this was only about sixpence and the passengers paid twelve pounds ten shillings each per voyage there was a fair profit margin for the owners. One good thing that arose from carrying passengers was that the food improved, and Officers and Sparks ate in the saloon with the passengers. As soon as *Sandsend* cleared the Bristol Channel she went through the usual pitching and rolling and there weren't too many passengers with good appetites, however we had strong stomachs and ate well.

The St. Lawrence river is frozen from November to April so all imports and exports have to be handled in roughly seven months, and speed in cargo handling is all important. Most sailors reckon the North Atlantic run is among the worst in the world - fog, icebergs, gales seem to be endemic - but in summer the odd sunny day can be encountered. The regular traders such as Canadian Pacific and Cairn Line were built for the job with extra heating internally, strongly constructed externally and ran like railway trains, but their ugly sisters, the tramps, took a fair hammering. On this first voyage we had to go south of Newfoundland as the Belle Isle Strait was still frozen with fog and icebergs everywhere, and once more we were on double watches navigating by radio direction finder (D. F.). We soon became experts in using this electronic wonderment and would have been in diabolical trouble without it. Radar, satnav and the like were still on the drawing board so we used the D. F. and the echo sounder to check our position, and our noses to smell the icebergs. The North Atlantic is a very matey place as regards human relations mainly because the weather conditions are so shocking that all sailors band together to fight the elements. Sparks seemed to work endless hours gathering the ice and fog reports whilst everyone broadcast their position, course and speed, ice and weather conditions every hour or so. The elegant Cunard and White Star liners were in constant touch with everyone and the airlanes had a 'clubby' atmosphere. Pushing our way past the pack ice and growlers we eventually reached Father Point on the Gaspe Coast, where we picked up the pilot for the haul up to Quebec. Apart from fog, this part was very interesting and our rather groggy passengers emerged to have the run of the ship in the calm waters.

At Quebec, with the magnificent Chateau Frontenac towering above the Heights of Abraham, we changed pilots and picked up the company's choice pilot, Captain Houd, a French Canadian with a great sense of humour. I was to be his helmsman on several occasions and we reached a great rapport in fighting the strong currents of the St. Lawrence. The ship had been on the Montreal run the previous season and the local stevedores, Louis Wolfe et Cie, knew the hatch dimensions and before we tied up, four huge grabs were taking coal from our holds. All hatches and beams had been removed on the way upriver and we were soon emptying at a rate which seemed alarming to me. It took less than 24 hours to unload the 5,000 tons of anthracite with very little dust. Towards the end, an army of stevedores, carpenters and welders descended upon us, sweeping out the last scraps of coal, and all of the dust from the ship's side and repairing the damage done by the grabs. Burlap and dunnage was laid and the shifting boards went up as if by magic. Another 15 hours and we were heading downriver for Sorel, Captain Houd hissing instructions to me as we moved from one set of leads to another down that turbulent river.

As we berthed at Sorel the carpenters finished fixing the last of the shifting boards with six inch nails, and if anything didn't look right out came the hammer and more great steel spikes to fix it. Eventually it took two days to take down what they had erected in 15 hours as they were 'nail happy', and I have seen a Chippy looking for somewhere to hang his hat, whip out a six inch nail, and smack into the nearest wooden structure. 'Built to last' seemed to be their motto, but this need not be true for shifting boards. Once under the grain spouts of Sorel, the golden grain of Canada's prairies came pouring into our holds together with a cloud of chaff, which formed a veritable fog of grain dust for the next twenty four hours. Speed is all important on the Eastern seaboard of Canada, and one day after arrival we were battening down the hatches and chugging down the St. Lawrence. So much for my first visit to Canada where I never set foot ashore except to read the draft on bow and stern.

We only had ten passengers so I retained my cabin and the inevitable confrontation was put on the 'back burner' for a while. We had the usual fog and slushy ice through the Gulf of St. Lawrence and were glad to get out into the Atlantic and clear of the heavy traffic and setting course for Barry Dock. Fred Hodgson had replaced Mac as Second Mate and we became extremely good friends sewing canvas in the mornings and afternoons. In addition to this little extra curricular activity I was asked to relieve the Mate from 1800 to 1900 hours so he could play deck tennis on no. 2 hatch. The bridge and I were well acquainted and the clean windows and shining brass attested to my industry. We discharged our cargo at Spiller's Mill at Barry and had two days in dry-dock for bottom painting then round to Swansea to load another anthracite cargo for Montreal. By now it was the end of May and the weather had improved somewhat. Nonetheless it was no picnic as the big icebergs were wallowing around the eastern seaboard and fog seemed ever present. We spent a lot of time stopping in mid-ocean knowing there were bergs nearby and were on double watches once more. It was a shorter voyage as we were able to use Belle Isle Strait to the north of Newfoundland but took two days longer due to fog.

Once in the St. Lawrence the fog cleared and we were able to enjoy the two days of placid steaming in brilliant June sunshine. A more pleasant trip would be hard to find as all the forests were in varying shades of green and the many villages added splashes of colour. There was enough traffic both ashore and afloat to make an interesting scene but we always had that nagging fear of fog at the back of our minds. Stark tragedy has struck in the St. Lawrence in maritime collisions during fog over the years. However on this particular voyage the weather was settled and the passengers gasped as each new village appeared amongst the trees. The bridges were all roofed over, which seemed curious until it was explained that the steeply pitched roofs shed the snow in wintertime. Snow falls on the Gaspe coast are so heavy that the weight of snow would have broken the bridges.

We were met by swinging grabs as we berthed in Montreal and having been out on the bridge or on top of the hatches all day, and then a three hour trick at the wheel with Captain Houd hissing instructions in my ear, I was told that I was to be up all night as officer of the watch. Such is the resilience of youth that I was up again at 1.00 p.m. and went ashore, determined not to let Montreal go unvisited this time. I managed to see many things and had ham sandwiches and a beer at Krausman's on Philip Square, shopping at Eatons and finally cinema before returning at 6.00 p.m. for my night shift. Cargo work finished by midnight so I was able to catch up on some sleep until 7.00 a.m. when the noise started again. The same procedure as on the last visit ensued with cleaners, carpenters, welders working with never a dull moment. By 6.00 p.m. most of the workers had gone and I was left in charge to see the welds on the tank tops tested. The Old Man, Willie the Mate, Fred the second Mate had all disappeared along with everyone else including all of the engineers. The foreman welder insisted on all the double bottom tanks being tested which didn't please the donkeyman who had to operate the pump in the engine room and keep steam on the donkey boiler up on deck. We were running around watching the results of tank testing, and having satisfied the foreman who departed into the dusk 'the rest of the day was my own'. I looked around for something to eat, having missed the 5.00 p.m. tea due to the pressure of business, but everything was locked away and the keyholders had gone ashore. I thus sallied forth ashore in search of sustenance. It was a lovely June night and I felt no qualms in leaving the ship as sometimes one watchman looked after several ships when laid-up.

I had a large plate of steak and eggs, washed down with a couple of glasses of beer, and strolled back at 11.30 p.m. feeling a lot better. I was met at the gangway by an apprentice and was told the Old Man wanted to see me an hour ago. Hastily changing into my khaki working gear I duly knocked at the Captain's door with fear and trepidation in my heart. 'Aaaagh' he said which meant 'come in and explain'. I sensed that he was not in the best of tempers and tried valiantly to explain that I had been left in charge, bullied by a welding foreman and a donkeyman, and had worked from dawn to dusk without food at the end of a traumatic 15 hour day! However he had me squarely in his sights and let go with both barrels 'You have committed the unforgivable sin of leaving the ship without a certificated officer on board'.

He made it quite plain that he considered me useless, and as a final straw he despatched my bruised and battered ego into the night with 'and another thing, you'll move into the Second Mate's cabin tomorrow as we have twelve passengers this trip and we'll require your cabin for passengers'. What was it that someone said about the 'cup of happiness full and overflowing ?' I spent a disturbed night - resentful at what I considered an injustice and fearful of the end result - a season ticket to the dole queue. However we were all involved in the loading which commenced at 6.00 a.m. and went on all day. I was out on deck amidst the dust and chaff created by five or more spouts pouring wheat into our holds, stores were being taken, moorings tended, and trimmers from Louis Wolfe & Cie were down in the holds properly trimming the wheat. Louis Wolfe's two sons were in charge on board and were decent enough to take Fred and I ashore for a couple of beers during a break in the loading. The passengers came aboard in the late afternoon with a large number of relations and friends to wish them 'bon voyage' or to make sure they got away from Canada. One of the two women who were to take over my cabin were in the latter category. There were the usual moans 'Outside yes, luxurious never' from more than half of them who had been conned by the company travel brochure into expecting luxurious outside cabins. It is very difficult to make an 8 x 10 cabin with two wooden bunks and an 18 inch wardrobe into 'luxury' accomodation and our crew didn't even try !

The three Mates being on deck were on the receiving end of the complaints and were constantly explaining that it wasn't their fault. The Chief Steward and his cabin boys were holed up in the pantry making themselves as inconspicuous as possible. The two ladies in my cabin were of uncertain vintage, one was a white-haired, motherly type and chain-smoked her way to the U. K. The other was an ex-Glaswegian, rough as bags, and it was soon evident how she had been making a living. Her 'husband' who came to make sure she sailed was an equally rough French Canadian who was obviously from the backwoods and glad to see her off. Also in our alleyway in the Fourth Engineer's cabin was a retired missionary and his wife. We christened him the 'Bishop' and he insisted on saying grace, long and loud, before and after each meal. The other eight passengers were housed under the bridge in two four-berth cabins and treated the Chief Steward to the rough edge of their tongues but he gave as good as he got. The passengers and their friends had come with a fair amount of liquor and fortunately it had a smoothing effect.

Loading finished in the early hours of the morning, the hatches were battened down, and we sailed at 6.00 a.m. with me at the wheel for two hours and after a hasty breakfast I was on watch again until noon. I was careful to keep out of the Old Man's way as it was obvious I was not in favour. Captain Houd the pilot was particularly matey and made kind remarks about my ability as a helmsman to which the Old Man was not receptive. Fred took over just after noon and I hopped into his bunk for a much needed sleep until he came off watch. We had agreed that I could use the proper bunk when he was on watch, so I slept well. The run down the St. Lawrence and through Belle Isle Strait is always, apart from the risk of fog, smooth and interesting in late June. We and the passengers enjoyed nearly three days of relative tranquility except that I was expected to work sewing canvas between 1.00 p.m. and 3.00 p.m. and then relieve the Mate from 6.00 p.m. to 7.30 p.m. so he could play deck tennis on no. 2 hatch with the Old Man and the passengers. I was putting in a twelve hour day and sleeping athwartships on a small bed of sorts in not exactly five-star accomodation but there was worse to come. Two days after leaving Fred and I were attacked by bugs which we traced to the lady passenger next door in my former cabin. Despite all of our efforts they kept coming and she became quite rude when we suggested she clean up her act and then decided to turn on her aged and fading charm. Some hope, we still reported her to the Old Man and a classic example of masterful inactivity followed !

Once clear of Belle Isle Strait we had five or more days of south-westerly gales which almost capsized the old *Sandsend*. I was constantly thrown off my settee bunk during the 4 to 8 watch while Fred was using the bunk. The Bishop and his wife were violently ill and hardly left their cabin, so Fred and I became chambermaids and general factotums to the poor souls. Everything had to be battened down and the stench was unbelievable as we lurched and staggered towards Europe. When the weather finally eased and things returned to normal, the Bishop after midday dinner insisted on saying prayers for 'our safe delivery' and praised the Old Man for bringing us safely through the storm and tempest. I was on the bridge relieving Fred and when he returned he regaled me with the whole incident and said there was no stopping the Bishop. Naturally I went off to get my head down in Fred's bunk but it was 1.30 p.m. before the Bishop finished his song of thanksgiving. Around this time I refused to work in the early afternoon as I was able to get a decent sleep in Fred's bunk from 1.00 p.m. to 4.00 p.m., and this endeared me further to the Old Man. What with killing bugs, fighting off the advances of the woman they came from, cleaning up the Bishop and his wife, we had a busy sort of life, considering that we spent a minimum of nine hours/day on the bridge. Eventually we reached our destination of Sharpness in Gloucester and a classic conversation ensued :-

Captain to Third Mate 'You are getting a new Captain next trip'
Third Mate to Captain 'Oh ! are you leaving sir '
Captain to Third Mate ' No ! You are - you're fired !'

So off to Bristol Shipping office where I was paid off, returning to the ship to pack my seabag and trundled it off to the left luggage office at the railway station. We had a hilarious party at the local pub with Fred, the apprentices and engineers, and then I had my first decent sleep for a fortnight. Next morning I had a brief and chilly interview with the Old Man who showed me a letter to the company saying inter alia 'Mr. Allen did not wish to remain in the ship due to the cabin being infested with vermin brought by the passengers'. I thought to myself that he would phone the Marine Superintendent later and tell him that he thought I was useless, and that is exactly what he did. I last saw the masts and funnel of *Sandsend* from the train leaving Sharpness and thought 'at least the wheelhouse brass is polished and the windows are clean'.

Being a lovely July day, the prospect of seeing my girl friend and being home, outweighed the fact that I was unemployed and fired with little hope of being rehired. At home I engaged in correspondence with Capt. Milner, the Headlam Marine Superintendent and he asked me for my version of affairs and I put pen to paper and awaited results. Towards the end of the month a letter came from him telling me to join their *Glaisdale* at Barry Dock. We all knew who was Captain of each ship so I knew that Capt. Robert Dixon was my new Old Man. He was a strict disciplinarian, non-smoker and teetotal with a reputation for giving Third Mates a hard time. My heart sank but off I went on the night train to the Bristol Channel. At 7.00 a.m. on 4th August,1936 I carried my seabag and bedding on board as clouds of coal dust wreathed the ship. I met Capt. Dixon after breakfast and he shook hands with me and expressed the hope I would 'fit in' with the ship. It was literally 'his ship' as he had invested a sizeable amount of money in her and was part-owner. He was strict on observing 'colours' i.e. the raising and lowering of flags at 8.00 a.m. and 5.00 p.m., and also had a 'no smoking between the masts' clause in the articles agreement when one signed on. Two days later we locked out of Barry Dock and headed for Rosario, with Mrs. Dixon on board and everyone agreed that her presence had a beneficial effect on her husband. He never slept in the afternoon, unlike most Captains, but was in bed by 10.00 p.m. every night. He was a keen carpenter and worked away making furniture all day long. The port side of the lower bridge was rigged up with a proper carpenter's bench and canvas dodgers to keep wind and spray away from the area. His sleeping cabin was on the port side, so the ladder from the lower bridge to the navigating bridge was off limits except in exceptionally bad weather. I made a canvas hammock for Mrs. Dixon to lie in and watch her husband planing away under the shade of the awning and the days passed very peacefully.

Recalada lightship came in view on 25th September and I spent my 22nd birthday practising my Spanish on the Argentine pilot to the amazement of my shipmates and the pilot. Most seafarers on the Plate run never learnt the language beyond being able to ask for a pair of boscoes (canvas shoes) or a dozen eggs. However I picked up a working knowledge of Spanish, French and Malay over the years. When we got to Rosario Capt. Dixon called upon me to interpret several times over the first two days - some of this was beyond my capacity but I was able to 'flannel' my way through, and then began to improve my vocabulary over the next four weeks while discharging and loading. We discharged our coal at Swift's frigorifico and after three grimy days cleaning holds, shifted up to the grain berths and started to load both bulk and bagged grain. We were about ten days loading until the end of October when we said 'adios' to the Plate and headed for Londonderry for discharge. A relatively uneventful month or so at sea, ten days in Londonderry, then back to Barry Dock to load more coal for the Argentine or more correctly Uruguay via the Plate.

Mrs. Dixon left before we sailed and we were then watching our manners in case Capt. Dixon returned to his old form. However he remained benign and positively avuncular as we sailed towards Recalada. Mind you it didn't stop him having his weekly roar and snort at the Third Mate. This time our destination was Fray Bentos and as in *Sandsend* they worked day and night discharging. So back to my nocturnal watch but this time it was different as our Second Mate was transferred to another Headlam tramp, the *Stakesby*. I was on pretty good terms with Capt. Dixon and he promoted me to Second Mate after a little homily on the duties and requirements of the position e.g. raising and lowering of flags. Just before sailing for Rosario to load grain he called me up and presented me with a handfull of pesos much to my amazement. He then told me that the coal receivers always pay overtime to the ship's officers, this time it was a sum equivalent to about six pounds, a vast sum in those days even to a newly-promoted Second Mate on £13 per month. He was a real expert at Charter Party interpretation and fought for every cent to which we were entitled, and from time to time little envelopes were given 'for services rendered'.

We loaded various grains in Rosario then down to Buenos Aires to top up as the Martin Garcia Bar was particularly low at that time. The Bar is upriver from Buenos Aires where the rivers Uruguay and Parana converge to form the start of the broad estuary known as the Plate. The depth over the Bar rises and falls with great rapidity, as we were to discover some months later, and it commands great respect and caution from pilots and regular traders. We had a pleasant four days in Buenos Aires, two nights at the Mission and two other good nights drinking in town. Capt. Dixon rarely went ashore and would always allow you to the opportunity to go. On 8th February,1937 we sailed from no. 4 Dock with the prospect of another thirty or more days at sea, and being short-handed were on watch and watch. Capt. Dixon always appeared at 7.00 a.m. and relieved whoever was on watch to get cleaned up before breakfast. It seemed a long trip, actually only 33 days which was normal, and the last three days up the Channel and across the North Sea were hectic and so we were glad to tie up in Amsterdam. There was no inward or outward lanes, no radar, a much larger fishing fleet and you steered by 'the seat of your pants'.

Mrs. Dixon and Mrs. Richardson, the Chief's wife, joined us at Amsterdam and sweetness and light were all around. From there we threaded our way down the Channel and up to Cardiff where we paid off on 23rd March,1937. We went straight under the coal tips and were covered in dust before we had time to count our 'pay off' money. We had also been paid two months 'short hand money' so the Mate and I received ten pounds each over and above our normal pay. During our absence in foreign parts several changes had taken place in the maritime industry and a lot more ships were on the move. It had become mandatory to carry a galley boy and a cabin boy when the crew numbers exceeded 24, so two young hopefuls joined us from Whitby. Another new regulation was that shipowners now had to supply bedding, sheets, blankets and towels to all Deck and Engineer officers. We reckoned that members of the Chamber of Shipping were having apoplexy and coronaries over these new expenses. However there was an interim period during which the officers could be paid an extra six shillings/month to supply their own. As we were already geared up to supply our own, the extra money came in very handy and saved the tramp companies a relatively large capital outlay. Freight rates were up and cargoes in good supply so we wasted no tears over shipowners' cries of poverty.

In Cardiff we loaded coal once more for Fray Bentos and the beginning of April saw us locking out of Cardiff and down the Bristol Channel into the broad bosom of the Atlantic. We were welcomed on our arrival by the citizens of the town as the coronation of King George VI and Queen Elizabeth took place during our stay and all work stopped as it was a British-owned company. An 'asado' or barbeque followed and the air was alive with toasts 'Viva Georgi' and 'Viva Lizabet' from their loyal subjects and several dozen Uruguayan citizens over a two day period. When all of the coal had gone, the holds were cleaned and we sailed further up the Uruguay river to the Argentine side and berthed at a small port caled Concepcion del Uruguay. There we loaded the first cargo of bulk linseed ever to be shipped out of the Argentine or anywhere else for that matter. Linseed in bulk tends to move very rapidly and once on the move runs like water, so a ship could very easily be put in an unstable condition in a very short time. We discovered this when we were three-quarters loaded and the ship had a barely perceptible list of a quarter of a degree. Twenty minutes later the list was five degrees and increasing rapidly, so we quickly brought all of the stevedores back to trim the linseed back to the high side and pour in more to bring her upright - it was a very close shave indeed !

Apparently tests had been carried out to prove the feasibility of carrying linseed in bulk but nobody had allowed for a stoppage of work when the ship had a list, no matter how slight.   There followed a high level conference with the management of the local grain Board, and as none of these spoke English I had to interpret. Eventually it was sorted out that we would carry on with the bulk but all of the main holds had to be finished off with layers of bagged linseed and nos. 2 and 3 'tween decks only had bagged cargo. In the event this worked out very well but we kept a sharp eye on the clinometer for the slightest suspicion of a list. We battened down hatches and departed for Montreal.

Approaching the Martin Garcia Bar about 2.00 p.m. I was on watch with Capt. Dixon and the pilot when a thick fog rolled in blotting out all of the marks and buoys. The Old Man dispatched me to the fo'c'stle to drop anchor, and off I went like a startled stag while he rang 'Full astern' and pilot said a brace of Hail Mary's. Down went the anchor but we were already aground forward, and the current carried the stern round and this too grounded. So there we were straddling the main channel aground at both ends. We couldn't see anything even if we had been afloat but this was a most undignified and dangerous position. The river level was dropping and the ship being fully loaded, there was the possibility of her breaking her back. Sparks was sending out warning messages to all other ships but Capt. Dixon was as cool as a cucumber. He merely remarked that this was the third time he had been aground here but never at both ends before, successfully blocking the channel for both inward and outward bound ships. The air started to hum with messages to and from the Buenos Aires port authorities, Lloyd's surveyors, our agents and other ships. The fog soon lifted to reveal three ships anchored to the south of us, waiting to proceed up river but fortunately no loaded ships trying to get out.

Later that night a small tug arrived with various officials on board but it was obvious nothing could be done until the river started to rise. Fortunately it had stopped falling and the weather remained calm. We kept sounding bilges all night but the ship showed no signs of strain and all seemed well. Next morning it was calm and sunny but there was no change in the river level so we went about our routine duties until just before noon when a big Lloyd Brasiliero ship *Alegrete* came up the river. She was in ballast and obviously thought her draught was shallow enough to pass round our stern. About 200 metres away she took a tremendous sheer to starboard, dropped both her anchors, then with a screech of riven metal ploughed into our starboard side, almost demolishing the galley in the process. Bill Rigden, the cook, in response to our shouts, realised something was wrong and shot out of the galley just before the impact. Fortunately the point of impact was on the transverse bulkhead between nos. 3 & 4 holds and this minimised the damage. There was a three metre gap extending from the galley down through the main deck to about four metres below the waterline. In addition the starboard after lifeboat on the top of the galley was dislodged half way towards the mainmast. A certain amount of shouting and gesticulating went on and *Alegrete* reversed her engines, trying to withdraw from the gap but she was securely locked to our main deck plates and stiffeners as her cast iron plates had shattered and were 'hooked' by the stiffeners.

The next four hours were confusing and exciting to say the least, *Alegrete* dropped a rope ladder from her fo'c'stle head and down came a very agitated Brazilian Captain and a very agitated pilot, both full of profuse apologies. Capt. Dixon and our pilot remained calm, their attitude being we're stuck and helpless as the two balls suspended from our rigging indicated. Eventually things calmed down, Capt. Dixon handed his Brazilian counterpart the usual 'Note of Protest' holding him responsible for the whole mess and we then had a belated lunch. The galley stove was clear of the gaping role in the galley so we didn't miss our steak and kidney pies ! Sparks was filling the air with morse code and signals flew thick and fast.

Several more attempts were made by *Alegrete* to free herself but to no avail so we settled down for the night, keeping the bilges sounded every half hour but not a drop came in much to our relief. Capt. Dixon sent me aboard *Alegrete* early in the evening to inspect his chart and get an English translation of their report roughed out but there seemed no satisfactory explanation why their ship had taken such a sheer and ploughed into us. She had possibly run into a mound of mud and canoned off into us. They were a friendly crowd, a lot of them cadets who seemed more interested in improving the performance of their two 'marimba' bands than in improving their skill as navigators. On the following morning the Buenos Aires port captain, Lloyd's surveyors and various officials arrived by tug. After more discussions the tug secured to the stern of *Alegrete* at 11.00 a.m. and the combined efforts of tug and ship going full astern were sufficient to break the locked steel and cast iron. Once more came the screech of riven metal and *Alegrete* was free and bowling down the river to Buenos Aires.

Glaisdale didn't even shudder as the uninvited guest departed and we were alone, stranded and far from home. Stages were slung over the side and we were able to make a closer inspection of the damage but no water seemed to be entering the hull. Arrangements had be made for tugs, divers and salvage equipment to come out the next day but the vagaries of the Plate altered the picture. We were sounding the bilges and the river depth regularly but there was no change until about 2.00 p.m. when the river depth suddenly started to increase. Calling Capt. Dixon and the pilot, I kept on sounding the river and sure enough the water was getting deeper and within an hour *Glaisdale* was free of the mud and swinging to her anchor - cheers all round !

A rapid consultation followed and it was decided it was 'Buenos Aires or bust' and away we went, sounding the bilges continuously and praying that nothing would come 'unstuck'. We need not have worried as by 10.00 p.m. we were safely berthed in Buenos Aires and invaded by hordes of port officials and the press. Colourful accounts of the incident appeared in several Spanish language papers and the two local English language newspapers, the B. A. Herald and The Standard. It was decided to discharge the linseed from no. 4 hold which would have the effect of tipping the ship by the head and bringing the hold out of the water. Lloyd's had worked out that the stresses imposed were acceptable so two days later all of the damaged area was out of the water. The dock in which we were moored was accessible to the public and everyday we had an audience, some being quite regular attenders. Work went on round the clock and it soon became apparent why Glaisdale hadn't taken in any water. The linseed round the hole had congealed with the first entry of the water and formed, in effect, a giant 'linseed poultice', stopping any further water from entering the ship. This aroused considerable interest so it was decided to let the local press have this fascinating snippet of information. This appealed to the various editors and once more we hit the headlines.

Soon the necessary amount of linseed was removed from no. 4 hold and welders, platers and rivetters set to and repaired the damaged hull, inside plating, stringers and strengthening pieces. The whole operation of discharging, repairing and reloading took over two weeks and we had a relatively easy time. Naturally, Lloyd's and the P. & I. Club insurers were grateful for the large amount of money we had saved them, and Capt. Dixon took good care that they expressed their gratitude in a concrete manner. From time to time the three Mates would receive little envelopes 'for services rendered' i.e. overtime on cargo discharge - all perfectly legal and above board. The Mate and I had three or four magnificent mixed grills at the old London Grill, now gone, in Calle Florida.

So in July,1937 we said goodbye to our many friends in Buenos Aires and resumed our interrupted voyage to Montreal. A peaceful and uneventful voyage, calling at St. John's (NF) for bunkers, then up the St. Lawrence to Montreal. Capt. Houd was still our 'choice' pilot and he guided us safely to our discharge berth. Montreal in early August turned on delightful weather and the stevedores were as hospitable as ever. Lloyd's surveyors were very interested in our temporary repairs which had held up well on the voyage, and the outturn on the linseed was most satisfactory as only 25 tons had been lost.

Our shifting boards were already in position but despite this we were invaded by hordes of carpenters who ensured that they came up to Canadian standards. This involved the driving in of dozens of six-inch nails into anything remotely resembling wood, and would add at least a day to the dismantling process. I wasn't particularly perturbed as I had my time in for my First Mate's certificate and would be leaving on arrival in the U. K. Although discharge was quite slow, the loading was the usual day's flurry and late August found us slipping down the St. Lawrence in perfect summer weather. We changed pilots at Quebec with the Chateau Frontenac standing high and regal on the Heights of Abraham, always a beautiful sight. Dropping the seaward pilot at Father Point we cruised north of Anticosti Island and through Belle Isle Strait, enjoying the scenery and the small amount of passing traffic. We had good weather all the way home and even the English Channel proved kind with no fogs or summer gales at any time.

Our cargo of wheat was destined for one of Spiller's flour mills in the heart of London Dockland and it was quite a thrill to come up the Thames and see the variety and size of British shipping. It was a panorama of houseflags, funnels and masts - Ellerman Lines, Blue Funnel Line, New Zealand Shipping Co. Ltd, Port Line, British India, P. & O., Royal Mail Line, T. & J. Harrison, Brocklebank and many more all resplendent in their company colours. Looking back it was a time when British shipping under the 'Red Duster' was at its peak, the Depression was over and our ships were moving all over the world. The forlorn ranks of laid-up tramps around British ports had been thinning out rapidly as commerce, fuelled in part by the Spanish Civil War, brought most ships out of idleness. Captain 'Potato' Jones and Jack Billmeir figured prominently in the news as 'blockade runners' whilst the Royal Navy manfully carried out it's thankless task of preserving British neutrality and protecting our Merchant Navy. Little did most seafarers think that in two short years the horrors of war would engulf us all.

On that sunny September day as we moved slowly through the Docks, the sights and sounds of the shipping occupied most of my thoughts. I paid off for the last time from a Headlam tramp and after a mildly riotous farewell party was on board the night train to the north. *Glaisdale* was the best and happiest ship to date, and I saw her once more many years later loading coal on the Tyne as *Sondica* under the Liberian flag and looking much as all tramps look when loading coal. Her lines were unmistakable and the Blue Cross of Headlam's could be distinguished on her funnel outlined in welding. It was still possible to decipher her original name, cut into the steelwork at bow and stern.

TANKER TRAINING

I was to do one more dry-cargo tramping voyage to the Plate before I switched to tankers. This time it was on the Sunderland tramp *Thistlebrae* owned by the Albyn Line of Allan, Black & Co. Ltd. The salary of fifteen pounds per month seemed like a small fortune to me. All bedding and linen etc were supplied and they even paid my fare and expenses to join. I just couldn't believe my good fortune and grabbed it with both hands. *Thistlebrae* was an 8500 dwt shelter deck ship with a raised fo'c'stle and had 'tween decks throughout and was quite modern. She had very good accomodation amidships and even a refrigerator for storing the meat, a big plus in my estimation. She had the unusual feature of three bridges, the upper or flying bridge only being used in extreme conditions of trim in the Suez or Panama Canals. Capt. Harold Meek lived on the lower bridge, as did Sparks, whilst the three Mates and Chief Steward lived on the main deck level. There was a big dining saloon, used only by the Captain whilst the Mates and Sparks had a separate, comfortable messroom nearby. The four engineers and the two deck apprentices lived further aft, grouped around the engine room with their own messrooms, bathrooms etc.

The crew of *Thistlebrae* lived aft in four berth cabins which was a distinct advance over old fo'c'stles with all the sailors in one room and all the firemen in another. They had separate messrooms and were well housed by the standards of the day. I was amazed at the available manpower as I was used to the economical manning of Headlams. The crew were a mixed bag with about five from Southern Ireland, including the Bosun and the rest came from all over Britain. Without any shadow of a doubt they were the best and happiest white crew I ever sailed with, and that's saying something as in my twenty years at sea I was lucky in having good crews. The Mate was Charlie Brown from my home town of South Shields whom I had known all my life, and he was five years older than me and had much more experience. The Third Mate was George Palfreyman from Sunderland, Sparks was a plump, jolly Irishman from Dublin and we were to prove an excellent team.

We sailed from the Tyne in December,1937 to load coal at Cardiff and expected to be back home in about three and a half months. Our cargo was destined for the Central Argentine Railway at their main depot of Villa Constitution, some forty miles down the Plate from Rosario. We picked up the pilot at Recalada in mid-February,1938 and two days later berthed at our destination. I was able to be a sort of tourist guide to my shipmates as they were not regular Plate traders and stressed the 'horrors' of the Martin Garcia Bar. A somewhat rosier picture was painted of the other bars in Buenos Aires and the Argentine. After ten days discharging at Vila we moved out into the roadstead and anchored, holds were cleaned, shifting boards erected and we awaited our next cargo.

However the Argentine grain harvest had failed and we spent five months at anchor at Villa Constitution. The available grain was given to scheduled cargo ships, the arrivals and sailings of which were well advertised in advance. This was known as 'loading on the berth' and a shipper would then know that his parcel of grain would sail on the date specified for the port or ports declared. The tramps were left out in the cold, as Blue Star Line, Houlders, Hamburg America Line, Louis Dreyfus and several others took what was available. Gradually the roadsteads of Buenos Aires, Rosario, Villa Constitution and San Nicholas filled up with idle tramp ships. British flag ships predominated but there was a couple of Jugoslavs and several Greek tramps all anchored forlornly. The owners of several tramps despatched them elsewhere in ballast but a lot hung on, including our own, hoping for the best. For a First Mate and a Chief Engineer it was a heaven sent opportunity to get maintenance work done and the deck crew were soon over the side chipping, scraping and painting with the firemen down below overhauling the main engine and auxiliaries. After a couple of days Charlie Brown suggested the three Mates attack the bridge and burn off the paint which had accumulated over the years. Sparks joined us too as he was bored, and we started on the first Monday after leaving the berth.

We soon discovered that all the woodwork was high grade teak, instead of the usual pine so day after day we scraped with gusto, then using sand and canvas, brought all of the woodwork back to it's original beautiful graining. We spent several months on this job and when it was oiled and varnished we regarded it as a work of art. None of us went ashore during the next six weeks except the Old Man to get the news from the agents, collect mail and order fresh stores. Our owners were far sighted and allowed us to buy paint and other stores even though they were much more costly than in Britain. The whole ship was scaled and painted both inside and out and was in a much better condition than an ordinary docking would have left her. After six weeks the arrival of the warship *Scarborough* showing the flag brought a little excitement, and the Senior Officers were invited to various functions on the warship and ashore. It seemed as good a time as any to have a run ashore so the Old Man arranged for launches to transport us all to and from shore. It cost about two shillings each but we felt it was worth the money as we all had a good time at the cabarets, bars and eating places.

One weekend we went up to Rosario, about an hour and a quarter away by bus, and this was taken up with enthusiasm. Our weekend forays became part of our lives and were extremely amusing in the bars on Saturday nights, followed by a few Sundays at the local racecourse. There were dozens of British seamen doing this as we were joined by many other crews including that of *Tymeric*, an Andrew Weir tramp. The long five month period of waiting became eventually rather boring and frustrating, despite our weekend frivolities and the maintenance work on ship, but at least my Spanish was becoming very fluent. We noted several smart new German motor ships coming and going, little knowing that they were designed to become commerce raiders in eighteen months time. Some ships left, seeking new cargoes elsewhere, and new ones came including several Headlam tramps, and there was a succession of meetings with old friends and shipmates.

In was mid-August,1938 before we finally loaded a mixed cargo of fifteen different parcels of wheat, maize, linseed, sharps, bran, middlings, oats and a few other unusual grains for Oslo, Gothenburg and Stockholm. We sailed in mid-August 1938 and bunkers were taken at Dakar. Oslo and Gothenburg were beautiful and the lovely late summer weather in the Baltic made for very interesting sailing. Stockholm was gorgeous and the work in port was not too arduous, finishing at 5.00 p.m. every day with a half day off on Saturday and Sunday. The stevedore supervisors were very kind to us and we had some enjoyable nights ashore with them. The same two supervisors worked both Gothenburg and Stockholm so we had good continuity and lots of laughs.

Early October, 1938 found us entering the Tyne some ten months after we had set off on our one round voyage and we berthed at Smith's Dock Co. Ltd at North Shields for a quick bottom scrape and paint. Our combined maintenance efforts during the long, boring period at anchor had paid off, and resulted in voyage repairs being practically zero, and only underwater surfaces required attention, much to the owner's delight. Unfortunately I had to go into hospital for the removal of a grumbling appendix. When I came out of hospital I had five weeks convalescence and the doctor refused to pass me fit until mid December. There were one or two Third Mate's jobs going but I wasn't keen on dropping back down the ladder if I could help it. I most certainly would have stayed in tramps, but for some time I had been considering trying oil tankers and knew I would have to start again as Third Mate but the tanker allowance would help to reduce the loss of income.

Tanker personnel were regarded with mild suspicion by the rank and file of the Merchant Navy, it being thought that the long voyages and short times in port tended to make them a bit odd. Quite erroneous, I hasten to add, as I was about to spend ten years in tankers and a further twenty-three years in the oil industry as a pilot/loading master for five years and eighteen as a Marine Superintendent for Shell. It started when I was offered a job as Third Mate of the steam tanker *Kennebec* run by the Anglo-American Oil Co. Ltd, the British marine arm of the American oil giant Esso and now called Exxon. I was to join at Modewheel on the Manchester Ship Canal on 30th December,1938. I still had to complete twelve months sea time to sit for my Master's certificate and figured that if tankers were not my forte, I could get out of them when I came ashore to go to school for Master. I had seen several smart-looking tankers of the British Tanker Co. Ltd of BP, known as B. T. C. or 'Better Times Coming', and of the Anglo-Saxon Petroleum Co. Ltd of Shell, during their refits on the Tyne and was expecting my ship *Kennebec* to be somewhat similar. I got a bit of a shock, standing on the dock at Modewheel to see, through the fog, this elderly dowager of a vessel with funnel amidships coming sedately alongside. I though tankers had their funnels aft !

This one was a WW1 standard tanker originally called *War Mogul*, and dozens had been built to the design but carried only 'low flash' cargoes such as heavy fuel and diesel oil. She had been acquired by the Anglo-American Oil Co. Ltd from the Government at the end of the war, and for the next twenty years had run across the Atlantic to load at Aruba or in the U. S.A., rarely being away more than two months and thus was a popular ship with the crew. Some had been in her for several years and if they completed two years service they were granted six weeks paid leave, a rarity then. It certainly ensured a steady and reliable crew, especially as their quarters in the poop had been designed for double the number and were extremely roomy and comfortable. Chippy was also the pumpman and had been in her for ten years and his cabin was a veritable home from home. He had over the years scrounged wood at various refits and panelled the entire room out. Chintz covers on the settee, matching curtains over the portholes and bunk space gave the whole cabin the air of a comfortable bed-sitter as I was soon to discover.

Capt. John Instone had been on leave and was waiting to rejoin and I met him in the agent's office on the dockside. A very affable gentlemen I thought, and indeed found him to be a thoroughly good type and an excellent shipmaster. No sooner was the gangway down then several off-duty crew members swarmed ashore and we were almost trampled underfoot. Eventually I found the guy I was relieving and was initiated into the business of taking ullages, temperatures and gravities, after which he departed and I was more or less left to find my own way around. By this time it was 3.00 p.m. and a cheerful youth accosted me and announced in a broad Ulster accent, that it was 'smoko' and the afternoon tea was in the saloon and would I hurry along as it was his turn to have a night off. I grabbed my tea, noting happily that there was an ample supply of sweet biscuits, then started to explore the ship. She had discharged part cargo at Glasgow and only had about 4,000 tonnes for Modewheel so this meant sailing at daylight - hence the run ashore. I briefly met the Mate, Mr. Poppleton, who had been Master whilst the Captain had been on leave, and Bill Broughton the Second Mate, then suddenly I was alone. Capt. Instone apeared as I was having my solitary tea in the saloon, wished me goodnight, and said 'If there's anything you wish to know ask Chippy' and disappeared.

I was like Coleridge's 'Ancient Mariner' but admittedly not on a wide, wide sea but on a dark, fog shrouded Manchester dockside apparently in charge of an 8,500 dwt tanker ! I had never been on a tanker before in my life and could scarcely believe it. However I was not alone and nonplussed very long before in came Chippy, wearing his pumpman's hat to give me a crash course in tanker operations and practices. A cheerful, competent character who hailed from Jarrow, he soon filled me in on the details and then asked anxiously if I could cook. I admitted to a certain skill in 'fast food' and seemed very relieved. Although cooking was not part of the First Mate's course at the Marine School, it obviously stood high on Chippy's list of priorities. I was then instructed as to what was going on, what to put in the log, shown the pumps in the engine room then a quick run round the deck valves. When this was completed, Chippy handed me a five pound note and told me to go to the nearest pub and get half a bottle of Scotch and three flagons of Brown Ale. I was a bit dubious about leaving the ship remembering my *Sandsend* experience, but Chippy assured me it was quite normal and anyway the previous Mate was still aboard - although he was not taking any interest as he had signed off that afternoon. It was a dark, foggy night and nothing moved in the Canal, Chippy was running the cargo operations so I made myself useful and shot off to the pub, returning laden like a St. Bernard in search of lost travellers.

There was considerable activity from about 7.30 p.m. and I was even allowed to open and shut a few valves under the supervision of Chippy and the Able Seaman on watch, who was his assistant. Things settled down by 9.00 p.m. and Chippy announced that supper was next on the agenda. He led me to the galley where I found an assortment of steaks, sausages, chops, eggs and bacon in sufficient quantities to feed the entire ship's company. Inspired by a generous slug of Scotch, chased by a glass of brown ale, I soon had two large plates of food flanked by crisp fried bread which I bore in triumph to Chippy's cabin where he had already set the table. It met with his approval and was washed down with a couple of beakers of brown ale. The appearance of Chippy's assistant indicated that a further flurry of activity was in the offing and it was well after midnight when we adjourned for a mug of tea and I was told to sleep until required, leaving the rest to the experts. I retired to what seemed the tiniest cabin in the Merchant Navy and slept until 6.00 a.m. when Chippy shook me and presented me with a mug of tea, announcing that ballast would soon be finished and we would be ready to sail at 8.00 a.m. Outside nothing stirred, the powerful decklights were hardly visible and there was an aura of calm around the entire foggy area.

As instructed, I called the Old Man at 7.00 a.m. and gradually people came from out of their cabins and a form of life emerged. I was in the saloon at prompt 8.00 a.m. as I was hungry and was served breakfast by the Chief Steward himself, Mr. Handley. He consistently dropped his aspirates, and was a large and imposing personality with a noble mane of white hair - a character in his own right ! He had been in Transatlantic liners for many years referring to them as the 'big boats' but promotion had been rare and he had opted for smaller vessels where honour and glory as Chief Steward outweighed the smaller financial reward - that was his story! He was good at his job and we fed very well so Mr. Handley (without the 'H') was a very popular member of the crew.

Around noon the fog cleared and we got under way, moving slowly down the Canal but after an hour or two the fog returned so we tied up at Partington - the last of our sea-going activities for 1938. Being New Year's Eve we went ashore to the local pubs to sample the brew and have a bit of a 'knees up' with the natives. It was a pretty hilarious evening, and we took supplies back on board to continue the party. The traditional sixteen bells were rung at midnight and little did I realise on the first day of 1939 that I would be in and around the oil industry for the rest of my life !

We remained shrouded in fog at dawn and it lifted sufficiently at midday for us to proceed. Once clear of Liverpool Bar Light we sailed down the Irish Sea and I was able to take stock of what I had let myself in for. The old *Kennebec* was a fairly basic ship, oil-fired triple-expansion steam engine amidships, abaft the bridge. There were three sets of cargo tanks forward and two sets aft. She had a centre line bulkhead running through the cargo section so there were virtually ten tanks with two big cargo pumps situated at the after end of the engine room. The second day out, old Poppleton collapsed on the bridge with stomach ulcers, and Bill Broughton and I had to go on watch which neither of us found too pleasing. The Old Man took a few watches and we put a brave face on it as the Mate was really ill. We were bound for Aruba in the West Indies and had a good run, and as soon as we were clear of the west of Ireland we started tank cleaning. It was all done by hand washing with hoses and brooms by the crew who were issued with overalls and seaboots for the job. A modern day conservationist would have had a blue fit but we pumped all of the tank washings straight into the sea and left a black trail of fuel oil half-way across the Atlantic. This was quite normal practice as there were no rules or regulations to prevent it. Oddly enough I can never recall encountering another tanker's washings although we all took roughly the same route. However pumping of oil soon became restricted with the outbreak of war as nobody wanted to leave a signpost for a lurking U-boat.

In the meantime I continued my career in this World War I relic, off duty we mainly slept or played darts with the Engineers and that was more or less our social life. Bill, the Second Mate, was much older than me and had been First Mate in his previous ship. However when his leave had finished only the job of Second Mate on *Kennebec* was available - take it or leave it - and being married with a couple of kids he took it but wasn't too happy with the deal. He had been First Mate with Andrew Weir & Co. Ltd who ran the 'mosquito' fleet as it was known bringing crude oil from Venezuela to Aruba. Esso bought the entire fleet and took over all the Deck and Engineer officers, merging them with their own fleet. There seemed no security of tenure, from which I gathered I wouldn't be staying too long.

We were in Aruba, loaded and out in 24 hours and had time for no more than two beers at the fine Marine Club as we were on watch and watch. So off we trundled bound for London and the Tyne where we were due to dry-dock. The Mate was taken to hospital in London but there was no sign of any additional help so we quickly left for the Tyne, still watch and watch. The ship settled on the blocks of Palmer's dry-dock at Jarrow some 34 days after signing on and we paid off. Capt. Instone asked Bill and I to stand by during the 18 day dry-docking and promised Bill the job of First Mate and me Second Mate when we signed on again. We didn't have to live on the ship but would be paid a 'lodging allowance', and as we both lived within a bus ride, we accepted and had a relaxing time which we felt was well earned. We got no extra pay for working watch and watch all of January and were a bit resentful about that. We signed on Articles on 22nd February,1939 and off we went on my third voyage from the Tyne in nine years, and I didn't know it then but I would be back soon afterwards.

Everyone else signed on again with the exception of Jock Reid the new Third Mate, and off we wallowed to Caripito in Venezuela this time. Two weeks later we were in the midst of the Venezuelan jungle loading diesel and fuel oil for Baltimore. Caripito takes first prize for 'Hicksville' as there is nothing there except a loading jetty and jungle. Being an elderly lady, the rivets of *Kennebec* were beginning to feel the strain and those on the diesel tanks began to weep copiously. Chippy and a couple of helpers were kept extremely busy during the loading, working over the side on stages, caulking leaking rivets. Rarely have I seen such unusual activities during loading operations but the crew had caulking mallets and chisels all laid out before we were alongside. Another unusual feature of Caripito was the berthing procedure - the river is about two ship's lengths wide so the procedure is to berth on the last of the flood tide. You steam past the berth then go hard to starboard and stick the ship's bow into the jungle which grows over the river. The current swings the stern round, you go astern and back off, then steam gently to the berth and tie up - saving a fortune on tugs !

We steamed up to Baltimore in good weather and picked up the pilot off Chesapeake Bay early in the evening. I came on watch at midnight and joined the Old Man and pilot on the bridge. They were both out on the port wing, watching a motor ship, laden with timber, running on a course identical with ours but about 400 metres off the port bow. We were overtaking so by International regulations we were obliged to keep clear. He was steering very erratically whereas we, being deep-draughted, had to keep in the channel, which had sandbanks on both sides. We gave several long blasts on the whistle to warn him of our approach but he took no notice so we proceeded to pass him. Suddenly he veered hard to starboard and steamed right under our bow. We rang full astern but it was too late and soon there was a dull thud as he crossed our bow and was hit amidships. We had been moving very slowly but even so 8,500 tons of oil can give a nasty dent and spoil the rest of your day ! Fortunately nobody was injured and he didn't sink and one of the tugs waiting for us towed him to a nearby dock while we went to our berth.

Later in the day we witnessed a scene straight from a Wild West movie. A gentleman wearing a Stetson came aboard, flashed a big silver star and announced he was the Sheriff and he had come to serve a writ on the ship from the owner of the timber barge. 'I'm supposed to nail this to the mast' he said, but we pointed out the masts were made of steel and he replied 'O.K., I'll nail it to the Captain's door' whereupon he produced a large revolver from inside his coat and used the butt to hammer the nails into the door, thus securing the writ which announced that in the name of the President, Congress etc he was 'seizing the steamer *Kennebec* until the owners had been compensated etc' - all great wild west stuff and made our day.

We phoned the Old Man at the agent's office and soon a battery of Esso legal eagles descended upon us and the writ was removed. We were all quizzed and made several statutory declarations covering the event. The Old Man, lookout, helmsman and myself were really given the old third degree and came out of it pure as white as we heard no more about it. We were finished by 7.00 p.m. and I went ashore to sample the pleasures of Baltimore. Jock Reid had agreed to stand the middle watch for me so I didn't feel too restricted. As it turned out it was a fairly quiet evening but I did get a chance to sample the famous 'Chicken Maryland' and have a couple of drinks of the local brew. My first legitimate drinks in the U. S. A. as my previous visits had been in prohibition days. We left the next afternoon, bound for Aruba to take on a load of fuel oil for London and Avonmouth.

We were regaled with a constant stream of radio commercials as we ran down the Eastern Seaboard as well as various types of music and soap operas. Some of the commercials became passwords for soap and the 'Lux' show produced a succession of would-be singers and entertainers whilst other soap operas assailed our ears the whole time. Everyone except me seemed to have a radio and we were kept up to date with the news courtesy of 'Exlax - the chocolate laxative' the virtues of which were extolled by some obnoxious brat saying 'Gee - I can't believe it's a laxative'. As some wag remarked 'Don't worry brother, you will soon' - all very entertaining and livened up our day.

In Aruba we had the usual 24 hour turn round which barely gave us time to go ashore, grab a couple of beers at the Marine Club, do some shopping and get back on watch. The tanker berths in Aruba were downwind from the refinery and the stench of sulphur was constantly in our nostrils, causing most of us to suffer violent headaches. Venezuealan crude was noted for it's heavy sulphur content and we got more than our fair share. Esso had some ships under the Panamanian flag owned by the Panama Transport Co. Inc., these were newish motor ships of 15,000 dwt built in Germany and manned by German crews which were replaced by American and Scandinavian crews in the months following the outbreak of war. Loading finished we headed through the Windward Passage and were on our way to London and Avonmouth. During the trip Bill, Jock and I speculated on our future once we reached home, and Bill reckoned that the previous Mate would rejoin and we would revert to our previous ranks and Jock would get his marching orders. It was agreed that if this happened we would quit and let Anglo-American get on with it ! In retrospect Bill was a bit of a stirrer and his own attitude was partly responsible for his lack of progress. Nevertheless he persuaded me to quit but Jock was not quite so sure.

We were in Purfleet less than 24 hours then off, round to Avonmouth but there was no news of any crew changes. However as we moved into Avonmouth locks there was Poppleton the Mate on the dockside waiting to rejoin. We only had about 3,000 tonnes left and expected to sail that evening. 'I told you so' said Bill after we had moored and sure enough the Old Man gave us the bad news. I could see he wasn't too pleased at the way this was sprung upon us, and we changed articles on board so as soon as Bill and I signed off we collected our pay and we refused to sign on again in the lower ranks. There were a couple of heavies calling themselves 'Marine Superintendents' down from the Head Office in London and they were quite rude about our decision. We pointed out that we had fulfilled our contract for the voyage and that was that ! Later I was taken to one side and told to hang about and I would get my old job back. Politely but firmly I refused and was treated to a tirade on loyalty to which I replied that it was a two-way street. Furthermore it was suggested that they all see a good taxidermist as I was going home. I demanded and got a ticket home which brought one of them to the verge of apoplexy.

When the sound and fury had died down and the aggravation had finished, the Old Man had me up and gave me a drink along with an excellent reference. He told me he thought I had done the right thing, and I had nothing against him or the Mate - it was just the half-hearted way the office had handled it. In fact I got on extremely well with both of them and I'm pleased to say that both the Old Man and the Mate survived when *Kennebec* was torpedoed and sunk on 8th September,1939 and both lived to a ripe old age.

JOINING SHELL AND WAR SERVICE 1939 - 1940

I had always considered that St. Helen's Court, home of the Anglo-Saxon Petroleum Co. Ltd - the English marine arm of the Royal Dutch Shell Group, to be a bit beyond my reach and indeed until 1939 they had only accepted men with Master's certificates - but times were a-changing. Somewhere high up in the Government, pressure was being brought to bear on Shell to transfer a number of tankers from the Dutch to the British flag. The founder of Shell, Marcus Samuel would have been delighted had he been alive ! None of this was generally known but it was an obvious precaution in view of the International situation. The Marine Staff department of Anglo-Saxon found it almost impossible to recruit staff for these tankers. The crews were all Chinese and they presented no problem for the time being, as they were used to servicing on either British or Dutch flag ships.

Recruiting around eleven Masters, thirty three Deck officers and eighty eight Engineer officers is very difficult at any time. After a riotous farewell to the crew of *Kennebec* in Bristol, I had got the train to London and a room at a boarding house for the night. Next morning, blissfully unaware of the reason for all of the frenzied activity going on around me, I stepped into the foyer of Anglo-Saxon to request directions to St. Helen's restaurant and was invited immediately to the Staff department. Rather bewildered, I got my cup of tea there and then - and was interviewed by a very courteous gentleman called Mr. Garland after producing my union card. He listened sympathetically to my story of why I had left Esso and assured me no such nonsense went on in Anglo-Saxon and they had a permanent rank system. This turned out to be true - he couldn't promise me a job as Second Mate (or Second Officer as he called it) but was sure promotion would follow. He wasn't kidding and I told him I was going north on the night train and was ushered out with good wishes for a safe journey. I felt that he really meant it.

At home, I was on my Uncle Tom's doorstep at 7.00 a.m., Mother being away, and at 8.00 a.m. a letter arived from Anglo-Saxon saying, subject to a medical examination, they expected to appoint me to their fleet very shortly. I was duly examined, passed, then on 3rd May 1939 I received a letter from Capt. J. Wilson, appointing me Second Officer of the motor tanker *Cymbula* currently in dry-dock at Grayson, Rollo & Clover's at Birkenhead and I was to join on 5th May. The first shock was the salary, nineteen pounds per month plus one pound per month in lieu of overtime. Laughable now but a fortune then. The second shock was seeing *Cymbula* herself, only a year old, sitting on the blocks, freshly painted, this 12,000 dwt tanker seemed to me the most elegant maritime object I had seen and the memory remains with me still. On board I was staggered by the luxury of the accomodation and fittings, especially after the old *Kennebec*. My cabin seemed huge, with a six and a half foot settee, kneehole writing desk, roomy bunk which was extendable, washbasin with running water, chest of drawers and an electric fan. My eyes must have been popping out like Chapel hat pegs, I was really in a daze !

I took my letter of appointment to the Master, Capt. Arthur Clatworthy, who gave me a warm welcome and filled me in on the background to taking over the Dutch flag ships. *Cymbula* had just been taken over and all signs were in Dutch but that was rapidly being changed. Anglo-Saxon had always had their forms and stationery printed in both English and Dutch so there were no problems there. She was a nine tank ship with each tank having three compartments - port, centre and starboard. There was a pumproom between nos. 3 & 4 tanks and another between nos. 6 & 8 tanks with two cargo pumps in each pumproom. The cargo pipeline down below was a 'ring' system, running along the port side, across nos. 1 & 9 tanks then down the starboard side. Nos. 2 to 8 tanks had crossover lines from port to starboard which meant she was able to segregate several grades of cargo.

The Chief Officer was Tom Kirk, a jovial Irishman from County Claire. He had an Extra Master's certificate but like me was basically a dry-cargo man. His previous tanker experience had been six weeks as Third Officer of the *Trochus*, another Anglo-Saxon tanker so we weren't exactly what you could call experts on the job. The Dutch Third Officer, Willie van Gorkham, was retained as were the three Dutch Fifth Engineers. Tom and I spent the next three days assisted by Willie in climbing up and down tanks and pumprooms familiarising ourselves with the layout. The Chief Engineer was responsible for setting the bewildering array of valves in the pumproom but Tom and I paid a great deal attention to them just the same. The Chief Engineer was portly Jack Mann from West Hartlepool with twenty years or more service with Anglo-Saxon and was the only other 'regular' apart from the Master. Davey Davidson, the Second Engineer, had been with the company about four years but the rest of us were all 'new chums'. At first we were viewed with some trepidation by the Old Man and the Chief Engineer, but were able to prove ourselves, even though we had 'humble origins' from tramp steamers. Tom Kirk had been Master of one of the blockade runners during the Spanish Civil War but had opted for a more established and orthodox firm to pay him for his endeavours.

All of the crew were Chinese as was the custom in Anglo-Saxon, sailors were from Foochow, firemen from Canton, and the catering department from Hainan. The custom of having each department from a different region of China was allegedly a carry over from the 1920s and early 1930s when piracy on the China Coast was not uncommon. The entire crew of a ship would be from the same area and the pirates were able to man and ultimately take over the whole ship - hijacking is nothing new ! We were about eight days more in dry-dock hands, during which time the after end of the stern boat deck was strengthened to take a 4.7 " gun. They also built a platform at the forward end of the poop on the port side to take a 12 pounder anti-aircraft gun. Considering Mr. Chamberlain's 'Peace in our time !' this seemed rather a waste of the taxpayer's money and the phrase entered the 'famous last words' category four months later. There was plenty of work to keep us occupied but we got a few nights ashore to sample the delights of such well-known hostelries as the 'Bear's Paw' and 'Ma Edgerton's' so life wasn't boring. Around midday on 15th

May,1939 we said farewell to Merseyside and headed down river and into the Irish Sea bound for Curacao in the Dutch West Indies.

Cymbula was propelled by an 8-cylinder Werkspoor diesel engine made in Amsterdam and cruised at a comfortable eleven knots. At that time the entire Anglo-Saxon fleet was diesel-driven and this was the fastest I had ever travelled on a ship and I quite enjoyed the sensation. We settled into a regular routine and I soon discovered what the one pound per month in lieu of overtime was in aid of. All Anglo-Saxon tankers had chart folios covering the whole world, literally hundreds of charts as I recall. It was the Second Mate, officially the Navigator, who had to keep these up to date from Admiralty Notices to Mariners and U. S. A. Coastguard publications. This took at least two hours a day, five days a week over and above normal watches, plus testing the fire-fighting equipment every week. The safety standards were very high and the Old Man took good care that they were maintained, so I was fully occupied.

The Old Man ran the 'bar' such as it was, ordered our drinks from the suppliers then issued each officer with his order. Gordon's Gin was three shillings a bottle and Scotch five shillings a bottle but hardly anyone drank beer at sea as it was considered too expensive at eight pence per can. Willie van Gorkham the Third Officer and I had a routine pink gin every night before dinner. All staff were issued with a bottle of beer every Sunday, courtesy of Anglo-Saxon, a custom of which we approved most heartily. The food was superb and I really felt I had come into another type of marine world.

Eleven days from Liverpool we entered the narrow channel leading to the huge inner harbour of Willemstad, capital of Curacao, and tied up to one of the many oil loading berths. The refinery processed Venezuelan crude brought in by shallow draft tankers known as 'mosquito' boats. There were always several of them coming and going like suburban trains plus a dozen or so assorted deep-sea tankers. So out went the ballast and in came the fuel oil cargo then three days later we sailed 'Land's End for Orders'. There didn't seem to be the near panic haste I had experienced in Aruba when I was in *Kennebec* and I had time to get into Willemstad to do some shopping and visit the excellent Club to which all Shell marine staff automatically became members. The Club was just outside the refinery gates and regular free transport was available from ship to Club - very handy and too handy sometimes as the war years were to prove.

We eventually arrived in Rotterdam on company instructions on 14th June, 1939 and discharged our cargo of crude oil. Once more a gentlemanly but efficient atmosphere, and during our stay I wangled a day off and guided by one of our Dutch Fifth Engineers took the train to Scheveningen, the delightful seaside resort near The Hague. Glorious sunny weather, lots of people enjoying themselves and a really colourful scene. There was a long pier stretching out into the North Sea but I passed that one up as I reckoned I could take a look at the sea at any old time. People in general and the girls in particular were much more interesting at the sandy end of the pier. So my guide Harmon and I wandered around taking in the scene, having the odd cup of coffee and joining in a dance at one of the beachside cafes.

I did not return to Scheveningen until July,1946 by which time the pier had been demolished during the German occupation of the war but it was still a lively town. Harmon and I got back about 8.00 p.m. just in time for me to grab some sleep before going on watch at midnight. Earlier in the voyage Willie had suggested that we buy our gin in bulk at Rotterdam and bottle it ourselves as required. I was rather staggered by the size of the enormous wicker-bound carboy which came on board but it worked out at about one shilling per bottle and lasted well into the following year.

After discharging the fuel oil we loaded a cargo of fresh water for Curacao where fresh water was always a problem and away we went. Another fine weather passage across to Curacao where we discharged our fresh water and then loaded fuel oil for Buenos Aires - back to the old stamping ground ! In July,1939 we weaved our way in to the South Dock at Buenos Aires and it felt a bit like coming home to me. Willie was a very keen daytime shoregoer whereas I preferred the night life, so we swapped watches so that each did an eight hour stretch, to our mutual satisfaction.

In 1939 the pipelines in Buenos Aires were very small, so to our delight, the discharge was very slow ! As a consequence we had three nights in town and I was able to take the boys around all of the better 'watering holes', seeing old acquaintances and generally having a ball. John Mann, the Chief Engineer, was particularly impressed with my tourist guide capabilities allied to my grasp of the language. Capt. Clatworthy and Tom Kirk, the Chief Officer, rarely went ashore and Tom was very good at doing a bit of extra watch time if necessary. However all good things come to an end and after a very enjoyable four days we sailed away. Little did I know that forty years would elapse before I saw Buenos Aires again.

Our destination was Long Beach in California and we were to go via the Magellan Strait which wasn't too thrilling a prospect as we would not take a pilot but go we must ! It was winter in those latitudes which oddly enough is the best time of the year as fogs are more prevalent in summer. Radar was still in it's infancy, as were gyro compasses so we had to rely on the old 'lead, log and lookout'. We had radio direction finder but there weren't too many shore stations down in Patagonia so there was a fair bit of 'By guess and by God' in our approach to the eastern entrance to the Magellan Strait. Overcast weather had rendered our sights of the sun a bit dodgy so we edged in slowly, sounding all of the time, towards the lighthouse named 'Dungeness'. Twice we moved in without sighting the lighthouse then back to sea again as the soundings indicated the water to be shallowing. Suddenly the skies cleared, the visibility improved and we found ourselves where we pretty well ought to be.

Dungeness lighthouse stood out against the dark mountains like a stick of Blackpool rock, red and white stripes shining in the sun. We soon had our bearings, rang down for full speed and were off into the main channel. Normally the main engine exhausts through the boiler combustion chamber and provides enough steam for the auxiliaries, but if engine manoeuvres are required the boiler is heated by fuel and the engines exhaust to the atmosphere. All eight cylinders exhausting up the funnel caused quite a noise, and one can safely say they bellowed ! The tide was in our favour and we must have been doing fifteen knots as we passed Punta Arenas and the meat packing factories. We stopped there briefly for clearance then off through the narrow winding channels towards the Pacific. It was the first time any of us had been through the Straits and it is quite an experience. Some 310 miles of narrow channels with bleak, dark mountains rising steeply from the water's edge to snow covered peaks.

There is no place to anchor as the water is too deep and very few places where a ship could be turned around in an emergency. In parts one felt one could toss a biscuit ashore, and there were no lights, buoys or beacons if visibility closed down. Fortunately there was a full moon which reduced the dangers of night navigation but even so it was a bit hair-raising. The bellow of the engine exhausts echoed back from the almost vertical mountain sides, creating a cacophony which almost deafened us and one could not describe this as a 'fun cruise'. It was a relief when morning came and we could at least admire the scenery even though it was bitterly cold.

Naturally the Old Man never left the bridge and it must have been quite a strain for him. As humble Second Officer I also heaved a sigh of relief when we emerged into the Pacific during the following afternoon and left Cape Pillar astern. Ten minutes after leaving it was impossible to see where the entrance was - just a continuous line of high, forbidding cliffs with huge Pacific rollers breaking at the base and sending columns of spray high into the air ! The Pacific Steam Navigation Co. Ltd ships which had traded here since the turn of the century probably took it in their stride, but we thought it was 'more like removing meat from a hungry lion'.

I found the Pacific to be very little different from my nine years of sailing the North and South Atlantic, so we settled down to some good navigation and obedience to the Old Man's orders. We were a very happy ship and I got on well with Capt. Clatworthy, who was a strict disciplinarian as well as very human. Both he and John Mann, the Chief Engineer, had over twenty years service each with Anglo-Saxon, and I got a great deal of pleasure and knowledge from listening to the pair of them reminiscing about the 'old days' - good, bad or indifferent. The Old Man had a good radio and kept us informed of the news as did the Radio Officer, Terence Mahoney, who was from Cork where his wife owned a pub. We reckoned he was crazy going to sea but he swore he would get out if war was declared.

Some time late in August,1939 we arrived at Long Beach adjacent to Los Angeles, and moored at a berth next to a factory rejoicing in the name of the 'Seven Mule Team Borax Manufacturing Company'. Somewhere beyond it lay a Shell installation but we never saw it, and loaded diesel for a place called Quepos in Costa Rica and topped up with fuel for Balboa on the Panama Canal. Long Beach was quite a town with oil wells lining the main street, and it seemed everyone had his own oil well in the backyard - an illusion we were assured ! War was almost inevitable at this time and we were warned not to talk about the ship or her movements.

I acquired my first radio in Los Angeles and then felt no end of a well-informed lad. When loading was completed it was the custom for all three Deck officers to calculate the amount loaded independently, then compare results. Tom Kirk had just acquired a primitive form of calculator but he was a brilliant mathematician, and unfortunately the confounded machine threw us all into confusion as it kept offering up different answers. As a result it was nearly midnight when we finally proved the machine wrong, so Tom decided to buy Willie and I a gin or two. We finished up having several, and Tom and I turned out for 'stations' leaving harbour at 6.00 a.m. with a very severe hangover. Willie had left early so wasn't too bad, and fortunately we were coasting so there was no need of morning 'sights' so we were able to sleep until lunch time.

The following morning I came off watch at 4.00 a.m. and after doing the mandatory 'rounds' of the ship, switched on the radio and discovered we were at war. I rushed back to the bridge and informed Tom and we decided there was not much we could do at 4.30 a.m. but we had better tell the Old Man in any case. He opened the sealed letter from the Admiralty which every ship carried and found there was no point in doing anything until morning so off I went to bed until the Steward called me with a cup of tea, after which I staggered up to the bridge for sights.

We carried a large supply of paint, known as Admiralty Gray, to be used in the event of war. All our deckhouses were white, with white painted bows, stern and top plate amidships so we were a very visible prescence. Immediately after breakfast all hands started on the job of painting all deckhouses, rails, bulwarks, funnel, masts, lifeboats, decks and overside plates gray. Lookouts were posted in the rarely-used 'Crow's Nest' up the foremast as we weren't sure if U-boats had already taken up station in the Pacific. They certainly were in the Atlantic and several commerce raiders and supply ships had been positioned, but we had no real way of knowing what the true situation was and were not taking any chances.

In two days our lovely white and buff paintwork had disappeared under dull Admiralty gray and that was the only colour we were to see for the next six years. Eventually we found Quepos, a brand new port just constructed for the export of bananas and we were not impressed. A long jetty sticking out into the Pacific with a perpetual swell, al least four feet high rolling in - charming ! There was a pilot who seemed impressed with our size then six hours later we moored, about twenty feet out from the jetty, held off by our starboard anchor forward and two ropes to buoys on our starboard quarter. Several heavy coir springs held us from moving longitudinally and a stirrup suspended from our derrick and a shore crane carried the cargo hose.

The ship was pitching and ranging up and down the wharf the whole time, and we were in a state of apprehension in case any of the mooring ropes broke and caused a chain reaction. We had a horde of burly American construction engineers coming on board to look at this 'limey' man of war. It was impossible to put a gangway out and those of us who were courageous or stupid enough to go ashore had to embark in a small launch and be ferried out to a little harbour further inshore. There was nothing much except the construction camp, five million mosquitoes and a pile of machinery to load bananas, but as yet there were none of the latter so we missed out on any free offers. The construction gang told us of San Juan, the capital of Costa Rica and it's many beautiful senoritas but there was no way of getting there in under two days.

Our main priority was to get the cargo out and clear off as we felt that at Balboa we were not so likely to be hurled on the rocks by a Pacific roller, and having got rid of their diesel we departed the next afternoon to everyone's relief. Some two days later Panama was a welcome change, although buzzing with rumours of U-boats waiting out in the Caribbean for Allied ships and German spies crawling all over Panama including Balboa where we berthed. I traced Ferdie Diaz, an old school pal of mine, and he and his family took me out to see the sights on both nights we were there and I really had a ball.

We sailed back again to Long Beach for another load of fuel, once more bound for Panama, with the U.S.A. making noises about neutrality and not supplying anything to either side. Nonetheless our forehold was filled with some form of patent fuel in drums consigned to Curacao, and when we got there it had been sold by the Dutch to Shell U.K. We got new Bills of lading and it was eventually discharged at Hull in November,1939.

A rather unpleasant surprise awaited us at Curacao in that we were to clean all tanks from fuel oil and convert to carrying motor gasoline, not a popular product to haul around the ocean in wartime. This involved a rather primitive and time-consuming procedure. First a perforated 40 gallon drum of caustic soda was lashed to the access ladder, halfway down the tank. Into this drum was inserted a steam hose, through which live steam blew the caustic soda all over the tank sides and hopefully the top. The tank was then washed for three hours, requiring relays of men as holding a hose spraying hot water is strictly a short-term occupation. The Americans had Butterworth tank-washing machines but the virtues of these machines had not yet reached the Technical Department of Shell. The whole operation would have turned the hair of a modern Safety Officer white in two days.

After about a week of this round-the-clock effort, the normal procedure was to load a tankful of kerosene and pump it from tank to tank and remove any remaining traces of fuel oil from corners, underneath beams etc. As war had been declared, it was decided to cut out this last operation and load the mogas direct. We informed the installation of the dangers of contamination but our protests were ignored and in came the mogas. The tests came out quite satisfactory but we pointed out we had yet to cross the Atlantic and the ship's motion would slop the mogas all over the tanks. Still no reaction from shore except to get on with it and shut up, and touching a respectful forelock we did just that. We delivered some 12,000 tonnes of straw-coloured mogas and the Manager of the receiving installation nearly had apoplexy - however this was only one of many procedures that were abandoned for the duration of the war.

Early October,1939 saw us leaving Curacao and heading up to Halifax (NS) to join a U. K. bound convoy. At that stage the U-boats had not ventured as far west as the U.S.A. but just the same we were extremely vigilant and kept as close as possible to the coast. Arriving at Halifax, we anchored in the inner harbour of Bedford Basin where dozens of Allied and neutral ships were at anchor. The Royal

Canadian Navy took us under their wing and supplied us with a 4.7" gun, two Lee Enfield rifles and ammunition. A barge brought out the gun and it was hoisted up and bolted on to the mounting which had been installed in the Mersey. It fitted perfectly to everyone's surprise, and ammunition lockers were welded around the gun and we were in business. The gun crew was at least seven men and here came a problem, as we only had thirteen Europeans aboard of which at least seven were required on the bridge, radio room and engine room during any action. Willie and the Dutch Fifth Engineers could hardly be expected to breach their neutrality although they all volunteered in case of necessity. Eventually we fooled the Bosun and two sailors into volunteering with the offer of sixpence per day for their services, with the Deck and Engineer officers doing it for the honour and glory. So the R. C. Navy took us all ashore every day for three days and gave us a 'crash' course in gunnery, and as I already done this the previous year I was appointed Gunnery Officer which suited me fine. The jobs rotated amonst the crew so that each was familiar with each function of gunlayer, projectile loader, cordite loader, rammer etc. Humping 4.7" shells on a cold winter's day in Halifax (NS) is not my idea of fun and games as I much preferred barking out the orders.

We had lunch in the Naval Officer's Mess each day and were the object of much attention from dozens of newly-recruited officers who had never even seen the sea before and regarded us as genuine war heroes. As it happened, they proved fine seamen and provided splendid escort groups for the North Atlantic convoys and elsewhere. We always had a couple of pink gins before lunch to give us strength for the afternoon's drills and were told to sign chits - no money changed hands in the Officer's Mess. Those chits never caught up with us, and I take this opportunity to thank the Royal Canadian Navy for six large pink gins. The guncrew were ready and willing when we put to sea for test firing. The Lt. Cmdr.(Ordinance) who was in charge of this practice disappeared when the time came to fire the gun, allegedly to check the movement of the mountings below deck.

As the gun was Japanese and made in 1917, I was apprehensive but kept fear to myself, and a 44 gallon drum was put over the side, a projectile and cordite stuffed in the gun and when the range was 500 yards I slapped the firing pad after which there was an ernormous bang ! We were about fifty yards off target but at least the shell came out of the right end. When we came to reload for a second shot, the Bosun, who was the rammer had disappeared so I rammed in the cordite myself, upped the range and off went projectile no. 2 - only thirty yards off the target this time ! In all we fired five shells and though we didn't hit the target we felt confident that we could scare anyone on the receiving end. Later we found the Bosun in his cabin muttering 'Me sailorman, me no gunman, too muchee bang bang !', and the Lt. Cmdr. emerged after the second shot having found the gun was not going to blow itself to pieces and announced our below deck mountings were in splendid shape ! As he had come through the previous war with a whole skin, I couldn't blame him for being suspicious of a 22 year-old Japanese gun, manned by a bunch of amateurs.

So suitably armed to resist the enemy, we sailed from Halifax (NS) early in November,1939 as part of the second convoy of the war. Our escort was an intermediate Cunard liner taken over as an Armed Merchant Cruiser. (A.M.C.), and I forget her name but she stood out like a mother duck in the middle of the convoy, with her heavily loaded ducklings around her. In retrospect it seemed ridiculous but we felt relatively safe with the A. M. C. in our middle. There followed a hair-raising few hours while we sorted ourselves out and formed up into seven columns each with about six ships per column. Keeping station was quite a performance, using sextants to measure distances between ships but eventually order prevailed and we soon became quite proficient at station-keeping. We zig-zagged all the way across the Atlantic with a few alarms but no casualties and steamed up the English Channel in mid-November. The Germans had just started laying the new magnetic mines, causing considerable mayhem amongst Allied shipping as we were to find out. We were now formed into two lines, with destroyers and minesweepers and motor launches as escort.

Our orders were to discharge at Hull and just before picking up the pilot to take us up the North Sea we received a signal saying 'All ships bound north of the Thames were to anchor at the Downs'. By this time we were in single file of about 25 ships, approaching the Downs where there were a dozen or so neutrals having passed contraband control, waiting their chance to tail on the end of the convoy and get some measure of protection in the event of attack. Neutrality meant very little from the outset. When the pilot boarded he was all for going straight on to Hull but the Old Man showed him the signal and we pulled out of the line and anchored. A Japanese ship *Terikuni Maru* was hovering around waiting to go to London so he slipped smartly into our slot - fifteen minutes we heard a loud explosion and he had fallen victim to a magnetic mine.

By this time we had received orders to proceed to Southend and anchor. Light fog had closed in and we seemed to be the only ship moving as we crept cautiously along. Suddenly a small patrol boat skippered by a young Sub. R.N.V.R. appeared out of the mist to hail 'I say - you're approaching mines - you had better stop and anchor' then disappeared. So anchor we did until half an hour later another patrol boat also R.N.V.R. came up and told us we were in the middle of a magnetic minefield, and to up anchor and steer for the Main Channel. This happened twice more before we reached Southend anchorage in a state of nervous collapse, and we anchored just on dusk at 4.00 p.m. - we had been up since 6.00 a.m. and had hardly left the bridge in that time. Willie and I treated ourselves to a double ration of Dutch gin before dinner that night. Floating around minefields on top of 11,000 tonnes of motor gasoline is not exactly a rest cure !

We spent a few days at anchor off Southend then the Old Man and I went ashore for the northbound convoy conference and we were to sail that afternoon. Once more lady luck had her eye on us because when we came to heave up the anchor, the windlass seized up and wouldn't budge. Seeing the gap in line where we should have been, the *Spaandam* of Holland America Line took our place and shortly afterwards collected a magnetic mine near the Sunk Light Vessel - fortunately without loss of life. When we finally sailed, two days later, the convoy was an 8 knot one and that was our critical speed where we vibrated horribly so we had to vary the speed a fraction above or below the 8 knots. A most exhausting exercise which kept us on the hop the whole time - to complicate matters further most of the convoy were coal-burning colliers. They had to clean fires every four hours causing a reduction in speed as the steam pressure dropped in the boilers, we thus altered engine revolutions the whole time.

Approaching the Newarp Light Vessel about 2.00 a.m. on 29th November,1939 the ship astern of us pulled out of line and passed us, then slid into the gap between us and the next ahead. She was the 14 knot *Ionian* of Ellermans and had only been in position about ten minutes when she blew up on a magnetic mine. The concussion seemed to lift us bodily out of the water as she was only about 200 yards away - fortunately thee was no loss of life but she sank eventually. She was bound like us for Hull, carrying general cargo including 15 tonnes of currants - Humberside was thus short of currants in their Christmas puddings that year.

Very thankfully we tied up at Killingholme jetty downstream from Hull and started discharge. As predicted the Installation Manager was rather cross at receiving straw-coloured gasoline but we referred him to his mates in Curacao, our letters of protest and left it at that. Apart from being sideswiped by a ship of the South American Saint Line which nearly gave us heart failure, the discharge was uneventful and we gas-freed in the river before proceeding to the Tyne where we berthed at Smith's Dock Co. Ltd, North Shields.

In addition to voyage repairs, bottom scrape and paint, we were fitted with pill boxes on the bridge wings for refuge when under machine gun attack. Plastic armour was fitted around the wheelhouse and radio room, and a 12 pounder anti-aircraft gun was bolted to the mounting on the poop and a retired Royal Marine, George Hancock, and two merchant seamen gunners joined. Our three neutral Dutch engineers were repatriated as was Willie the Dutch Third Officer. Terence Mahoney departed to help his wife run an Irish pub and Arthur (Jumbo) Alexander joined us as Third Officer - an Anglo-Saxon apprentice so he was well versed in tanker procedures.

We had a pleasant three weeks in dockyard hands and I was able to get home most nights and saw a lot of my girlfriend Celia, which pleased both of us. Unfortunately we sailed on Christmas Eve which put a damper on things and we spent Christmas in another 8 knot convoy of mainly colliers of 2,000 dwt. We stood out like a sore thumb in this period of the 'phoney war' and there was little air or U-boat activity - not that there weren't heart-stopping moments keeping to the narrow swept channel with strong tidal currents sweeping across the channel. We formed up in convoy off the Isle of Wight and left on New Year's Eve for Constantza in Roumania via Gibraltar. A relatively uneventful passage and after Gibraltar we were on our own and relished the warmer weather for a few days. Coming up to the Greek islands en route to Istanbul and the Bosphorus entrance, we were challenged one night but it proved to be a British A. M. C. and our heartbeats returned to normal.

At Constantza it was as cold as charity with snow everywhere. A very slow loading rate about 100 tons/hour, so there was ample time to sample the night clubs and restaurants. As there was a very favourable exchange rate we were able to take full advantage of the facilities and I bought a beautiful Leica camera at one-tenth of English prices. Capt. Clatworthy was a really keen photographer and so infectious was his enthusiasm that he got me quite involved. A curious situation arose as we were on one side of a pier loading petrol for the U. K., and the other side was a Russian tanker discharging lubricating oil into rail tank cars bound for Germany. Russia and Roumania were neutral at this time so there was nothing really unusual in this, however returning one night from a foray we were full of drink and patriotism in roughly equal proportions.

Seeing the spectacle of all this lube oil going to the enemy was too much for our alcohol-fuelled minds, and once on board *Cymbula* we changed into dark working gear, pinched some sand from the fire boxes intending to pour it down the loading plugs of the tank cars. This would bring the German war machine to a shuddering halt, thanks to the heroic efforts of us British sailors. We made so much noise getting on to the tank cars we woke up the Roumanian Army guards who fired shots in our general direction. Fortunately one of our crew had the sense to pull the switch and put out our deck lights so we were able to scurry back on board before the Army arrived. Fortunately the Constantza Port Authority were not over generous with the lighting, so the Army could no see us properly if at all, so we protested with injured innocence and went back to bed - so much for our valiant effort to sabotage the war machine of the Third Reich !

We sailed unescorted with a full cargo to Gibraltar where we had four days waiting for the convoy to assemble. Jumbo Alexander and I had a run ashore and foolishly went to the races, lost all of our money of course, then found that the launch service back to the ship had been cancelled due to bad weather. Luckily we had been chatting to some naval ratings from one of the destroyers whilst at the races and we ran into them just after leaving the wharf. We in 'civvies' were considered ideal to act as lookouts for their 'black market' gambling activities to warn of the approach of Army M. P.s or naval shore patrols. They had a fairly successful night and our share enabled us to hire a couple of beds at the Salvation Army Hostel, thus obviating the indignity of being apprehended on a vagrancy charge. The weather had cleared up during the night and we were able to get back on board by breakfast time to a very chilly reception from the Old Man and Tom Kirk who had shared the anchor watches during the night. The Old Man then cancelled all further shore leave due to the unreliable weather so we were held responsible for this by our shipmates. We were not exactly popular but as we sailed the next day the situation was short-lived.

We were bound for Shellhaven on the Thames, and we were not very thrilled at the prospect of playing with magnetic mines again. However after a few bangs from depth charges and a couple of false alarms from air-raids, we tied up at Shellhaven and started to discharge our mogas. This time the colour was correct and we had no hassles with installation managers. Several of our Chinese crew were paid off for a variety of reasons, and we were left three men short of a full complement required by Government regulations. By this time the Board of Trade had been changed to the Ministry of War Transport (M.O.W.T.) but the rules remained the same and the men had to be replaced. Anglo-Saxon had no men officially available, but our ship's agent Tubby Wheatly from Davis & Newman reckoned he could find a few men given a ship's officer to assist him. The cargo was almost finished and the Old Man reckoned I could be spared, so Tubby and I set off into the gloom of a late February afternoon.

I was extremely pleased with this unorthodox expedition and the prospect of seeing a bit of London was an exciting change. It was old stuff to Tubby and he knew his way round better than a London cab driver. We disembarked at Fenchurch Street station about 5.00 p.m., Tubby led the way to the Three Nuns hotel where we booked two rooms, had a quick meal then off into the stygian darkness of a blacked-out, wartime London. We must have visited at least a dozen Chinese boarding houses where Chubby was greeted with enthusiasm by the landlords. We drank many little bowls of Chinese tea, talked incessantly but the deckhands had all vanished. Cooks, firemen, stewards and mess boys in profusion but never a deckhand in sight, however our luck changed at 1.00 a.m. when we found one lone sailor willing to accept the Shell 'shilling'. We also found two more who had been sailor's cooks and showed enough willingness to be promoted to sailor. It must be explained that the sailors and firemen had a cook and a boy for each department. We left our recruits in 'protective custody' and returned footsore and weary to the Three Nuns. The night porter, a friend of Tubby's from previous similar expeditions, had taken the precaution of having several bottles of Toby Ale available for the weary recruiters and these went down well with a couple of beef sandwiches. It was my first and only experience of 'press gang' activities and I really enjoyed it, as Tubby was a genius at persuading people to see things his way and it was most instructive to watch him at work. After distinguished war service later in submarines, he rose eventually to be a senior marketing manager with Shell.

We were aroused at 6.30 a.m. by the arrival of our transport and we left with our three recruits for Tilbury Shipping Office, pausing for breakfast on the way. The Old Man was waiting for us and after a lengthy argument with the Shipping Office bureaucrats, Tubby's inexorable logic prevailed, the recruits were signed on as sailors and we had our full complement. We sailed the next day in convoy, picking up ships from the Solent and the Bristol Channel, then on to Gibraltar without major incident. The convoy split up at Gibraltar and we proceeded solo through the Mediterranean once more to Constantza, where we were careful not to repeat our sabotage efforts and really enjoyed the night life. We had three days waiting for a berth and another four days loading so weren't exactly overworked.

We sailed back unescorted to Gibraltar, but from there on it was convoys, zig-zag courses and a series of alarms both from U-boats and air attack. Nevertheless we arrived safely at Avonmouth and discharged our cargo of mogas, and reloaded with 8,000 tonnes of aviation gasoline for R. A. F. Coastal Command at Plymouth. We reached there in early April, having been escorted from Avonmouth by an armed trawler flying the White Ensign, armed with two Lewis guns and a twelve pounder ! Anglo-Saxon had moved their head office to Plymouth on the outbreak of war, and a curious system prevailed there regarding tankers. We were moored to buoys and access to the shore was via a small boat operating on a pulley system. The ship was fully manned from 6.00 a.m. to 6.00 p.m. but after that all hands went ashore, leaving only one Deck and two Engineer officers, one quartermaster, one pumpman and one fireman on board. The slow discharge went on during the night but the six shipkeepers were going to be very busy in an emergency. However none arose and the rest of us were delighted to have a couple of nights ashore and sample the nightlife of Plymouth. It didn't compare to Constantza as it was all blacked-out but was still pleasant.

No. 10 Squadron of the Royal Australian Air Force were stationed there, having come over to the U. K. to take delivery of Sunderland flying boats. When war broke out they remained there, carrying out anti-U boat patrols over the Bay of Biscay and out into the Atlantic. We met several of the aircrew in their distinctive dark blue R.A.A.F. uniforms at the hotel next door to our boarding house. An extremely cheery bunch of lads and one of them was a Flt. Lt. W. M. Garring, whom I next met at the United Services Club in Geelong sixteen years later. By that time he was Air Commodore in charge of Point Cook R.A.A.F. station in Victoria. We eventually departed on a lovely Spring day in a convoy to Gibraltar, then on our own to Constantza for more gasoline. A week there and we headed back to Gibraltar for another convoy which left on 27th May,1940. By this time the German armies were advancing everywhere in Europe, although we were not really aware of the gravity of the situation and the coming significance of Dunkirk.

We were detached from the convoy and anchored in Brest roads on 3rd June but nobody seemed to know why we were there. No shore leave was allowed but we took the opportunity to drop the lifeboats and give everyone a bit of experience of rowing - it was a time when such skills could be of great value ! After a couple of days we were told to proceed south to the River Gironde where once more we were the orphans of the storm. We watched a couple of American liners sail past, evacuating their citizens, fished unsuccessfully, then two days later were ordered up to Donges, a small port on the Loire river about 24 km above St. Nazaire.

Arriving at St. Nazaire on a glorious sunny Sunday the 9th June,1940, it was difficult to believe war was so close or that we were to have a rather traumatic departure. The good citizens of St. Nazaire were promenading along the waterfront and there was an amorous young couple on the seaward side of the lighthouse having a cuddle at the end of the Mole. They were invisible from shore but in full view of *Cymbula* some 150 yards away, and every pair of binoculars was in full use. We had picked up the Anglo-Saxon padre Rev. Derek Tyrie in Gibraltar and he was nonplussed at the attention given to the lighthouse at first, but he soon caught on ! A great man was our Derek and worth his weight in gold during the days to follow. This light relief over, we had a gin and tonic and went to lunch.

We moved up to Donges the next morning and berthed at the installation and started pumping our cargo ashore. There followed seven days of varying degrees of excitement, fear, hope, joy and just about every other emotion. This has all been covered in a separate story and proved a saga in itself, suffice to say that after air raids every night we left Donges on 17th June with the Panzer columns of the Wehrmacht just up the road, spearheading what we felt might be an attempt to appropriate *Cymbula* for their own devices. On the way out we picked up the last 241 survivors from the trooper *Lancastria*, which had been bombed and sunk with great loss of life an hour or so earlier. This created a somewhat crowded situation, coupled with a hefty demand on the Chief Steward's store of groceries. Nonetheless we made it to Plymouth where we only just managed to find a spot to anchor among the dozens of other ships - it had been a sort of 'ocean-going' Dunkirk.

Next day we landed all survivors including 24 stretcher cases, then started the job of cleaning up the ship. All of the survivors had been saturated with fuel oil when they came aboard and we had cleaned them off with kerosene and then hot soapy water. All of their soaked gear was piled up on the after deck and the whole area was a shambles. I now had sufficient sea time to sit for my Master's Certificate and my application for leave had been sent in two months previously. As Anglo-Saxon was now in Plymouth my relief was easily arranged and after an interview with Jerry Walters, the Chief of Staff under Capt. Jimmie Wilson, I bid farewell to my shipmates and another ship passed through my life.

Jumbo Alexander had his time in for First Mate so we travelled home together. The train was crammed with hundreds of survivors as the balance of the B. E. F. were lifted by deep-sea ships from St. Nazaire to Plymouth, and at every stop the locals turned out to give us tea, sandwiches and cakes and a real hero's welcome. So the end of June,1940 found me back in South Shields enrolled at the Marine School and reunited with my family and girlfriend. Some of my friends had been lost at sea but there was still a group of us who studied four nights a week until 9.00 p.m. then nipped off to the local pub for a couple of jars before closing time. My girlfriend Celia was a tremendous help, going over the 'Rules of the Road' in which you had to be word perfect, three times a week. By the time I felt ready for the examination she could almost have got the certificate herself.

During this time we had several unwelcome visits from the Luftwaffe and one bomb hit a house three doors from our own, and mother and I sheltering under the stairs thought ours was coming down. Fortunately the bomb fell in soft soil but caused a considerable crater which we gazed at in awe after the 'All Clear' had sounded. Fortunately nobody was injured but all were extremely shaken and several houses were damaged. The owner of the bombed house kept hens and they had become casualties but not necessarily from the Luftwaffe as there was a strong smell of chicken soup in the area for a couple of days afterwards. I felt ready in October,1940 to do battle with the examiners, and contrary to the opinion of post-war young Third Officers, they were not 'giving away' certificates. Quite the reverse as there was a surplus of both deck and engineer officers due to the mines and the activity of U-boats in the Atlantic and Western Approaches.

By October 20th,1940 I had convinced the examiners that I was a fit and proper person to command any ocean-going ship from the *Queen Mary* downwards. I got 87% for my written work but was given a real going-over in the orals by Capt. Dowdy, the Head Examiner. He was a hard man who didn't suffer fools gladly and I feel he was only just convinced and no more that I didn't come into the fool category. So there I was a Master Mariner and did my 'ritual' dance on the bar of the Queen's Head in Newcastle, flogged my Leica and bought a ring, so Celia and I became engaged - the world was my oyster !

During this time the BP tanker *British Officer* hit a mine and sank between the Tyne piers, and the big Norwegian liner *Oslofjord* was also mined and sank just off the South pier. Every house on the seafront was very badly shaken by both explosions, and caused some consternation among the Minesweeping Flotilla based at North Shields who had swept the channels a few hours earlier. These were the new acoustic mines which were activated by the noise of the ship's engines and propellers. Motor ships were the most susceptible, and this was cold comfort to Anglo-Saxon as all of our tankers were motor ships.

I duly informed Head Office who congratulated me but were in no position to offer me employment and said they would be in touch. It was obvious that a number of ships had been sunk but it was not in the national interest to let it be known. You had to complete two years service to be granted leave on pay and as I had only done 13 months and 20 days it was my bad luck. I went off and did a week's extra gunnery course and was drawing the dole, with several friends in the Minesweeping Flotilla, R.N.R and R.N.V.R officers, so at least I got my gin and tonic at duty-free prices.

WAR SERVICE 1940 - 1941

Normally obtaining a Master's Certificate in Anglo-Saxon meant a further year or two as Second Officer but time were a changing as early in December I received a telegram telling me to join the motor tanker *Opalia* at Swan Hunter's dry-dock at Wallsend as Chief Officer. I felt a mixture of elation and satisfaction - elation at getting a job and apprehension as to whether I had sufficient experience. Nevertheless I quickly got up to Wallsend to view my new posting and wasn't disappointed. *Opalia* was of 9,000 dwt some 3,000 tons smaller than *Cymbula* but similar in every respect as regards tanks, pipelines and accomodation. She had just been in dry-dock for repairs following bomb damage from a near miss whilst in convoy fromn London to Methil. The whole convoy had been subjected to a fairly heavy air raid and Opalia had been given special and unwelcome attention. Most of the East coast convoys were composed of colliers around the 2,000 dwt mark so the larger cargo ships and tankers were the prime targets for the glory seeking, trigger-happy Luftwaffe pilots for obvious reasons.

Opalia in this action was using her 12 pounder A. A. gun and in the general excitement and desire to defend her honour, loosed off a round at an approaching aircraft. Fortunately the shell was time-fused as the trainer was following the aircraft's movements when the gunnery officer hit the button. The shell went straight through the main topmast, continued its trajectory and burst right under the nose of the aircraft. Doubtless the pilot was upset by this hostile action and promptly dropped his stick of bombs, did a sharp turn to starboard and flew straight back to Germany. The bombs dropped about twenty yards from *Opalia* along her starboard side and the explosion lifted her bodily a couple of feet in the sea. In addition to smashing both standard and steering compasses, and putting out the lights in the engine room, the ship's entire upperworks and lifeboats were peppered with shrapnel and the steering gear went haywire. Fortunately nobody was injured which was quite miraculous and the steering gear was soon under control, but steering without a compass was pretty tricky and they put into the Tyne for repairs. I hadn't the faintest idea she was in port as wartime censorship was in force.

She was almost ready for sailing when the Captain fell ill and had to be hospitalised. Arthur Lodge, the Chief Officer and known as Oliver, was promoted to Captain and as I was only six miles away became temporary acting probationary Chief Officer. As often happens in these rush jobs, it was a further ten days before we actually sailed, and the enemy came over every night and dropped their mines. Dutifully our minesweepers went out and swept north to meet their colleagues from the Firth of Forth and south to meet those from Hartlepool. By the time they got back it was too dark for the convoy to sail as there was only about seven hours of daylight. Then around midmight the sirens would sound to herald the return of the enemy to lay mixed bags of acoustic, magnetic and orthodox mines. Life in the 'sweepers was more hectic and we were always glad to see them return with none missing. By this time we had moved downstream and were moored near the Fish Quay 'Trawler base' as the minesweeper flotilla H. Q. was known, ready to depart when the channels were clear. This day came on 17th December and, being a motor ship, we had to be towed out as the engines hadn't to start until we were well clear of the piers and into the swept channel. Chippy and I felt very alone and unwanted as we stood at our stations on the fo'c'stle head, complete with life jacket, breathing dense smoke from the leading steam tug. At the designated point, the engines were started and as no bang ensued we all breathed a collective sigh of relief and cast off the tug.

Our first stop was Grangemouth for bunkers, and going under the Forth bridge we were amazed to see what seemed to be the whole Grand Fleet at anchor. Closer inspection showed them to be big cargo ships, camouflaged with wood and canvas to look like battleships, cruisers and aircraft carriers to fool any high flying reconaissance planes - they certainly looked the part. Following a night out in Edinburgh we went off in convoy through the Pentland Firth and down the Minches to Oban which was a convoy assembly port. During the night of 23rd/24th December the Luftwaffe arrived with unwelcome Christmas presents in the form of high explosive bombs which badly damaged a cargo ship and sank a drifter. The Scandinavian cargo ship had a racehorse on board in a loose box as deck cargo, which took exception to the way things were going and kicked its way out of the box and swam ashore. It was found next day quietly nibbling the grass outside a local hotel - 'horse sense' seems to be the apt expression. Two days later we sailed out with a local escort then were taken over by two new corvettes and two former U. S. Coastguard cutters, with the Senior Officer Escort (S.O.E.) in an old 'V & W' class destroyer from the previous conflict.

We were a forty ship 8 knot convoy and this was quite a task for our watchdogs as the weather developed into a typical Western Ocean winter gale, and our hearts bled for those poor souls on the escorts as they seemed to be more under the water than on it. At 30 degrees west the convoy was dispersed and we proceeded independently while our escorts picked up an eastbound convoy. We zig-zagged our way to Curacao and soon picked up fine weather and sunshine. At that time there was not much U-boat activity west of 30 degrees but we kept our lifejackets on just the same. Two days later we were ordered into Bermuda where the Navy put us alongside the Vichy French tanker *Scheherazade* which had been captured as a war prize. The crew had been slapped into the local bastille with only an engineer, four shipkeepers and a cook on board. She was of 15,000 dwt but we were told to take as much of her cargo as possible. Anxious to load my first cargo as Chief Officer I repaired on board with Bud Watson our Second Officer to plan the operation. Unfortunately the Admiralty had got their lines crossed and she was loaded with heavy fuel oil which was heated by her heating coils. We in *Opalia* were not similarly fitted as we were a gasoline and light oils carrier. Considerable discussion followed during which Capt. Lodge showed a great deal of patience and after a sharp couple of signals to the Admiralty (copies to Shell) he won the day. So we sampled a bottle or two from the ample stock of wine of *Scheherazade* and sailed into the sunset and our original destination of Curacao. Still, it made a pleasant change in the routine and at least we got a couple of good nights' sleep.

We loaded at Bullenbai a few miles west of Willemstad and were in and out so fast we barely had time to scratch ourselves. By this time we had a coal-fired galley so all meals had to be cooked ashore. The reason for the coal-fired galley was that originally the oil tank for the galley was immediately behind the 4 " gun on the poop. One of the early casualties was *Telena* attacked by a U-boat off Spain on the surface, with the first shell hitting the galley fuel tank setting it alight so that the gun was unable to be used. The galley tanks were removed in the rest of the fleet and in went coal bunkers - a wise precaution but sometimes a source of annoyance and delay. Coal is in short supply at an oil refinery, and it took a long time before coal was available especially in the Pacific. So back we sailed to Bermuda, where we spent three days waiting for the convoy to assemble, and then we sailed for Loch Ewe.

We had the *Clea* another Anglo-Saxon tanker abeam to port most of the way but nearing the Western Approaches the weather deteriorated to such an extent that keeping station was impossible. The Commodore ordered the convoy to disperse and proceed independently. *Clea* was never seen again and was torpedoed and sunk by U 96 on 13th February,1941 with the loss of all hands. Eventually most of us got to Loch Ewe and anchored very thankfully. There followed an East coast convoy through the Pentlands to Methil where we formed another convoy to Shellhaven. We had several staff changes and lost our apprentice Denis English, and Second Officer Bud Watson who was due for leave. Denis had been in the ship a long time and knew where everything was and how lots of things should be done Anglo-Saxon fashion. He had four years service with the company to my one and had been a tremendous help to a brand new Chief Officer. His replacement was Paul Spencer, another splendid lad who had only two months seatime to qualify to sit for his Second Mate's certificate. Alan Nelson took over from Bud Watson, and we also got a new Chief Engineer, Arthur Morgan Evans but the team spirit remained.

Capt. Lodge had a vast experience of tanker life and was a splendid Master and a marvellous ship handler, and during the long hours on the bridge I had learnt a lot from him. He had been an Anglo-Saxon Master many years previously but had left to take a job ashore. This had ended, unfortunately, and Anglo-Saxon had got him a job with another outfit as there was no return to Shell pre-war, but the rules had been altered by the war and the rapid fleet expansion of 1939. He had done one voyage as Chief Officer of *Opalia* when the chance came to push him 'upstairs' and this opened the door to myself. By now the Dover Straits were virtually closed so all supplies for the East coast came in through the Pentlands to reach London, which the Germans continually announced was closed by radio. We discharged our cargo of mogas and avgas and lingered not a moment longer than was necessary at Shellhaven.

We sailed back to Loch Ewe via Methil and the Pentlands where we stayed several days awaiting convoy. Loch Ewe had almost replaced Oban as a convoy asembly port and it was a very wise policy, as it was difficult to reach on the surface and must have been almost impossible from the air. It seemed to be perpetually shrouded in fog, mist or rain and was surrounded by mountains, each looking exactly like the next one. There was good fishing and lots of sheep but we were not impressed, however in the course of fishing we honed up on our lifeboat handling skills and slept soundly at night. The time came to depart and we slid out of Loch Ewe in mist and light snow bound for Baltimore. The second morning out we were attacked by a Dornier which sneaked up from astern and sank *Benvorlich* of Ben Line and badly damaged two others. He flew right down the next line to us, machine-gunning all the way, just above the mastheads. As he came abeam I gave him a burst from our bridge wing Hotchkiss machine gun but I might as well have used a peashooter. The ship abeam of us was the tramp *Dan-y-Bryn* from Cardiff and our bullets probably did more damage to her than the Dornier, and we would have been better armed with an Oerlikon or Bofors gun. It was all over in seconds and our 12 pounder gun crew hadn't time to load as they had been at the 4 " anti-submarine gun when the plane approached.

The *Benvorlich* had a load of ammunition including 400 mines for Cape Town and burned fiercely for about five minutes then went up with a tremendous explosion which gave our eardrums a hammering even though we were at least two miles away by then. Our engine room ventilators were facing in the direction of the blast and Jack Dunleavy, the Second Engineer and his Fifth Engineer were standing between the ventilators and were both quite deaf for several hours afterwards. We all felt very sick as we were sure nobody colud have survived that lot. Some three years later I learned that about half the crew survived as they got two boats away as the ship sank by the head, and both boats were under the lee of the stern when the mines blew up and the blast went right over their heads. The convoy dispersed at 30 degrees west and we headed for Chesapeake Bay and up to Baltimore where we were treated as genuine war heroes.

We completed loading and waited two days for the convoy to Halifax (NS) so our Senior Sparks and I had a run ashore for a change of scenery and to do some shopping. We visited a night club and our 'limey' accents attracted some attention and we weren't allowed to pay for a drink or meal all night. We stayed in a hotel and the waiter, at breakfast, turned out to be a Geordie from my home town so we got a free breakfast too - Baltimore was very pro-British and we loved it ! Halifax had changed somewhat since my last visit in October,1939, and the town was now bulging at the seams with service personnel in April,1941. The Royal Canadian Navy administration and non-seagoing ratings used to parade up and down the main street called Barrington Street in the evening. There were no pubs but dozens of 'sly grog' houses which we avoided like the plague, but all our officers were made Honorary Members of the City Club and each was allocated a little locker in which to keep a bottle or two of his favourite tipple. The Stewards brought us soda, ginger ale or tonic, for which we paid and we able to have a drink in a very civiliosed manner. Our main target was of course shopping for clothing and food which were severely rationed in the U. K., and the merchants of Halifax did a roaring trade from the ships of the Allied convoys as thousands of ships passed through.

We were sent off in a ten knot 50 ship convoy to feed, cloth and fuel the beleaguered occupants of Britain, and were originally destined for London so we were on the northern flank of the convoy in order that when we reached the Western Approaches we could peel off with the Clyde-bound ships and then head up the Minches. We plodded along behind the motor tanker *Oilfield* of Huntings of Newcastle, which like ourselves was loaded with mogas and avgas. Immediately astern of us was *Port Hardy* of Port Line loaded with frozen meat, then behind her was the Norwegian Texaco tanker *Caledonia* loaded with lubricating oil. The day before we reached the N. W coast of Ireland we were met by the local escort and the Commodore signalled us a change of orders. We were to go to Swansea instead of London so we were directed to a position on the southern flank of the convoy. Capt. Lodge skilfully jockied us out of line, dropped back between columns to the stern of the convoy, increased revolutions and we roared across the back, then up to our designated station. In the calm sunny weather this took less than an hour and we were on station by noon and back to ten knots. So far, so good and we were all interested spectators on the bridge to this smart example of ship manoeuvring.

I came on watch at 4.00 p.m. on 28th April,1941 and had just nicely settled in when there came a series of loud explosions over on the northern side of the convoy right where we had been until that morning. To our horror *Oilfield* was one huge ball of flames and both *Port Hardy* and *Caledonia* had been hit and were sinking. We saw one of our sister tankers *Ensis* enveloped in smoke, but it was from *Oilfield* and soon *Ensis* emerged unscathed. Destroyers, corvettes and armed trawlers were dashing every where and depth charges were sending up huge columns of water. Although we didn't know it at the time the U-boat was severely damaged and was later sunk by R. A. F. Coastal Command. Amazingly the Second Officer and several Chinese crew escaped from *Oilfield* by sliding down ropes from the fo'c'stle head and they were picked up by a very courageous armed trawler skipper who steamed under the bows, picked them off the ropes then backed off smartly, but everyone else had been killed in the blast. We had lost one ship the previous day but this tragedy shook us all and the smoke from burning *Oilfield* was still visible three hours later. Tankers are not so easy to sink due to their many watertight compartments, especially in ballast, but when carrying gasoline or similar light oils they usually blow up and few, if any, personnel survive.

We reached Swansea a couple of days later and were very thankful to get rid of our mogas and avgas. We were there several days and Capt. Lodge gave me a couple of days leave so I took the night train north and spent a very uncomfortable night, punctuated by a couple of air raids which added to the discomfort. Trains were always packed in wartime with service personnel going on or coming off leave, all suitably armed with liquid refreshment, and we became quite resigned to the bombs. A joyful reunion with my fiancee and my family and three days of catching up with the local scene, finding out who was still alive, and the change was most soothing and enjoyable. During this time I ran into a friend who was a navigator in Coastal Command and learned of the fate of the U-boat which had wreaked such havoc on our convoy. The U-boat had been sunk and a special 48 hour pass was issued to the Catalina's aircrew.

Celia was able to wangle several days leave and come with me for a couple of days to Swansea, after which she went to London to visit her sister and was unlucky enough to be in London when the fire-bombing started but was unscathed on that occasion. We sailed next day for Milford Haven, then on to join a convoy from Liverpool and were escorted to 30 degrees west once more. During 1941 the Army formed the Maritime Anti Aircraft regiment for coastal voyages only, but soon their Lewis guns assisted the Navy gunners on deep-sea ships. After we dispersed we had a fright one night when a light cruiser challenged us. She was one of the units seeking the Scharnhorst and scared the living daylights out of us, we never found out who she was but presumed she was one of 'ours'.

In Curacao once more we had a quick turn round at Bullenbai then off to Bermuda for convoy with the usual load of mogas and avgas. During our stay in Bermuda, waiting for convoy to assemble, in came my old ship Cymbula. Alan Nelson our Second Officer had served in her briefly after I had left so we decided to lower the jolly boat and visit her. Tom Kirk was still Chief Officer and Jack Mann still Chief Engineer plus a few assorted juniors so we had a very happy and boisterous reunion, rowing back about 2.00 a.m. feeling very happy. We sailed in another ten knot convoy of about fifty ships and Capt. Lodge took the ship out himself. There was a shortage of pilots and the Commodore had asked those Masters with piloting skills to do their own piloting. It was quite an experience watching him jockeying the ship into position and reaching our proper position in convoy. The ship was supposed to be dry-docked at home and Celia and I had arranged to be married during that time. We had a reasonable crossing from Bermuda and arrived in Oban mid-July but there were no instructions about the docking. I was able to telephone Celia from Oban and tell her to get down to London, stay with her sister and I would arrange for us to get married by special licence when we arrived at Shellhaven.

We duly departed from Oban and had a trouble-free trip through the Pentland Firth to Methil, however from there the enemy tried everything in its power to stop my marriage. Firstly we had a summer gale, then U-boats, followed by several attacks by the Luftwaffe. Our 'ack-ack' boys had a spare 'strip' Lewis gun which I borrowed and I had this with me for two days, as I felt this was all very personal and took a poor view of the enemy's efforts to mess up my arrangements. After several angry exchanges of fire we emerged unscathed except that one night while changing course we had a minor colision with the ship abeam which had failed to notice the alteration of course. Sparks, both actual and verbal, flew everywhere but thankfully no real damage was done. It would have been most undignified to go up in flames from a collision with a friendly ship. Collisions were not infrequent on the East coast run due to the narrowness of the swept channels and the strong cross currents. We berthed safely at Shellhaven on 20th July, 1941 and having seen the cargo discharge started, I left Second Officer Alan Nelson and Chief Engineer Arthur Evans to do the rest and left for Blackheath to join my beloved.

Next day we all went up to town, Celia, her sister Bea and brother-in-law Mick, to what was to be a very busy day. We found out we could not be married in a registry office as it required 24 hours notice, so off we went to the sanctuary at Westminster Abbey where we obtained a special licence to marry at Greenwich Parish Church from the Archbishop's secretary. Meanwhile I had been in touch with Thomas Cook for rail tickets and a booking at the Wellington Hotel in Tunbridge Wells. The taxi driver seemed as enthusiastic as we were and eventually brought us back after four hours of frenzied activity. We contacted the Vicar and by 3.00 p.m. the knot was tied and we were man and wife - best thing that ever happened to me in my whole life. Things then went smoothly and we got the train to Tunbridge Wells and were welcomed at the Duke of Wellington, then went for a walk in the nearby woods. It was a balmy summer evening and the war was a million miles away as we sipped a Pimm's at a nearby pub and made plans for the future.

We came back to earth on Tuesday as we travelled back to *Opalia* and work, arriving in time for dinner that evening and the crew had presents for us and a party in the cabin of Jack Dunleavy, the Second Engineer. A really delightful evening with laughter and songs, sweetness and light all the way, and as a bonus we learnt that we were to go into dry-dock in the Tyne after all. Celia and I would get a proper honeymoon. We had a further three days at Shellhaven gas-freeing and cleaning tanks so Celia was able to stay on board during that time then returned to Shields by train. The trip to the Tyne was uneventful relatively speaking except that they gave us a barrage baloon to trap dive bombers. This was flown from a special fixture attached to the main mast and was fine for the first few hours. After that it developed a leak and sank lower and lower until it was right under the bows of the ship astern. Some of the things the 'boffins' devised to protect us were more lethal than the enemy, first kites then the Holman projector to name but two - but we survived. I saw Opalia safely settled on the blocks at Smith's Dock Co. Ltd, North Shields and then took off with Celia for a lovely, peaceful week at Ford near Berwick in the Border country.

Celia had a reserved occupation and had to go back to work on our return but was able to come over to the ship every night while we underwent repairs. We had a few air raids but nothing too dangerous and the work went on apace, with new plastic armour round the bridge and a couple of extra machine guns as well as an engine overhaul. We had several parties with our friends in minesweepers and left after three weeks for Loch Ewe and a week at anchor waiting for the convoy to assemble. The whole area was under military control as Capt. Lodge found out when he tried to go home for a couple of days, as he was in 'civvies' he was taken in by the Military Police and slapped in the local bastille until his identity was established.

We fished and did lifeboat drills, visited other ships and consumed large quantities of rum and generally bemoaned our fate. We sailed in convoy and for the first time when we dispersed at 30 degrees west there was a reassuring American destroyer hanging around all the time. We were bound for New York which made a pleasant change from Curacao and offered much better shopping opportunities. There was quite a delay getting a berth so I managed to have a couple of runs ashore and stacked up with nylons and tinned food for my forthcoming leave. I was now earning £ 27 / 5 / 0d per month plus seven pounds per month war bonus so money was no object - well, not much ! We managed a few nightclubs and the Americans seemed kindly disposed to us and were the object of generous hospitality. After all, we were in the forefront of the war although by 'force majeure' but we were there. We left New York in September with an American escort to Halifax (NS) then three days in Bedford Basin before setting off home. Our escort was part R.N., R.C.N., and U. S. Navy and once more Uncle Sam was giving his boys a bit of practice for which we were duly grateful. We had some shocking weather in the form of autumnal gales but more or less held together and all arrived in Loch Ewe in one piece. We lingered there only one day then round to Methil where we re-grouped, picked up a few colliers and once more down the East coast swept channel, collecting colliers off the Tyne, Sunderland and Seaham Harbour then on to London. A few months earlier on 9th April the H. E. Moss tanker *Lunula* had been mined just as she tied up at Shellhaven and 26 crew were burnt to death as well as the crew of the tug *Persia* and all personnel on the jetty. Gloomy and daunting thoughts as we approached the next available berth, but we made it !

Sparks had rigged up a loudspeaker in the wheelhouse at Methil, and we were able to hear all of the conversations between the escorts on the auxiliary radio all the way down the coast. We found this to be most helpful and informative and often could anticipate the Commodore's orders. We secured alongside and the relieving officers came aboard and next day I was on my way home to my beloved Celia and my family - so another ship passed through my life. I was due to two months leave which meant I would not go back to sea until Christmas, and as luck would have it there was no ship available so I was on leave until late January, 1942 - a great source of joy to us all.

Celia had to remain at work but despite that we had a blissful leave and survived the air raids, rationing, blackout and the cold weather with the resiliency of youth and enjoyed ourselves enormously. On 7th December America joined the war after the attack on Pearl Harbour and we felt the beginning of the end of the war had come. We were now more optimistic, especially those of us who had witnessed the industrial capacity of the U. S. A. and their industrial production reached unprecedented levels before the end of the war. Anglo-Saxon had moved back to St. Helen's Court by the end of 1940 and withstood the blitz and the fire-bombing remarkably well. During my leave I was granted the permanent rank of Chief Officer, and the 'pooling' system of manning ships came into being. This decasualised the whole system of marine employment, and shipowners took on staff and ratings as permanent employees or relied on the 'pool'. Anglo-Saxon opted for their own permanent Officers and Chinese crews but used the pool for European ratings. This was most satisfactory to us and remained in force until after the end of the war when the contract system came into being.

PACIFIC VOYAGING 1942

Around 16th January,1942 I arrived in Portsmouth, scruffy and weary after a 24 hour journey to find a snow covered, heavily blitzed city and no ship (E.T.A. unknown) and was put into a hotel with very few amenities and a long walk to the loo from my bedroom - not one of the major hardships of war but annoying in the middle of the night ! There were three junior engineers and myself joining Cardium and we spent a miserable few days walking in the snow and slush-covered streets in search of amusement without success. As this was a naval base there was a military tailor and I took the opportunity of having a battledress made in navy blue to save wear and tear on my doeskin uniform. I figured that if battledress was good enough for the Army it was good enough for the Merchant Navy. I also had shoulder flashes with 'Great Britain' sewed on, as the place as crawling with Free French, Dutch, Belgian, Polish not to mention Canadian, Australian, South African and New Zealand - all with shoulder flashes proclaiming their country of origin. I felt that it was only fair to inform the populace at large that there were also one or two British engaged in the contest.

Eventually we got a call from the agents that the ship had arrived, so we hastily got our gear together and took a taxi to the Naval Dockyard where *Cardium* was about to commence discharge of her cargo of Admiralty fuel oil. I reported to the Captain, John Hughes who hailed from Anglesey, greeted my predecessor then was back into the old valve whirling routine. *Cardium* was a twin-screw motor tanker built on the Tyne in 1931 and was a seven-tank ship (21 in all) and one pumproom so was much simpler than *Cymbula* or *Opalia*. She was on long-term Admiralty charter and designated Merchant Fleet Auxiliary (M.F.A.) and a sort of illegitimate sister of the Royal Fleet Auxiliary (R.F.A.). We were engaged in oil transport to Admiralty depots and R. F. A.s while the latter actually delivered the oil to H. M. or Allied ships. We were fitted with gear to oil at sea but were not encouraged to carry out this task, being considered amateurs. This picture was to change dramatically later in the year but the reader must contain his/her excitement for a while. Sufficient to say we brought 'Shell Service' to really mean something for the Allied navies. A nice blend of private enterprise and Goverment bureaucracy with all of the virtues of both and none of the failings. Marcus Samuel must have been smiling benignly down on us, and even Henri Deterding may have raised a chuckle over the operations of *Cardium* over the next two years.

The Chinese crew had joined two months previously and were well familiarised with the job so there were no worries there. George Robson, the Second Officer had been nearly a year in the ship as had Robin Gray, the Chief Engineer and Syd Murie, the Second Engineer. The Senior Sparks was a morose, anti-social lad but his two juniors were excellent as were the rest of the juniors. The R.N. electrical officers were swarming all over the ship as something had gone wrong with the degaussing system. This had been installed on all ships during the previous year, and it's function was to neutralise the ship's normal magnetic field and thus combat magnetic mines. It was a very successful system but some times temperamental, and after a thorough investigation the Navy decided a major overhaul of at least a week was essential, so after discharge we were to go to Southampton for the electricians to get to work. This was an unexpected bonus and I immediately phoned Celia and we were able to have an extra week together. We finally sailed at the end of January and this time the escort took us well west of 30 degrees west as U-boats were expanding their areas of operation.

We had a relatively peaceful trip to Curacao where we loaded a cargo of fuel oil for Brisbane and Noumea, proceeding unescorted all of the way. Coming through the Panama Canal we had about twenty U. S. guards on board as an anti-sabotage precaution. They were fully armed and stationed at every strategic part of the ship, fortunately they had brought their own rations. By this time virtually all of the Far East was in Japanese hands and things were not looking so good - the prospect of a solo voyage across the Pacific didn't exactly thrill us.

We had orders to call at Wellington for bunkers and routing instructions so virtually had no news for three weeks. Private radios were forbidden but we had a big radio called a M. N. 100 on which short-wave programmes and news could be received. This allegedly broke down after leaving Panama and Sparks reckoned it couldn't be fixed - this turned out to be a load of nonsense but we didn't find out for about four months until the new Sparks got it going within half an hour. Cardium had some inherent fault in both engines as one or the other seemed to break down every few days. Something mysterious to do with telescopic pipes which kept snapping, it only took about two hours to fix but we had to stagger along on one engine during the repair time. Fortunately the two engines never broke down simultaneously - well not during the two years I was in her. Eventually we arrived at the eastern side of Cook Strait, making up for Wellington when we received a signal to stream paravanes as a precaution against mines. Now minesweepers do this all of the time and it looks easy but with a bunch of inexperienced amateurs like us and it can be a lethal and damaging catastrophe. Capt. John Hughes and I got on very well but we had a friendly disagreement over the interpretation of Admiralty instructions for streaming paravanes. A bottle of gin was the wager and I finished up with a bottle of Gordon's juniper berry-flavoured spirit.

John Hughes reckoned the wire had to be paid out slowly but I reckoned it had to go out with a rush and the ship's speed would take the paravane out to the correct position. I am not often right but I was this time, John took the port side and I the starboard side, each of us with his own party of sailors plus all available hands as interested spectators. At the critical moment, I knocked out the holding pin and off sped my paravane taking the sixty fathoms or so of wire in about five seconds and settled nicely into position. John's paravane on a slow pay-out started to perform like a playful porpoise, turning round and smacking back into the ship's side at 30 second interval with a noise that sounded like a depth charge or mine exploding. They could hear it in the engine room and George on the bridge phoned down to reassure them that it was only the 'Old Man playing silly buggers with his paravane' to set their minds at rest. Despite flying wires, sparks and lurid Welsh oaths, no physical harm came to anyone except a few blisters and some near amputations of the odd finger. We recovered the paravanes when we stopped to pick up the pilot at Wellington, and the nose of John's paravane was decidedly the worse for wear and a lot of paint was missing from the ship's side. However John gave up gracefully and got his fair share of the gin but he never forgave the Admiralty and their stupid instructions. He had a pathological dislike of the R. N. and the R.N.V.R. in particular and it did cause problems from time to time - we reckoned he left a trail of apoplectic N.C.S.O. s around the world.

Arriving at Wellington we looked very travel-stained and rusty as *Cardium* had been to and fro across the Atlantic all winter, followed by two long ocean passages, but the good folk of Wellington came down in hordes to view this war-torn veteran. We were two days in Wellington during which time Syd Murie and his boys toiled over the engines and my gang slapped a coat of paint along the top two strakes of the hull plating. We took fresh stores aboard, sent food parcels home, sampled the local brew which was in short supply and generally enjoyed the luxury od sleeping in pyjamas and not having a life jacket to hand. There appeared to be no danger of Japanese submarines so we sailed over to Brisbane without escort, although we were told there would be some friendly corvettes along the route. We never actually saw any which produced a flow of abuse in fluent Welsh from John, and we berthed in Brisbane around 22nd April,1942.

Brisbane resembled an American Armed Forces camp as General McArthur had his headquarters there. A continuous stream of war material was coming through Brisbane and heading north in huge quantities, so all cargo berths were fully occupied. The Shell Company of Australia did their own agency work and we were well looked after by their staff who took us to their homes and on trips during our three days there. We were able to stock up on beer and galley coal although it had to be manhandled in bags along a 300 feet long track. We gave the Navy some 7,000 tons of fuel oil then set off for Noumea, once more on our own. If Brisbane was like an American Army camp, Noumea was like an American Army fortress. We tied up to R.F.A. *Dingledale* but she could only take about 3,800 tons leaving us with 350 tons on board. As all of the Allied naval ships had just been refuelled, some on their way to the Coral Sea, the problem was where to put the 350 tons. The U. S. Naval Officer in charge was reluctant to let any fuel escape his grasp so we finished up pumping it into one of the new 'Liberty' ships stationed in Noumea. She was certainly an eye opener to us as every officer had his own shower and toilet, with refrigerators in every messroom (we still had iceboxes in the deck and engine messrooms) and cold water drinking fountains in every alleyway. About sixteen gunners, all U.S.N. ratings and petty officers under a Gunnery Officer, to man two 4 " guns and six anti-aircraft guns, compared to our six gunners for one 4 " gun and twin Colt 0.5 " anti-aircraft guns - one of our gunners remarked 'Gawd, those Yanks don't muck around' !

The 'Liberty' ships were the brainchild of Henry Kaiser who eventually produced them in dozens by a sort of assembly line process, some were assembled in three days flat. They were the answer to the appalling losses suffered by the

Allies in the North Atlantic and were not exactly 'built to last', and some were lost due to bad weather, however quite a few fulfilled their purpose with many still in service twenty or more years after the war ended. We were then ordered to return to Panama routed via Cook Strait, then eastward across the Pacific almost to South America where we turned to port and up to Panama. We saw nothing but seabirds and dolphins until almost at Panama when we were boarded by the U. S. Navy and escorted through the Canal, then on our own to Curacao arriving 12th June,1942. This time we loaded fuel and diesel oil for Freetown, and had several cocktail parties aboard other tankers in Curacao harbour and from Shell while waiting for a convoy. As ships were loaded they were moored to buoys, in tiers of three or four alongside each other and at least twenty ships could be moored in this way. If your ship was moored on the inside and you had to cross two or more others to get to the launch, the chances were pretty good that you'd had a couple of 'warmers' in before you even reached the party. We were a 'matey' lot and a good time was had by all !

We left in a small convoy which took us as far as Trinidad after which we were on our own. We had to zig-zag all of the way as well as follow various instructions which allegedly brought us to positions where the Admiralty had some sort of naval prescence. This added about two days to the voyage but we assumed the Navy were better informed than us, the fact that we arrived safely indicates this but we heard enough S. O. S. signals to keep us all a bit 'twitchy'. With hindsight, some of them may have been the imagination of our Sparks, who by this time was at loggerheads with everyone including his two juniors. At Freetown, John Hughes got him removed and his replacement was a magnificent Irish lad, Paddy Keilly, who was with us for the next eighteen months and ran his department with splendid efficiency. The Navy commended us several times on the excellent quality of our signalling, all due to Paddy and his two boys, especially during the North African campaign which lay ahead of us.

Freetown was a major convoy assembly port and we were there ten days, much to our disgust. We had to take Mepachrine (or some such name) for malaria and our skins all turned yellow (except the Chinese crew who had a start on us). A false rumour was it would make you sterile and as ex-officio Medical Officer I had big problems in making the boys take their ration. In the event, only George Robson the Second Officer got malaria but that wasn't until we got to Trinidad two weeks after leaving Freetown. The enemy by this time had his U-boats strung out in singles, pairs and packs all the way from West Africa to the West Indies and the Eastern seaboard of the U.S.A. - it may have cost him a bit in 'penalty rates' but it was certainly paying dividends as we were soon to discover. We left Freetown in a four-ship ten knot convoy with two escorts, and various courses were steered presumably to avoid U-boat concentrations, but our telescopic pipes broke down half way across and reduced our speed to seven knots for three hours. After this happened twice, the Senior Officer came close alongside and said he was sorry but if this occurred again we were own our own as they had to rendezvous with stronger escorts at a certain time and place. It was the very next day when the same fault occurred on the other engine, up came the S. O. E. and said he was sorry but he had to proceed without us and wished us the best of luck. John Hughes was furious at what had happened and was almost foaming at the mouth, fortunately we didn't have a loud hailer only the old-fashioned speaking trumpet so the S. O. E. only heard part of what John was calling him. He was only obeying orders and had three other ships to consider, but nothing we said could control the flow of John's Welsh and English ruderies. Anyway, this particular repair took longer than usual, so at seven knots the convoy had long disappeared over the horizon.

We had various courses to steer and positions to meet but John was having none of it and drew a straight line from our position to Trinidad and said that was our new course. Next morning just south of Barbados, Sparks sent up the 'situation report' of suspected U-boats - eight in all and I plotted them on the chart. They made a perfect circle about 50 miles in radius around us including one two miles away. He must have submerged for breakfast as we saw no sign of him, but no matter which way we had gone it appeared someone was lurking with 'felonius intent'. When I called John to show him the 'Sitrep' he chortled and said 'There you are, Robert, those buggers in the Admiralty are up the bloody pole again' - it could well have been in the category of 'famous last words' but we fortunately reached Trinidad without incident to sighs of relief all round !

When we came to anchor at Trinidad we discovered that the harbour entrance was covered by some form of ASDIC and a couple of nights earlier a U-boat had crept into the harbour, torpedoed two ships and then quickly cleared off. The story went that the operator saw a 'blip' on his screen and thought the equipment was faulty so called a technician to check it out, and when the U-boat beat a hasty retreat said 'Look, there it is again - must be a fault somewhere !'. History does not record what happened to the unfortunate operator but he certainly did his career structure a lot of damage. Ivor Harris replaced George Robson the Second Officer who came down with malaria, Ivor was with several others on his way to replace members of the 'mosquito' fleet at Curacao. The 'mosquito' fleet of the Curacaosche Scheepvaart Maats (C.S.M.) were Dutch-flag vessels of shallow-draft transporting oil from Lake Maracaibo to the refinery at Curacao, much as the Lago fleet did for Aruba. We had a mini-convoy with escort from Trinidad to Curacao, where we tied up at buoys for three days awaiting a berth. Ivor Harris and the other Welsh singers aboard including Capt. Hughes, and Taffy Loyn and Herbie Ham from other ships, set-up a male voice choir which kept the whole of the Lesser Antilles awake until 4.00 a.m. - they all survived the war but they certainly murdered 'Men of Harlech' and 'All through the night'. We had about a week in Curacao and got a new Second Officer called Anton Blinkhoff who was from the C. S. M. and going to the U. K. on leave. He had never been in a real convoy before and was a bit loathe to cruise along with his bow only a couple of hundred yards from the stern of the ship ahead, but got used to it. We left in a convoy towards the Mona Passage with an escort of one old 'V & W' class destroyer, a corvette and an assortment of fast American P. T. boats.

At dawn on the morning of 13th August,1942 the Convoy Commodore's ship was torpedoed and sunk, so Taffy Loyn as Vice-Commodore in *Standella* took over. *Standella* was Taffy's first command so it was a heavy responsibility for him, and we were to the north of Cuba in four lines. Reading from starboard to port, *Standella* was 31, we were immediately behind in *Cardium* as 32, abeam of *Standella* to port was *Empire Corporal* as 41 and to starboard as 21 was the *Michael Jebsen* an ex-Danish ship but under the British flag. The Shell tanker *Rapana* under senior

Capt. Bob Allen in 1947 when Master of NEWCOMBIA.

Celia & Bob on their 53rd Wedding Anniversary at the Sheraton Towers in Melbourne on 21st July,1994.   Model of yacht LANDFALL in glass case behind them, Bob sailed in her for three years at weekends as a deckhand during 1958/61 with the Royal Geelong Yacht Club.

The view looking aft from the bridge of CYMBULA, having just cleared the Straits of Magellan in July,1939.

Headlam tramp SNEATON, in which the author served his apprenticeship, loading timber at Gulfport on the Mississippi in 1931.

CARDITA of 1931 was a sister of CARDIUM.

STANDELLA of 1936 was a sister of OPALIA.

Dutch-flag Merchant Aircraft Carrier 'MAC' GADILA seen in 1945.

Shell's NANINIA of 1943 was the former Tyne-built 'MAC' EMPIRE MACMAHON.

master Capt. Syd Goodrich was position 14 and he more or less took over as Commodore. Next morning just before dawn U 598 (Holtoff) fired a spread of torpedoes from the port side of the convoy and *Empire Corporal* was hit in the engine room. The gunner and I moved sharply into the wheelhouse as we knew she was loaded with gasoline, but fortunately she did not catch fire. By the time we had got into the wheelhouse, there was another loud explosion and *Standella* right ahead of us was hit on the stem, unfortunately killing a lot of her Chinese crew but also did not catch fire but the air was thick with gasoline fumes. John Hughes rushed out of the chartroom as *Michael Jebsen* was hit by the remaining torpedoes and was capsized and sinking by the time she was abeam of us. John was still sightless in the pre-dawn darkness and bellowed 'Robert, what the bloody hell's going on ?' but I was too busy conning *Cardium* through the debris of *Standella* to reply immediately, and the gunner and the lookout were able to enlighten him.

When the sound and fury died down we were able to take stock and Standella was still with us albeit with a great deal of bow missing. Syd Goodrich took over and patrol boats were circling around dropping depth charges right, left and centre like confetti, so we closed up on Syd and order was restored. Syd ordered Taffy to make for Havana the nearest port to get repairs done, and we moved steadily on to Key West where we thankfully dropped anchor on 16th August,1942. What appeared to be half of the U. S. Navy came on board and we had to make many reports before we sailed in another convoy for New York - lots of escorts and Navy 'blimps' flying overhead until we reached New York on 25th August.

Due to extensive U-boat activity offshore, it was decided to send us to Boston via the East river, Long Island Sound and the Cape Cod Canal, a most unusual route for ships of our size. So off we went for a very pleasant, interesting and safe two days sailing close to the shore all the way and beautiful scenery with never less than four P. T.s as escort. We transitted the Cape Cod Canal without hitting anything, then on to Boston and arriving it looked like a re-enactment of the Boston tea party. Ships everywhere with launches criss-crossing the harbour in all directions. We were there two days and every six hours as the tide changed we had to manoeuvre the engines to avoid hitting other ships as we swung. We were all very experienced in manoeuvring and needed this practice like a hole in the head. We left on 30th August heavily escorted and anchored in Bedford Basin at Halifax (NS) on 1st September, thankful to have enough room to swing. Four days later, having stocked up with groceries, nylons and bond stores, we sailed for the U. K. in a large nine knot convoy. Fortunately the telescopic pipes held out and we arrived in Loch Ewe after an eleven day passage which was free of incident - presumably the enemy was still in the Caribbean !

Lingering only for one day we took off for Sheerness and we stood out like a sore thumb amongst the small colliers, although there were two or three biggish ships scattered up and down the two mile length of the convoy. I distinguished myself off Lowestoft by not allowing enough for the tidal drift and collected one of the dim, flashing channel marker buoys under the port quarter. It lodged under our elliptical stern and stayed there for about three miles winking away, and apart from losing some paint and getting a pithy reproach from the S.O.E. no harm was done.

We moored at Sheerness on 23rd September,1942 and I was soon joined by my beloved wife and we forgot all about the war and past headaches. By this time Celia was working in the War Office, London as a confidential secretary to a Colonel Miller in Signals (4), having been snatched up by the War Office two days after moving to London earlier in the year. She shared a flat with her sister in Blackheath and was working a 13 day fortnight in an office that was four levels below street level in Whitehall. We had four blissful days together then off we sailed to the Tyne for dry-dock and general overhaul. The War Office people were very good and granted Celia leave to join me on the Tyne for most of the docking period.

I managed to avoid collecting any buoys on the way up the East coast and apart from a couple of minor skirmishes had an uneventful run arriving at Smith's Dock Co. Ltd, North Shields on 28th September,1942. Come the dewy dawn of the next day, we were invaded by hordes of citizens, all of whom thought they had priority over everyone else. Not only the normal dockyard assortment of electricians, welders, platers, rivetters, fitters, turners and general dockyard hands, but Navy, Army, D.E.M.S, R.A.F. (the latter to remove the anti-aircraft balloon) as well as Anglo-Saxon superintendents and agents. All clamoured for attention and at times like this Chief Officers have been known to go quietly crazy and gaze longingly at the machine guns. However by the time the yard hooter went at midday to signal the lunch-break, most of them had vanished and those remaining were gaily tearing the ship and engines to pieces. Amongst the Anglo-Saxon personnel were representatives of the Staff and crew departments with sheaves of notes to disturb the relatively even tenor of our ways.

MEDITERRANEAN SERVICE STATION 1942 - 1944

I was to stand by *Cardium* during our month long refit at North Shields, during which we were torn apart and put back together again, new liferafts installed, new guns mounted, stores taken aboard, bottom scraped and painted. I also had to attend an Admiralty court of enquiry into a minor collision we had in *Opalia* with a coaster during the previous year. The new Captain joined before John Hughes had left and John was able to fill me in on him so I was forewarned. Capt. D. B. Edgar was a dapper little man who sometimes wore a monocle and had a penchant for the ladies, but whose knowledge of ship handling was somewhat limited. He was amenable to flattery and really quite harmless, and I laid it on a bit thick as I thought I would not be sailing with him and thus hoisted myself by my own petard. Halfway through the docking I was told the enquiry had been settled and I was to stay on the ship. Having spent two weeks showing him what a crash hot Chief Officer I was, I had to keep it up for the next fifteen months. However, in the event, he left everything to me, sometimes too much, and we got on very well. Chief Officers usually make it their business to get on with the Old Man, and Capt. Edgar was the opposite to Capt. Hughes in his attitude to the Navy, which was just as well in view of what lay ahead.

Our new Second Officer was Roly Tinn from Newcastle with a Master's certificate, a good sense of humour and very competent. J. 'Mac' MacMillan came as Third Officer and he had a First Mate's certificate plus a wealth of experience. We even got a fourth year apprentice, Sutton, who was a good addition to the team. Our new Chief Engineer was Geordie Brooks, a very senior Chief who was to be a strong supporter of mine in the months ahead, as was the new Second Engineer 'Stonewall' Jackson. Unfortunately all of the Chinese crew were replaced, although they had only been in the ship about thirteen months and were really good. We got a new crew who had done their normal two year contract plus nine months of a third year, for which they were paid extra. According to Anglo-Saxon we were to do a short voyage to the West Indies and back. The Admiralty had other ideas but omitted to mention it to Shell, doubtless in the interests of security, considering our ultimate destination. We had a magnificent deck officer's steward called Yip Yeung, who initially was replaced with the crew change, but his replacement was so lazy that he was given the push after a week, and to our delight back came Yip Yeung.

We sailed at the beginning of November, 1942 for Loch Ewe where we arrived after a few days and went alongside an American Esso tanker and were told to load a cargo from her - all very mysterious and hush hush ! The Americans seemed to know where we were going but weren't saying and everyone was as talkative as a pack of oysters. It wasn't until we were fully loaded and at sea on 8th November that we heard the news that the Allies had invaded North Africa and we had been invited to the party, joining convoy KMS 3. There were forty or more ships, mostly 'Liberties' and all of us fully loaded and ready but not keen for action. We received several signals, telling us of the importance of the convoy, what splendid chaps we were etc - but we were not impressed !

Coming through the Straits of Gibraltar during the night of 21st November we frightened the life out of a Spanish ferry boat crossing from Spain to North Africa. He suddenly found himself surrounded by menacing grey shapes, all with guns manned and heading his way at ten knots. He was lit up like a Christmas tree so we knew exactly where he was and took the necessary avoiding action. As it happened we passed so close to him in *Cardium* we could almost spit down his funnel, and we heard the Spanish captain let fly with a string of Spanish oaths mingled with a few Hail Mary's - made a change and relieved the monotony a bit !

On 23rd November,1942 we moored in the shambles that was Oran harbour, with two anchors forward and our stern tied to the breakwater in what is known as a Mediterranean moor. And shambles it was ! Wrecks everywhere with funnels, masts and deckhouses sticking out of the water at all angles. Flotsam and fuel oil everywhere with divers and salvage crews from American, British and French navies working round the clock to clear all of the wreckage and make the port usable. When H.M.S. *Walney* and H.M.S. *Hartland* crashed the boom in the early hours of 8th November,1942 the French armed forces were alerted and ready. Both ships were sunk with tremendous loss of life and every ship in the harbour plus three floating docks were scuttled, some 28 ships in all.

The Allies advanced from Arzew in the east and Les Andalouses in the west, and were predominantly American forces as the Allied High Command realised that the British Navy's action in bombarding the French fleet at Mers el Kebir in June,1940 would still be remembered with rancour - Allied H. Q. were quite correct ! We were promptly inundated with various members of American, British and French armed forces, plus douaniers (Customs). Like their British counterparts the douaniers never missed an opportunity to extract tribute from any passing traveller, war or no war ! As far as we knew, we were to deliver our fuel oil cargo then return to somewhere else to reload. R.F.A. *Abbeydale* came alongside and we began discharging part of our cargo into her, she had been there several days and during one of her moves had hit one of the wrecks, to the detriment of her bottom plating. Operations had already started when up came two British destroyers who berthed on our disengaged side and demanded fuel. That was the moment the Anglo-Saxon rule book went out of the porthole and stayed out for nearly 18 months !

However we soon learnt the ins and outs of our new role. Before the arrival of the destroyers we had salvaged three huge puncheons of Algerian red wine which had been floating around the harbour from one of the scuttled French ships. This red wine proved valuable barter currency in the weeks to come. We had left the U. K. with sufficient food and stores to take us to the U.S.A. or West Indies where we would be stocking up, but being lumbered with this North African caper it became apparent we would soon be in a parlous state especially in regard to groceries. Your average, friendly neighbourhood Algerian grocer had very little to offer in the way of exotic (or even plain) food and a diet of dates washed down by Algerian red wine was not a prospect we viewed with any favour. However Mac was also victualling officer, and he was soon to take care of the situation !

Capt. Edgar proved very useful, dashing around in uniform, monocle at the ready, chatting up the ladies and impressing the Americans in the public relations fields. Meanwhile surveyors were swarming all over the *Abbeydale* and after three days they decided that her bottom damage was not repairable in North Africa and she would have to return to the U. K. As she had been designated Base Oiler for the area you have one guess who got stuck with the job - *Cardium* - experience nil thus bringing a fresh, uncluttered mind to the job. We hadn't enough hoses, spanners, reducers and other requisite gubbins to cope with the various types of ship connections but *Abbeydale* happily unloaded all of her garbage on us and left us shortly in time to be home for Christmas !

Next thing we knew another M.F.A. *British Chivalry* came alongside, topped us up with fuel and we were back to square one. Next day we moved round to Mers el Kebir, the ex-French and now Allied naval base about four miles west of Oran. The Captain of *Abbeydale* acted as pilot and we berthed on the cruiser *Scylla* to oil her, and more destroyers berthed on our other side and we had a busy 24 hours. Next morning at 7.00 a.m. we had to leave *Scylla*, move around the wrecks and anchored ships, then berth on the battleship *Nelson*, the flagship of Force H with Admiral Burroughs as F.O.H. in command.

Capt. Edgar appeared on the bridge as we went to stations, dapper and well rested and announced he was going to let me do the piloting. 'Good experience for you, Allen, and I'll be here to watch you and help if you make any mistakes' he said. 'Charming' I thought ' here goes my career structure ', however the theory worked and we got away from *Scylla* and moved up to *Nelson* without hitting anything. Just as were warping gently alongside and I was feeling pleased with myself, despite sweaty palms and wobbly knees, a party of Royal Marines decided to train a 4 " gun barrel outboard and punched a neat hole in Stonewall Jackson's cabin on the starboard side of the forward end of the poop. Rather spoiled my glow of achievement as someone on *Nelson* had forgotten to tell the Marines that an oiler was coming alongside at the critical moment. However, everyone on board was very nice about it and they sent a team of artificers on board and patched up the hole as soon as oiling was over. We moved from *Nelson* to the aircraft carrier *Furious* then on to an even bigger carrier *Formidable*, where we stayed two days. At each capital ship, destroyers would berth on our disengaged side so we were getting rid of a lot of fuel and doing calculations that were mainly inspired guesstimates, but we balanced the books and the Navy were satisfied. Capt. Edgar had lost interest in this sort of practical operation as it obviously involved getting oil on one's hands, plus squalid arguments with Chief Stoker Petty Officers over quantities of oil received, so he fixed himself up with a flat ashore and showed up now and again with extra provisions, checked on progress, had a chat and then departed. He mostly didn't bother to come aboard for various moves, which I found rather disconcerting.

Leaving *Formidable* on 4th December we moored alongside the Norwegian tanker *G. C. Brovig*, which topped up our depleted stocks of fuel, then we were off the next day and moored to *Vindictive*, a destroyer depot ship and topped up her fuel tanks, then back to the *Brovig* to collect the balance of her oil. Finally on 7th December everyone in sight seemed to have enough fuel, the *Brovig* left and the U.S.N. port director allocated us an anchorage berth and we settled down to a little peace and quiet and catch up on our sleep. We had been on the go for seven days non stop and were beginning to feel a little weary. I had done some twelve pilotage jobs, we had issued 8,000 tons of fuel, received a similar amount from the *Brovig*, received no complaints, so felt we had done rather well for amateurs. Little did we know that we had only started and eventually would be handling more than ten ships a day - but that was some time away.

As previously mentioned, Mers el Kebir had been the French naval base which the Royal Navy had bombarded in June,1940 to prevent French ships falling into German hands. I don't propose going into the rights and wrongs of this decision but the local population were not terribly pro-British. This was the reason for the whole of the area centred on Oran being under American control. The harbour was formed by a breakwater, about a mile long, running south east from a north west corner and covered a very large area. Unfortunately the French battleship *Bretagne* sunk in the 1940 bombardment was slap in the middle of the harbour and restricted the movements of big ships to a great degree. In the following months *Cardium* narrowly avoided hitting *Bretagne* on several occasions due to bad weather and crowded conditions, but for the moment had plenty room to spare. Force H had departed to harry the enemy leaving *Vindictive*, ourselves and a small French tank steamer of 1,000 dwt named *Benzene* with bags of manoeuvring room. There was a R. N. boom defence ship and a couple of flotillas of M.L.s huddled away in their base at the north west corner under Fort Santon. Various buoys were scattered around the harbour for mooring ships, and the breakwater was in great demand as various cargo ships came and went, discharging a variety of war material, plus food and supplies for the armed forces and civilian population.

We needed a small launch to service the crew's shore leave, carry stores and for general communication, but were reluctant to use our motor lifeboat as this type of service launch is likely to get knocked about a bit. We persuaded Capt. Edgar to hire a small fishing boat but the best we could get was manned by two direct descendants of the original Barbary Coast pirates. The U. S. Marines had allegedly stamped out piracy during the previous century but the spirit was alive and flourishing in 1943. The launch was a typical Mediterranean fishing boat painted in blues, reds and yellows, and smelt of long dead fish. Pietro and Jacques, the owners, were defrocked speedboat drivers who considered 'first to the gangway' to be of prime importance and seemed to delight in shouldering senior officer's boats to one side. This caused us considerable trouble but it was exciting while it lasted. It is not often that a junior Merchant Navy officer gets a chance to beat a Royal Navy Admiral to his own gangway, as happened to Mac one day on an errand to *Nelson*. After that we parted with Pietro and Jacques who went back to chasing pilchards and we used our own motor lifeboat. *Vindictive* promised to keep it in good repair, we lashed an old 8 " manilla mooring rope along the gunwhale to protect it and thus we had a service boat.

Ships of all shapes and sizes came and went, we were topped up by other tankers a couple of times and by Christmas Eve all of Force H had departed on their lawful occasions, so we looked like having a peaceful Christmas Day. However Admiral Darlan was assassinated in Algiers and trouble once more flared with U. S. forces confined to barracks. We managed to have an excellent Christmas dinner with various friends from the British forces, Capt. Edgar having made the initial contacts and Mac had followed up swiftly so we we got rations from the U. S. Army and Navy and from *Nelson*. We had access to the local markets for fresh fruit and vegetables so fared very well on the whole - surplus of some things and shortages of others, especially rice for the Chinese crew. This problem was overcome by one of our chummy destroyer Captains being able to produce several hundred kilos in Gibraltar and bringing them back on his next escort run. The American rations were extremely generous and we were able to help several French civilian families with whom we had become very friendly. Happily the original anti-British feeling soon died down and we were absorbed into the local scene.

Our relations with the U. S. port directorate were extremely cordial, as indeed they were with our own Navy and the Polish, Greek and French units who were part of Force H. It was business as usual after 26th December for three days and our stocks of fuel were running low when alongside came the U. S. tanker *Bennington*. Our signals had once more got mixed up as she was loaded with motor gasoline, and while this was being sorted out we had a pleasant 24 hours socialising with her officers. She was a 'dry' ship, they appreciated our hospitality and brought Coca Cola to make 'Cuba libres' plus assorted goodies such as chocolate bars which were in short supply on the Barbary Coast. A sudden Mediterranean storm blew up which whipped the sea into a nasty swell and we dropped anchor and managed to ride it out but had to move on New Year's Eve morning. This was easier said than done as an extra strong squall blew up just as we were clearing *Bennington* and we were blown athwart her bows. Sparks were flying and we were deeply conscious of the 14,000 tons of gasoline in *Bennington*. The tow rope broke on the after tug and the forward tug wasn't powerful enough so things were a bit dodgy for a while. The wind took us back alongside *Bennington* and we had every available fender slung between us. We managed to hold on for another couple of hours until the wind eased, but by this time we were only about 30 yards from the wreck of the *Bretagne*. We only had about 6,000 tons of cargo on board so were fairly clear and moved over to the main breakwater and tied up at 2.00 p.m. *Bennington* hastily hove up her anchor and departed for the comparative safety of the open sea.

There had been several cargo ships discharging at the open breakwater but they had hastily sailed the previous evening, leaving huge piles of cargo on the wharf. The seas were sweeping over the shore side of the breakwater so it was impossible to get trucks along to pick up the cargo. Being relatively sheltered we decided to salvage some of the gear and did ourselves quite a service. There were cases of rifles, truck parts, bolts of cloth, tinned food and various other items which we managed to save from being washed into the harbour. Next day the Americans told us we could keep the cloth and tinned food and only took the rifles, truck parts and other war material so we finished up with enough gear to set up a clothing shop and a delicatessen. The crew got most of the loot and made a small fortune later in the year flogging it to the locals.

On 1st January,1943 there was great activity with blacksmiths and other artisans repairing our plates and guard rails with a couple of warships in for fuel and it was business as usual. Our life was an ever changing pattern and we gradually developed into a sort of maritime 'corner shop'. In addition to handling thousands of tons of fuel oil, in and out, we acquired stocks of coal for one little coal-burning minesweeping trawler, various grades of lube oil and kept a couple of hundred tons of fresh water in the fore peak to replenish the two flotillas of M.L.s. On one of their forays eastward, one of them discovered an unguarded Army stores depot which contained, inter alia, hundreds of cases of rum in two gallon jars. Fearing the enemy may counter attack and capture the rum, they patriotically liberated a number of cases and we got our share. We were able to get concentrated Coca Cola from the Americans and *Vindictive* had a machine for making soda water. Lemons were in profusion, so instant rum and coke, Viva Cuba ! Day after day we serviced dozens of warships, R. N. at first then U. S. troop transports, assault ships, hospital ships, minesweepers, minelayers etc. Although we did not know at the time, the total stock of fuel oil between Gibraltar and Malta was 7,000 tons and we had it. The situation had been foreseen and a convoy assembled in late December in the West Indies to fill the gap. This was the ill-fated TMI which consisted of nine tankers, all loaded with fuel, diesel or gasoline and sailed from Trinidad on 28th December. This convoy was attacked by nine U-boats betwen 3rd and 10th January and seven tankers were sunk, the last was *British Dominion* commanded by my own father-in-law Capt. J. D. Miller, who was subsequently awarded the O.B.E. for his gallantry and splendid seamanship in saving the balance of the crew not killed as the torpedoes struck.

The two surviving tankers, the Shell *Cliona* and Norwegian *Vanja* subsequently reached Algiers and Oran respectively and on 23rd January,1943 we took on part of the cargo of *Vanja* at Oran. We got back to Mers-el-Kebir two days later, gave 800 tons to our friend *Benzene* and were then beset by Force H escorts. February brought in another rush of customers and a rather unique situation arose. Firstly a Norwegian tanker *Thorsholm* came alongside to top us up then three destroyers stacked up on our disengaged side, so there we were merrily loading down one line and happily pumping out on the other - strictly against Anglo-Saxon rules and regulations. Then in came the fast minelayer *Abdiel* and moored alongside the free side of *Thorsholm* having returned from laying mines around Italy with fuel problems. Capt. Pleydell-Bouverie of *Abdiel* sent a polite message saying 'We have water in a fuel tank but cannot find which one - can you assist ?' Our Chief Engineer Geordie Brooks and I went over with some water-finding paste (*Abdiel* had run out of that valuable commodity) and soon were able to trace the offending tank. Where to put the ten tons of offending fuel was a problem, but we persuaded the master of Thorsholm into accepting the oil. In the meantime a dozen or so brawny R. N. stokers were stringing hoses over the decks of *Thorsholm* so we could refuel *Abdiel*. We had every hose in the area in operation and it looked like spaghetti junction, three strings to destroyers, one string from *Thorsholm* to us and the balance from *Abdiel* to *Thorsholm*.

It happened to be Chinese New Year so the crew were not exactly happy at humping all those bloody great 3 " and 5 " copper hoses around on what should have been a day of rest. However judicious application of a little rum kept the peace but what made their day was Capt. Pleydell-Bouverie's trump card. He was an old China Station hand and sent over a bottle of Johnnie Walker Red Label for the boys together with a 'Happy New Year' signal - that really made their day ! Fortunately we finished by 5.30 p.m. and the boys were able to have their traditional feast and several officers of *Abdiel* came over to join in the celebrations. Everyone was gone by noon the next day and we were lucky to have a few days rest and clean the ship up a bit. So it went on with familiar faces coming and going, and troopships like *Empress of Australia* and *Franconia* to be oiled and another Norwegian tanker to fill us up. In mid March 'Mac' MacMillan developed ulcers and had to go ashore to hospital - fortunately we had all become interchangeable so his departure was not as serious as it might have been. However it meant Roly Tinn and I had to share the burden, although Sutton the apprentice was extremely competent and it's a pity he was not able to take over the role of Acting Third Officer. Mac was still on Articles and technically part of the ship's company.

So we pressed on regardless with refuelling Force H as required, and often we had to up anchor and put to sea whilst Force H came in and settled down for a day or two. At that time Force H was composed of *Nelson, Rodney, Formidable* and a gaggle of destroyers ranging from old veterans through Tribal class to new fleet destroyers and Hunt class, plus minesweepers, minelayers, corvettes, sloops and miscellaneous craft from all parts of the Dominion - South Africa, Australia, Canada, India, Free French, Polish and Greeks. We became a sort of crossroads, a meeting place to exchange news and views, as *Cardium* sat there like an old mother hen waiting for her thirsty brood. We never stayed long in one spot in the harbour as we had to go alongside all of the big ships in turn and give them their quota of fuel and lube oil. When Force H was in, we never lacked for invitations out to dinner as Mac, Roly and I were blessed with the ability to tell a good story and embroider the incident to make it interesting. Capt. Edgar used to bring aboard an assortment of visitors from ashore and the U. S. Military Police were constant visitors along with U. S. and French Army officers, various shore-based R. N. people and their attendant ladies. I started a Visitors Book which I still have, and Sutton, who was a gifted artist, decorated the cover with cartoons of the various visitors. We became firm friends with many members of the U. S. port directorate and they relied on us for nautical information especially in the early days. In addition, a few R.A.F. officers used to visit us and stay the night when they were on leave from La Seina or Tafaroui, the air bases south-east of Oran - made a change from hurtling through the air at 150 m.p.h. or more for them.

There was an attempt by Italian midget submarines to penetrate the boom defence system but this was foiled by the M.L.s who patrolled to seaward the whole time. Just the same U. S. Naval Commandant (known as COMNOB ORAN) was taking no chances and every night we had our own boom defence towed out and strung around us. This was wire netting suspended from a series of 44 gallon drums and took about two hours to put in place. Trouble was that the destroyers and escorts had a habit of coming in during the night for fuel. They had to back and fill whilst the French tugs were roused to remove the mini-boom - my knowledge of French improved daily and nightly.

Most of the French Algerians were completely bilingual in French and Spanish but English was a little lacking, so much so as to be completely non-existent. However my mispent youth in the Argentine had left me with a very good working knowledge of Spanish, which I used to full advantage. The locals were so surprised on finding 'un Anglais' who spoke good Spanish and we were able to establish a rapport which was extremely valuable. Since Capt. Edgar was ashore most of the time, my shore leave was rather restricted. On quiet days I would pop ashore and go for a stroll along the quay into the village and chat up the locals. This way I became friendly with a dear old gentleman who was the civilian guardian of the French Navy ammunition storage dumps, drilled into the rock below Fort Santon. Our first exchanges were in Spanish, about twice a week and I learned of the food shortages the locals were experiencing. Having a surplus of some commodities, I brought across some tins of spam, coffee, crackers, tinned fruit and chocolate bars for his grandchildren which sparked a reaction akin to receiving the Holy Grail. On my next visit, two weeks later, I was invited in to meet the family and regaled with excellent red wine and lots of Spanish chatter. On leaving, I was presented with a bottle of vin rouge and six fresh eggs, which was something we never saw and I enjoyed them to the full.

My visits were limited then to every three weeks or so but it was always a pleasure to visit them. One night we were chatting away in Spanish when he asked me about my ability to handle the French language. The sum total of my linguistic ability in French was only average but he suggested we change from Spanish to French and I acquired a reasonable working knowledge of French and have been a mild Francophile ever since. As the enemy was gradually being forced to relinquish their positions in North Africa, so a build-up of men and materials began, with the object being to have a smack at Mussolini on his home ground. We got predominantly U. S. transports as we were an American-controlled port but the R. N. still had a very visible prescence. Naturally, the build-up attracted the enemy's attention and airmen popped over to drop bombs from time to time but only one ship was ever hit - a Norwegian tanker in Oran roads which was damaged and returned to the U. K. for repairs.

Mac returned from hospital on 19th March to collect his gear and left the next day to join a hospital ship for repatriation to the U.K. As luck would have it, we oiled 22 ships in the next four days, so Roly, Sutton and I were rather the worse for wear. However we had a two day break after that, and bright-eyed and bushy-tailed we faced our next set of customers. We were fairly busy until the end of the month when we moved round to Oran to load from the shore installation there, and had five days alongside. I was fairly free after completing the loading on the second day and Capt. Edgar had me up to his flat for dinner one night. A most amusing and enjoyable evening with an assortment of his mates, both male and female. He was a fairly abstemious man as regards the demon alcohol but that night he let his hair or rather what was left of it down, and kept telling me what a wonderful Chief Officer I was. On leaving he insisted on pressing several hundred francs into my hot, moist palm as a good behaviour bonus. All his mates seemed to have lots of money and I was definitely the 'poor relation'. However as I seemed to be from the right side of the tracks and had a glib tongue, I became 'persona grata'. Fortunately it was only for a couple of days and we were back in Mers el Kebir on 5th April surrounded by our thirsty offspring. My old scrap log records that we refuelled *Nelson, Formidable* and ten destroyers in the next four days.

It was around this time that we were able to top up the wardroom of *Formidable* with red wine, as a result of which I was invited to dinner on her and met Lt. Cmdr. Tommy Woodruffe, Laurence Olivier and Ralph Richardson. The Government were making a propaganda film about the crew of a Fleet Air Arm Fairey Swordfish. Tommy was a BBC commentator pre-war and was back in the service as a liaison officer, and Laurence Olivier was actually a Lt.(A) R.N.V.R. and a qualified pilot with Ralph Richardson having the same temporary rank and played the part of the aircraft observer. It was a typically uproarious F.A.A. guest night with no flying the next day and most entertaining. As in all capital ships, the bar shut down promptly at 10.00 p.m. but as we had no bar to shut on *Cardium*, Tommy Woodruffe came back with Roly and I, and we soldiered on until 4.00 a.m. Tommy was a most gifted raconteur and we had a hilarious time listening to his experiences as an outside commentator for the BBC. He was still able to sign my visitors book with a firm hand on departure.

So life went on, some days busy then two or three days clearing up, then receiving other tankers to top up our fuel supplies, then more fleet replenishment activities. Sometimes we were bored out of our tiny minds but not often. I learnt a bit about the American Civil War from the crews of *George B. McClelland*, a 'Liberty' ship and the *Antietam* a U. S. Navy tanker. I recall the *Antietam* clearly because after receiving several thousand tons of fuel oil, her supply officer handed me a bill for several thousand U. S. dollars. Something to do with Lease Lend protocol, I was told, so I blithely signed the paper assuring Uncle Sam I would pay him a sum of money I would never acquire in two lifetimes - so far Uncle Sam has not asked for repayment. We were being topped up by the American tanker *Gulf of Mexico* and reached our plimsoll mark with our supplier still having one thousand tons left on board. The British naval liaison officer and U. S. port director were keen to get her to leave the next day and asked me to take the extra thousand tons. I pointed out I was already loaded as far as I dare even though there was still room in our tanks. After much discussion they assured me that Force H would be back in two days and they wouldn't send me to sea in an overloaded condition. We finished up with 13,400 tons of fuel - not bad for a 12,000 dwt ship. Our lords and masters in London would have had a collective coronary if they had but known. I tried to get in touch with Capt. Edgar but of all things he was visiting the French Foreign Legion in Sidi bel Abbes. As luck would have it, he came back the next day around noon and we were so low in the water the gunwhale of the lifeboat and our maindeck were level. When we got the signal to send the boat over I thought we were in for some rude words on overloading, but he merely gazed around, smiled benignly and said we seemed to have got a good cargo into her. Fortunately, when I signalled in my daily 'fuel available' report the previous evening, the B.N.L.O. and Port Director both signalled back 'Thanks and well done' instead of the usual 'Acknowledge'. I waved the two signals under the nose of Capt. Edgar and he was delighted.

Next day in came the fleet and slowly *Cardium* threw off her resemblance to a half-tide rock. By mid-May 1943 the Allies had successfully clobbered the enemy who had retreated from North Africa. At the end of May the place began to fill up with U. S. N. Attack transports and five magnificent fleet oilers, complete with power-operated gun turrets and 'all mod cons'. We were green with envy but to our surprise we were flooded with officers from them anxious to gain experience and watch us operate. It soon became apparent that although the ships were technically light years ahead of us, only very few of the officers and ratings had any experience of oiling. However, they were extremely keen to learn and soon caught on, and we made some good friends, and also on the twenty destroyers and two cruisers with them. On average we could oil and despatch three destroyers (R. N.) whilst they were doing one (U.S.N.). They referred to their destroyers as 'cans' (short for tin cans) and one Commander remarked in my presence 'Gawdammit ! How in hell do those gawdamned limeys turn round those cans so fast when they haven't anything like the equipment we have ?' - we soon found out when we came to handle the U. S. Navy 'cans' ourselves.

The average destroyer has a dozen compartments or more, interconnected with a common pipeline and a filling valve to each compartment. The term 'manifolding' was used in the R. N. and once you connected to the manifold in a British ship that was that ! You just kept pumping and the destroyer ratings just shut and opened valves until all compartments were full and then shouted 'Stop' - plenty of experienced men was the answer. However the U.S.N. was short of these, they moved the hose from tank to tank so there was a series of stops and starts. Once we started oiling the U.S.N. ships. Geordie Brooks seconded a couple of his junior engineers on to the 'cans' to assist. Soon all went well and the Yanks caught on very quickly and the crews of U.S.S. *Bernadou, Cole* and *Dallas* were no bother at all. They were old World War I four-stackers and they were more frequently oiled than any other ships so we became very friendly with them.

Often they stayed alongside all night after oiling and would show movies to which we were invited, and being a 'dry' navy they would pop over to us for a couple of nips of whatever we had but I took good care to see there was no repeat of the H.M.S. *Meteor* incident, of which you may have heard, and warned my boys accordingly. This is not to say they didn't do a discreet but profitable drinks trade when we were alongside oiling transports. However, their entrepreneurial qualities had improved so much by this time that they were masters of discretion. The going rate at the time was one bottle vin rouge for one carton of cigarettes. As the American G.I.s were issued with free cigarettes in a combat zone everyone was happy. The Bosun and carpenter took pains to see that nobody messed up the system - I often wished I had got in on the act but prudence indicated otherwise.

By the end of June,1943 we had a terrific build-up of U.S.N. and U.S. Coastguard Attack transports and attendant escorts and all the oilers were going flat out. Force H had been joined by the battleships *King George V* and *Howe* and the harbour was a constant scene of activity as small landing craft practised loading then landing on various beaches by day and night. Our private boom defence was withdrawn whilst all this was going on and it was obvious that some big operation was about to take place - it was the invasion of Sicily but we humble folk in the cheap seats didn't know that. There was more frenzied activity on 2nd and 3rd July as gradually the transports and their escorts put to sea, then six fleet destroyers came alongside early on 4th July and were gone before lunch 'Whew - that's Shell that was' !

The jumbo-sized version of the Spithead Naval Review had vanished, leaving three U.S.N. oilers, *Cardium* and *Benzene* as the sole occupants of many hectares of harbour. One of the U.S.N. oilers *Winooski* (nicknamed the Polish battleship) had arranged an inter-ship boxing competition on her big afterdeck by way of celebrating 4th July. All of the senior officers of the three oilers came over to us for drinks about 11.00 a.m., and Capt. Edgar played host as only he could do and used up a month's drinks ration by 1.00 p.m. when we all went over to *Winooski* for a magnificent lunch with roast turkey and all the trimmings. I got lumbered with the job of M.C. between the various bouts and had to keep a couple of hundred sailors entertained. By this stage I had accumulated a fairly comprehensive array of stories and having been forewarned had chosen them carefully. As any professional comedian will tell you, what has them rolling in the aisles in Glasgow leaves them cold in Philadelphia. In addition, there were several nurses from the U. S. Army hospital as guests but the entertainments officer of *Winooski* and I decided they must be pretty broad-minded. There are plenty of interesting alternatives to four letter words that can be even funnier and not give offence. They laughed louder and longer than the guys and it turned out to be a riotous afternoon. As one American sailor remarked 'Shore glad we licked you limeys otherwise I wouldn't have gotten so many laffs from you Chief' !

The leftovers from lunch served as dinner, then a select few came back to *Cardium* to round off the day with a few glasses of 'cleansing ale'. The ale was drawn from another source of our supplies, the British Army Commando Training school some twenty miles west of Oran. They had NAAFI supplies coming out of their ears and were kind enough to let us draw from them. The Americans were extremely generous and as we were officially on their 'ration list' were able to shop at their PX canteens on the ships and use their PX facilities ashore. At one of their shows I met the legendary Al Jolson who was entertaining the troops. Amongst the American naval officers we met was President Roosevelt's son and Douglas Fairbanks jnr., both serving as Lt. U.S.N.R. In all of this activity prior to the Sicilian landings, we were joined by Mac's replacement. He was R. E. Bobbie Annett with the ink barely dry on his Second Mate's certificate and no tanker experience. He was a bright, willing and cheerful lad and soon caught on, making a valuable addition to the team. A relatively peaceful time followed with a couple of days in Oran to load from *Empire Viscount* then back to Mers el Kebir and the odd destroyer or corvette coming in for fuel. During the entire time we were in North Africa Paddy Keilly and his two juniors handled all the visual signalling and they were really first-class at the job. We had many complimentary reports on the efficiency of our signalling and it was due to Paddy and his boys. At the end of July, Roly Tinn had to have his tonsils out and was sent to the American Army Hospital at Ainel Turk where he was duly operated on. He nearly won a Purple Heart, the American award to wounded soldiers. He was in a ward full of wounded from the campaign and was still under anaesthetic when an American Senator came into the ward and started to pin Purple Hearts on the soldiers. He was about to pin one on Roly when some G.I. called out 'Hey Senator - that guy's a limey and he ain't wounded - he's only had his tonsils out' - so Roly missed out on a gong.   When he finally recovered consciousness he had a fair amount of good-natured ribbing from his fellow patients.

It is interesting to note that at this period of the war, there was not one Campaign Medal struck by the British Government whilst the newly arrived Yanks seemed to have at least three apiece without hearing a shot fired in anger. It was only towards the end of 1943 that the 1939 star was struck and most of us were lucky to get it by 1945. Early in August about 10.00 p.m. four Australian sloops appeared out of the darkness and were fuelled. They had been in the Red Sea on patrol when they were suddenly lumbered with a convoy to Gibraltar and had to refuel with us. They had no cold weather gear and the Mediterranean can be quite chilly even in August. *Cessnock, Cairns, Geraldton* and *Wollongong* were their names and they were glad to receive orders to return to Suez. Twenty years later I met one of their C.O.s in Northern Queensland, Capt. Bob Smith, who by that time was a Torres Strait pilot.

By early September,1943 an increase in business indicated some activity was in view, and our days and nights were an endless procession of moves from transport to transport with escorts and other smaller craft occupying our disengaged side. This was all a prelude to the invasion of Italy in general and Salerno in particular, from 28th August to 4th September we oiled nine transports, thirty escorts and gave *Benzene* three loads. We were topped up three times ourselves by ocean tankers and issued fresh water to thirty M.L.s. Business could be termed brisk to say the least, and Roly, Bobbie, Sutton and I were beginning to feel the strain a bit. Chief Engineer Geordie Brooks was a tremendous help and would sometimes take over operations and let one or other of us grab a bit of sleep. Often we would be oiling five or more ships at one time and three pairs of hands were essential, things began to ease up towards the end of September when it became evident that Italy was out of the war and the surrender documents were signed on *Nelson*.

There had been a Victory Parade much earlier in Oran to celebrate the end of the North African campaign. The stars of that show were the Royal Marines who did their celebrated 'fix bayonets' whilst on the march. The locals went wild with delight at the sight of this impressive and difficult manoeuvre - Capt. Edgar attended but we were too busy oiling. As the workload eased and some blackout restrictions were lifted, we were able to have a couple of concerts on our after deck when we had a couple of destroyers alongside for the night. These went down very well as the cramped conditions on the small ships were very restricting and the after deck of a tanker must have looked like a football field. There was some amazing talent amongst the crews and we always played to packed houses. We even wrote a radio play for the nights it was not advisable to put the floodlights on and broadcast it from our wheelhouse, hooked up to the sound systems of the ships alongside. One memorable night when alongside *Formidable*, with two destroyers alongside her and two on our other side, we reckoned we had an audience of nearly two thousand men. Amongst the troops there were several ex-BBC operators of various types so we were able to put on a fairly professional show and the troops lapped it up.

By this time the barnacles and weed on our hull had reached alarming proportions and in October,1943 we were relieved by *Spondilus* another Anglo-Saxon tanker which was on her way home, having been out east of Suez for three years. They were not amused at this move but as we were only five days on the floating dock in Oran soon recovered their good humour. I suspect they thought they were going to get lumbered with the job permanently. The amount of garbage that was scraped from our hull was absolutely amazing and we reckoned that prior to docking old *Cardium* would only have managed about seven knots flat out with a following wind. After five days billeted in the Continental Hotel in Oran which was virtually a services barracks run by the U. S. Army we took it badly going back on watch again. *Spondilus* gave us back all her remaining fuel and the necessary gear with indecent haste and left for the U. K. Only ourselves, *Benzene* and *Vindictive* were the sole occupants of many hectares of harbour.

This situation didn't last long and we were soon up to our necks with troop assault ships and their escorts heading eastwards. We were joined in early November by another oiler *Yankee Arrow*, a Socony-Mobil tanker that had come off second best in an argument with a couple of torpedoes off Algiers. She had been holed in two of her forward tanks but could only carry about 7,000 tons in the undamaged tanks so had joined us as a 'back-up' ship, the idea being to eventually carry out temporary repairs when hull plating was available. About this time our two flotillas of M.L.s left and moved eastwards to Italy, and Lt. Ralph Cole was one of the skippers and had arranged with the NAAFI in Algiers to allocate stores for the M.L.s and ourselves but transport was the problem. At this juncture enter Pierre one of the civilian drivers/interpreters for the R. N. who had a friend who owned a magnificent big Delage limousine but it had no gasoline and no tyres. Capt. Edgar had a word with the British naval liaison officer and gas and tyres were soon forthcoming. However he nearly had a fit when he realised I was going with Ralph, ostensibly for lifeboat stores, and he would have to stay on board for three days. However we soon convinced him of the rightness of our thinking, and we departed one dewy dawn with Pierre and his mate, in this enormously long Delage beloved of Presidents and the Mafia.

A most interesting trip to Algiers through the Atlas mountains, stopping at a village called Minas for a delightful lunch of delicious lamb chops and lovely local vin rouge, then down to the plains for the run into Algiers. However about 3.00 p.m. an ominous spluttering noise developed and the engine packed up, apparently it was the bobbine (distributor) so Pierre and I thumbed a lift in a truck to a village which boasted a sizeable garage. The owner of the garage turned out to be a French lady of formidable aspect, who semed to take a dislike to Pierre and declared she didn't have a bobbine in stock. A little charm was the order of the day by myself and it worked, but in the middle of this up came the Delage harnessed to three terrified horses with its engine roaring despite all efforts of the driver to throttle it back. Arabs, goats, dogs, melons and vegetables scattered in all directions and a general air of mayhem prevailed. Apparently Ralph had tired of waiting and hired a passing farmer to tow the Delage to the village, and switched on the engine just as they entered the village and the wretched thing had burst into life and screeched to a halt at the garage. Soon the garage foreman found a spare bobbine (actually borrowed from another car under repair) and several hundred francs changed hands and we were on our way.

All this delay meant it was dark when we got to Algiers and we had to hunt around for lodgings. This was easy as Algiers was under British jurisdiction and the naval duty officer found us a couple of rooms at a commandeered hotel, with Pierre and his mate staying with relations. In the morning we obtained a complete set of lifeboat stores and other navigational equipment including a loudhailer from the Dept. of War Transport. We visited the NAAFI and were able to organise a reasonable quota of gin, whiskey and English cigarettes, the latter made a welcome change from the American ones available from the U. S. Army in Oran. This took most of the day and the springs of the Delage began to creak with the weight of stores, and it was obvious there would not be room for both of us, so Ralph decided to go to Maison Blanche airport and thumb a lift to Oran - always very easy in wartime if you were in uniform and able to tell a good story. We stayed the night at a huge four-bedroom apartment of one of the Dept. of War Transport boys after a very pleasant party, and next morning we topped up with gasoline, requisitioned a few spares for the Delage, and set off back heavily-loaded. Our progress was very slow and it was dark when we got to Orleansville with still 100 miles to go. Everything seemed shut so we stopped at the French Foreign Legion sergeant's mess to try our luck and hit the jackpot. We were welcomed with open arms and they rustled up a meal for us although dinner had finished, and we had a riotous couple of hours and departed humming rude French Army songs having firmly cemented l'entente cordial.

It was midnight when we arrived back in Oran, we dropped off Pierre and the driver invited me to stay the night. He was a retired jeweller and the three days seemed to have been quite an adventure for him. His charming wife accepted this travel-stained Englishman with the utmost aplomb and made me very welcome, quickly providing champagne and sandwiches. We sat up until 2.00 a.m. whilst her husband regaled her with a full account of our odyssey. After a good night's sleep they gave me breakfast, then took me to the M. L. base where our precious cargo was unloaded and handed out. Ralph was already back courtesy of the R. A. F. and we agreed it had been a very worthwhile exercise, and Capt. Edgar was pleased to see me and the 'loot' when I got back to *Cardium*.

On 20th November,1943 Mers el Kebir had a memorable visit by the American battleship *Iowa* carrying President Roosevelt, General Marshal and other high-ranking officers on their way to the Teheran conference. We had been vaguely briefed previously by two of the U. S. assistant port directors that we were to give 3,500 tons of fuel with a similar amount from the *Yankee Arrow*, only trouble was that they didn't tell us we only had seven hours to do it. The entire harbour was cleared of everything that floated except the two oilers, while the shoreline was swarming with service personnel armed to the teeth. Into all of this heavy security steamed the Royal Navy cruiser *Sheffield* homeward bound for a refit with a number of service and civilian passengers on board. The U. S. port director was furious as nobody had told him *Sheffield* was coming and it almost required an act of Congress to let us go alongside and refuel her. She left before dawn of the big day, then in steamed the huge *Iowa* and seemed to fill the harbour. Through the binoculars we could see President Roosevelt, General Marshall and other staff members disembarking into a convoy of Army vehicles which sped off to the airport. We had most of the port director's staff on board to see the events and one could hardly move on board. As soon as the President had departed, we berthed on the forward end of *Iowa* and *Yankee Arrow* berthed on the after end - she was so big there was plenty of room to spare. *Iowa* had a huge crew but not too many knew what they were doing. We pumped rather slowly at first giving her 100 tons in the first hour, but when her Chief Engineer came across to us and told us we only had four hours refuelling time left we upped the pumps to full speed. Ten minutes later came howls to slow down, and eventually we reached an acceptable speed and by delaying her departure by half an hour gave her the required amount so honour was satisfied and she steamed off into the sunset. Mers el Kebir had its finest hour, and it is interesting to note that *Iowa* was still in commission in 1991 during the Gulf war with Iraq.

By the end of November things were very quiet and the 'galley wireless' came to life with rumours that we were to go to the States for overhaul and refit, of which we were in dire need. Confirmation soon came and Capt. Edgar was asked if he would be Commodore ship of the convoy. This would mean all hands 'doubling up' in our cabins to accomodate the Commodore and his staff, but this would be a small price to pay for the joy of not having to keep station and not having to read flag signals and Aldis lamp signals which were part of every convoy. He put the proposition to us and it took less than a second for us to agree, so on on 15th December,1943 Capt. Thomas H. Taylor U.S.N., Lt. W.L. Glass and six signalmen came aboard with their gear and were duly installed. We had transferred the balance of our fuel to *Yankee Arrow* and *Benzene*, and were rushing around getting enough stores and victuals for the Atlantic voyage. At least two ships in the convoy had to have food put aboard by the escorts near the end before we reached New York. We had cases of spam, dehydrated eggs, potatoes, onions, masses of coffee and canned fruit but were very light on fresh vegetables and fresh meat except for a small amount of boneless beef. The balance was Algerian mutton which we reckoned was ancient goat, plus a few chickens - in fact we had quantity but not quality. Two bottles of gin and one questionable bottle of French brandy was the sum total of our bond store.

We sailed on 6th December,1943 just after noon then half an hour later one of our famous telescopic pipes snapped, but Geordie Brooks and his boys had us going again in three hours. We joined our convoy GUS 23 by 7.00 p.m. and Capt. Taylor and his boys were in action. Things had changed for the better since we were last in convoy twelve months previously and we enjoyed the feeling of freedom and having competent signalmen doing all of the hard work and everyone keeping station on us for a change. We seemed to have masses of escorts, moving Spanish fishing boats out of our way and generally keeping order, and dropping the odd depth charge to remind us there was a war on. We were through the Straits of Gibraltar by 8th December and were joined by more ships from Casablanca to give a convoy of 45 ships mostly 'Liberties' and a couple of tankers. The Senior Escort Officer in *Wilkes* came to deliver mail for the Commodore but unfortunately got caught in the turbulence of our port propeller and poked a hole in the engine room with his starboard anchor. Luckily it was in the 'tween deck and we were able to put a cement box over the hole so no real harm was done.

Next morning I got star sights and a position for Capt. Taylor then we gave him a longitude at 8.00 a.m. followed by the noon position so the Commodore was well supplied with accurate positions. As there were so many Liberty ships which had much better accomodation than ours, we asked Capt. Taylor why he had picked on us for Commodore ship. His reply was 'Hell Captain, you boys know how to navigate and that's what I need, 90% of ours have only the Captain who can take sights properly and if anything happens to him you're up the creek without a paddle. A lot of those guys out there don't know the stern end of a ship from the bow, besides I checked the records of you boys and safety is more important to me than comfort'. Not that Capt. Taylor was badly off as Capt. Edgar gave him his bed and slept on his dayroom settee. I gave my signalman lodger my bunk and slept on my settee, not that I was particularly noble, my settee was nearer the door in case a rapid exit was necessary.

In the event we had a peaceful crossing as regards enemy action but the weather was rather bad and it took us seventeen days to reach New York. We dropped anchor in New York harbour late in the evening of 24th December,1943, close to a mass of loaded ships which were due out in the next convoy. Lt. Glass produced a bottle of bourbon to his eternal credit and we gathered the signalmen into my cabin for a stirrup cup with only one bottle of brandy left in our medicine cabinet. They were a splendid bunch of men and we had reached tremendous rapport during the voyage, and two of them came back to visit us during our repairs. Capt. Edgar went ashore with Capt. Taylor and his staff, promising to send some Christmas dinner, but as it was after 10.00 p.m. we treated this with much distrust. However we were happy enough to be in a safe harbour and have a good night's rest. I was up at 4.00 a.m. on Christmas Day to take over the anchor watch and was not the most happy person in the world. Disgruntled would be the word as I surveyed the dozens of grey shapes around us, wreathed in a cold, clammy mist and all laden with fresh food.

We were still officially in quarantine but could not, in any case, go ashore until we had been issued with American I.D. cards complete with picture and thumb prints. Our monotonous diets had us all longing for some fresh meat and vegetables as our beef had run out five days previously and only stringy Algerian goat, dehydrated cabbage and spuds was left for Christmas dinner. A motor launch appeared bringing a young Coastguard seamen and our agent from Furness, Withy & Co. Ltd. They listened with sympathy to our tale of woe and the agent mentioned there was an Anglo-Saxon tanker anchored nearby. It was *Empire Alliance* owned by the M.O.W.T. but managed by Anglo-Saxon and she was loaded and due to sail in the next convoy on 27th December. The agent had a crew list and on perusing this found I knew Capt. Freddie Vines, and his Chief Officer, Chief Engineer and the Chief Steward. Hope springs eternal as I broached the one bottle of medicinal brandy, called it French cognac, and proceeded to work on the Coastguard's sympathy. This coupled with large cups of American coffee had the desired effect and we all agreed that although I couldn't go ashore there was nothing to stop me visiting another ship. I received a very warm greeting as I climbed the ladder of

Empire Alliance, and rapidly I explained the situation and although it was too late to thaw out turkeys, I was given two magnificent smoked hams, a case of eggs, two sacks of spuds and four cases of beer - thus assuring my shipmates of a good Christmas dinner. I was about to leave with this manna from heaven when Freddie said 'Why don't you come back and have dinner with us and stay the night, there are sure to be boats in the morning'. So back to *Cardium* bearing gifts which were hastily hoisted inboard by my shipmates. After another drink the Coastguard saw no reason why he shouldn't drop me back on the *Empire Alliance* on his way ashore. I left my shipmates preparing a good Christmas dinner and had no qualms about returning for a riotous day with Capt. Freddie Vines and his hospitable crew.

I slept on Freddie's settee and was back on *Cardium* by 9.30 a.m. on Boxing Day just in time to be photographed, thumb-printed and issued with the Coastguard I.D. pass. I had brought a bottle of Scotch and a bottle of gin so I was able to gather my fellow officers together for a wee dram of something better than Algerian red. Gradually the citizens of New York emerged from their Christmastide activities, and we moved to our first berth at Staten Island where an army of workers began removing the stains and scars of our months in North Africa, straightening guard rails and generally repairing the ravages of ill use. Anglo-Saxon's own Engineer Superintendent together with a gaggle of dockyard officials, D.E.M.S. officers from the R.N., U.S.N. officers who assumed an almost proprietarial air, and other marine people with nothing better to do descended upon us. Our greatest joy was fresh, decent food along with cases of beer and other alcohol for our leisure hours. The shore gangs worked 24 hours a day or at least made a noise for 24 hours a day and as Chief Officer I seemed to be at the beck and call of everyone, but Roly Tinn and Bobbie Annett and Chief Engineer Geordie Brooks all got their fair share.

Half of the Chinese crew deserted within two days of berthing at Staten Island including the Chief Cook - not that he was much of a loss - taking their North African 'black market' proceeds with them. Practically every one of them had made a small fortune trading with the troops and locals at Mers el Kebir and they decided an extended holiday was the order of the day. Gradually over the next two weeks all but eight of them disappeared, never to be seen on *Cardium* again. They had all been playing Mah Jong and other gambling games for high stakes in the fo'c'stle on the voyage across. As it was, Ellis Island was full of Chinese ex-sailors as we were to discover when we finally sailed. Capt. Edgar made a brief appearance, expressed horror at the dockyard-induced shambles, and departed leaving a telephone number. Our agents Furness,Withy & Co. Ltd were very good, making sure we were paid a victualling allowance to eat ashore at the local diner. The assistant steward Yip Yeung was a tower of strength and both he and I had been in the ship for two years and he took a fatherly interest in my welfare. The Chief Steward had decamped with the chief cook, but Yip had all of the keys which he used to great advantage. Every morning we got a full breakfast and if we were too busy to go ashore at lunchtime, some ham sandwiches or similar nosh would appear as if by magic.

In addition to the normal repairs, a further horde of workmen were erecting a 'spar' deck over the main deck to carry aircraft in boxes to the U. K. but on our next voyage we didn't load any, but at least the structure was in place for future voyages.

It consisted of vertical steel posts welded to the main deck, across the top of which horizontal steel bearers, both athwartships and fore-and-aft, were welded at five feet intervals.   Diagonal strengthening posts made walking along the main deck a hazardous procedure and once more Heath Robinson would have been delighted. When we finally came to load a cargo of fuel oil, getting from tank to tank for valve opening and shutting, was difficult.   By this stage of the war our old, heavy brass and copper hoses were very old-fashioned and , to our joy, we were issued with lightweight neoprene hoses with aluminium 'snap' couplings.   A continuous platform was constructed from the fo'c'stle to the poop along the starboard side, and two lengths of hose each 400 feet in length were laid.   The idea was to oil the escorts over the stern and obviate the old 'alongside' method which had caused such mayhem and damage in the past.   Modern Replenishment by Sea (R.A.S.) is by the 'alongside' method thanks to the advances in technology but in *Cardium* we didn't even have a gyro compass and things were primitive.   The sight of an escort vessel veering away from an oiler with the hose still connected is something never to be forgotten.   Stirrup wires parting with loud twangs, endless fathoms of copper hose unravelling in strips across the horizon, fuel oil calming the angry seas as it gushes from the ruptured hose, terrified crew members frantically trying to unscrew the hose at the manifold while dodging the shreds of broken wire, and the Chief Officer mournfully watching as his career went down the plughole - all stirring stuff and conducive to ulcers ! But oiling astern is a much simpler procedure and before the war ended I had done literally dozens of astern oilings and never spilt a drop. It can be said quite safely that the North Atlantic had hundreds of satisfied Shell customers by V. E. day !

We moved over to Brooklyn Navy yard from Staten Island with work on the spar deck proceeding and the addition of steel racks to carry several dozen depth charges, without detonators and thus safe (we were assured).   The idea was that when the escort ships ran out of depth charges they nipped alongside and we swung the depth charges out on our derricks and the escort hove them on board with a wire previously fired by a Coston gun.   Quite simple really but not so easy on the heaving gray wastes of the North Atlantic, but more of that later.   After a few days of extreme activity we got used to it all and set out to recharge our social batteries.   There were a couple of dozen Anglo-Saxon officers in New York mostly staying at the Great Northern Hotel in which the late Jack Dempsey, one-time world champion heavyweight boxer, had a financial interest.   They were all waiting to pick up new ships under the Lease/Lend scheme and many of them were old acquaintances.   We managed to get a couple of them to relieve us for a few days so I was able to spend New Year's Eve with friends in New Jersey and had a wecome four-day break.

The port authorities were hot on anti-sabotage precautions and we were supposed to have three shore watchmen on duty round the clock.   In addition one officer had to be patrolling the ship 24 hours a day.   Our three radio officers were lumbered with the night patrols after some equitable financial arrangements were made, but also one Deck and two Engineer Officers had to be aboard.   This latter was no hardship as it was normal Anglo-Saxon practice in any case.   The British Consul also had a number of security officers whose function was to patrol the New York dock system and do spot checks on all British ships.   It goes without saying we christened them the 'gestapo' but saw only one in four weeks so they must have been thin on the ground. Our particular visitor was an amiable English gentleman who had spent 35 years in the Shanghai Customs service. He probably knew little about security but he gave us a good report - so he should considering he managed to knock a big hole in my bottle of Scotch. We also encountered some of our U. S. Navy friends from North Africa and were quite overwhelmed with hospitality and met dozens of officers and ratings we had dealings with over the previous year.

My father-in-law Capt. J. D. Miller OBE came into New York on his ship while we were at Brooklyn Navy Yard and came to visit me. On the same day an old friend Lt. Cmdr. Bill Blore U.S.N.R. was driving past the yard when he spotted *Cardium* tied up alongside and did a sharp U-turn and pulled up at the gangway. He joined us for a drink and stayed for lunch as old Yip Yeung was able to rustle up a little extra food. Bill invited us to his home and the three of us had a delightful evening around the piano, with my father-in-law having a god tenor voice. Bill brought us back about midnight and Dad and I retired to bed feeling happy. Next day I took a day off and we went shopping, after which Dad bought me an expensive lunch and departed to his ship. Dear old Joe Miller OBE was a splendid father-in-law and had recovered from his injuries sustained when he was torpedoed in the ill-fated TMI convoy, and went on to survive until retirement.

The weather was mostly sub-zero and all the toilets and pipes froze up to our great discomfort. Toilets and showers were provided ashore for us but this involved trudging many yards through the slush and snow so we devised a 'portable dunny'. Looking back we could have made a fortune if we had known how to market the bloody thing - alas, opportunity doesn't knock too often. There were never less than a dozen welding machines and compressors on the dockside and they were going 24 hours a day. The noise was horrendous but after a few days the spar deck and depth charge racks were finished and the decibel level dropped a bit. We moved berth one day to lie alongside the old Esso tanker *Iroquois*. She was the brainchild of one of John D. Rockefeller's minions and quite unique, at the time of her building, in the magnitude of her operation. She carried about 10,000 tons of oil and on her poop was an enormous towing winch for towing the 10,000 dwt barge *Navahoe*. *Iroquois* used to tow *Navahoe* to and fro across the Atlantic between U.S.A. and the U. K., and if the wind was favourable *Navahoe* would hoist fore-and-aft sails resulting in a decrease in fuel consumption on *Iroquois*. The operation was phased out in 1930 after 23 years of operation and *Iroquois* sailed on alone until scrapped at Dalmuir in 1946.

We finished our overhaul after four weeks, took on stores and bunkers and loaded a cargo of Admiralty fuel oil. A couple of quartermasters, the deck storekeeper, pumpman and two engine room ratings still remained on board. They were probably those who had come off second best in the mighty Mah Jong sessions, but they were a big help when it came to loading. With all the uprights and diagonals of the new spar deck, visibility on the main deck was almost zero and loading was carried out with a vast amount of whistle blowing. We had promoted Yip Yeung to Chief Steward and when the collection of Chinese ex-deserters from the Immigration Department's luxurious apartment block on Ellis Island arrived, he soon whipped his new crew into shape. Our new crew of thirty came aboard the night we were sailing with an equal number of security guards to make sure the crew didn't desert again. These 'guards' were the toughest bunch of hombres you could expect to meet anywhere and looked like mafia capos in training. All with suspicious bulges under their left armpits, we reckoned they were leftovers from the Al Capone days but were too scared to express an opinion. They spent the night playing poker and consuming large quantities of liquor but a few patrolled the decks and our new crew were sufficiently impressed to stay indoors and keep their heads down.

In late January, 1944 we hove in our frozen mooring ropes and managed to avoid maiming our new crew, then proceeded up the East river into Long Island Sound and then through the Cape Cod Canal, which we had traversed some 16 months previously, and joined a convoy at Boston for escort to Halifax (NS) where we anchored in Bedford Basin. As usual, Bedford Basin was crammed with Allied merchant ships but were not there long enough to count them. Alongside came a Navy barge which transferred about fifty depth charges which were secured in their racks. They were the size of a five gallon paint drum and from memory contained about 250 lbs of Amatol, an explosive guaranteed to blow the tripe out of anything within fifty metres range. We were assured once more they were quite harmless as they had no detonators. Promptly we departed to practice oiling and depth charge transfer with a poor, unfortunate R.C.N. corvette and spent a hazardous and nerve-wracking day at sea. Oiling with the new gear and 'line of sight' control was easy and we were all finished and had the gear recovered by lunchtime. We then went on to depth charge transfer, and the winch on the main deck at the depth charge racks was invisible to me on the bridge so Sutton was lumbered with repeating my signals to the winchman. Bobbie Annett stood by ready to pounce if the winchman got it wrong.

There was a fair swell running and up came our corvette on the port quarter, rolling as only those little ships know how. It was always said that you could put a corvette in the middle of a paddock and if there was a heavy dew she would roll. Anyhow, they fired a line across with a Coston gun and my back-up team of six Chinese sailors hauled aboard the transfer wire which was duly shackled to the short bridle to which our wire winch runner had already been shackled. The procedure was to hoist the charge from the rack, then the seamen on the corvette would haul it across whilst we paid out the runner from the derrick and winch - sounds simple ! However the R.C.N. had decided the exercise would be good practice for some of their new recruits, so we had the blind leading the blind. Fortunately there were enough experienced hands among them to preserve some sort of order. As the two ships surged apart, then came together, the depth charge was in the sea one minute then ten seconds later was dangling in mid-air with *Cardium's* wire and the corvette's wire twanging away. As the corvette was rolling heavily this blasted can of Amatol was being tossed around like a bag of lethal chaff. Roly was on the bridge making soothing noises to Capt. Edgar who was becoming concerned at this carry-on. On the spar deck we had to watch our footing as there were large gaps between the girders and we could easily have fallen eight feet to the main deck. After what seemed an hour but was actually three minutes the depth charge arrived aboard the corvette but not before clouting her ship's side putting a nasty dent into it. When this happened our hearts stopped for a split second but the corvette did not disappear in a cloud of smoke and proved that the tale about them not exploding without detonators was correct. One supposes the escorts had enough room in their magazines for spare detonators. We spent another hair-raising couple of hours transferring more, then just for laughs, brought them back aboard and restowed them in their racks. The naval oficers who were observing all of this fun expressed great satisfaction at our efforts and one Lt. H. Rainey was kind enough to write in my vistors book 'Mr. Allen's superb good nature is unshaken in the face of oiling at sea and depth charges being added to his many duties. 22nd January,1944' I have to add that my superb good nature was all on the surface, inside I was quivering like a jelly.

When we got back to Bedford Basin Capt. Edgar celebrated in no uncertain fashion and we all felt very pleased with ourselves as well as relieved. After about four more days during which we had a couple of runs ashore to stock up on groceries for home and give the City Club a visit, we departed once more for the gray, heaving wastes. By this time thanks to Capt. Walker R. N. and his fellow Allied naval vessels and some odd hybrid ships called Merchant Aircraft Carriers (MAC)s the U-boats were not nearly so successful as they had been so we had a good run across from Halifax to Glasgow in a fifty ship convoy. Apart from the usual odd depth charge attack carried out by the escorts, there were no untoward incidents and we anchored at the Tail of the Bank on 14th February,1944 - extremely glad to be home once more and in one piece. I was on watch at 0400 hours next morning and as dawn broke I could make out the shape of two of these MAC ships anchored nearby. They were both Anglo-Saxon tankers converted for the purpose and I remember thinking they might be interesting ships to serve on and a challenge.

We moved up to Bowling later that afternoon and had all been sending messages to our wives announcing our safe arrival, unfortunately I didn't know whether Celia was in London or South Shields but had sent messages to both places. The agent gave me a lift into Glasgow and I started a shuttle run between both railway stations hoping to catch up with my wife as the London train came into one station and the Newcastle train into another. Everything was blacked out of course and after four fruitless hours of searching without success gave up with the last train arrived at 9.00 p.m. The problem of where to stay the night was solved when I phoned my mother and got the name and number of the guest house where she always stayed when she worked in Glasgow. I then rang the guest house and they put me up on a bed settee in the lounge. A good evening was spent talking to several of the guests including two American soldiers on leave who were quite interested in my North African stories and a reasonable rapport developed after a few whiskies. I was loaned an alarm clock and got my weary head down on the pillow and was roused by its jangle at 6.00 a.m. and staggered out into the cold gloom of a February morning in Glasgow. A passing milkman gave me a lift back into the centre of Glasgow and at 8.00 a.m. I pinned a note for Celia on the door of the agent's office, requesting her to meet me for breakfast at a cafe across the road.

I was enjoying a pair of kippers when I really felt Celia's presence and sure enough when I turned around there she was in the doorway, scanning the assembled diners and we were together at last. Life took on a new meaning and we had breakfast together for the first time in 15 months. A very joyous reunion, and we had missed each other in the blackout with Celia spending the night at the Y.W.C.A. We went back to *Cardium* to finish discharging cargo then we were scheduled to go to Greenock for voyage repairs, degaussing and other Admiralty matters. My relief had arrived but Capt. Edgar asked me to stay on for a few days while he nipped home with his wife for a short leave. I was quite happy to stay as Celia was with me so we moved into his accomodation leaving the new Chief Officer to do the work. We had a lovely few days then off to London for a well-earned leave. I had been in *Cardium* for 26 months and knew every rivet !

MERCHANT AIRCRAFT CARRIERS 1944 - 1945

I was to see *Cardium* again five years later when I was a pilot for Shell Sarawak Oilfields in Miri. She had been sold to London Greeks and rechartered under her new name of *Hawthorn Hill* owned by Counties Ship Management. Her Captain was an Irishman, 80 years of age with a mane of white air, a flowing white beard and bearing a remarkable resemblance to an old Testament prophet. He was over six feet tall with hands like hams and forearms as thick as the lower limbs of an oak tree. He ruled the ship with a rod of iron but the crew seemed to love him for it as charisma was the operative word. He seemed to be at odds, on occasions, with his Chief Officer, who was in his mid-Sixties and I heard him refer to him as 'that stupid boy' - but once more I digress.

So the end of February,1944 saw me on leave, quite a new experience, in London with two months of relative leisure, dodging bombs and scouring S. E. London for extra rations. Anglo-Saxon called me up for interview at St. Helen's Court on a couple of occasions with Capt. Jimmie Wilson, Head of Personnel and Jerry Walters, his Chief of Staff. They took me out to lunch and told me to enjoy my leave as I wouldn't be required until April. Some of the more unorthodox schemes for improving M. N./ R. N./ U.S.N. procedures must have reached receptive ears at the Admiralty as I was twice called in for a debriefing conference and twice taken out to lunch. This was almost equivalent to a knighthood, extracting two lunches from the Admiralty, but I was only too happy to oblige. Celia still had to keep working at the War Office as her work as a confidential shorthand typist was considered extremely important. However they were very sympathetic as they allowed her to work part-time and finish at 1.00 p.m. every day. As she had been working a 13 day fortnight for fifteen months it was the very least they could do.

All Merchant Navy officers wore uniform when ashore and this had a most beneficial effect. In our native North East coast, where everyone and his dog had sea-going connections, the Merchant Navy was as commonplace as fish and chips, thus arousing no particular interest. However in London we were held in very high esteem and one only had to appear at the back of a queue in uniform to be ushered to the front, ahead of old pensioners and pregnant women. It was a bit embarrasing at times, especially when a lot of shopkeepers wouldn't even take ration coupons, but who was I to thwart the will of the people ? After all I had helped to get the bloody stuff here in the first place. All in all we didn't do too badly and I consoled myself with the thought that I had earned it as I was always hot on self-justification.

There was a Merchant Navy club in Rupert Street just off Piccadilly Circus, run by a blonde lady called Doris Hare, who was quite a singer and ran a programme for the BBC especially for the Merchant Navy. On the days when the proceedings were being broadcast the BBC provided free beer for M. N. personnel, and it didn't take me long to catch up with this little lark, and I wish to thank the BBC for several jars of the old 'singing syrup'. They also served reasonable meals if you were there on time, but one had to be quick as everyone shot off to lunch at noon. I would meet Celia at 1.00 p.m. when she finished work by which time most restaurants had the 'Sorry - sold out' signs in their windows. We regarded each lunch as a challenge and usually obtained something, with our favourite places being the Merchant Navy club and Lyons Corner House in the Strand but one day we finished up at Frascati's, an upmarket restaurant in Oxford Street where we dined on jugged hare as that was the only item left on the menu. We were the only diners left but the staff were extremely courteous and solicitous of our welfare. It cost me the thick end of a wek's pay but the general ambience was worth it.

We were sharing a flat with Celia's sister Bea and her husband Mick at this time. Mick had been called up and was a R. N. rating in the Fleet Air Arm or 'Branch' as it was called - a hangover from the days when the service was the 'Fleet Air Arm Branch of the Royal Navy'. Flyers, never ones to stand on ceremony, called it the 'Branch' and that was the normal expression during the war. One fine morning the four of us decided to have a walk to a local pub called The Dover Patrol and have a quick drink before lunch, after which we would go up to the M. N. Club for a dance they were putting on. Approaching the bar of the pub I noticed some small bottles of stout. My mind flashed back to New York where one of our American friends had introduced me to a mixture of champagne and stout called 'black velvet'. I only had one but had found it extremely palatable, and as I was on leave and relatively wealthy I gathered four of these lethal potions and distributed them. We probably had three of these and waltzed back home giggling like a bunch of schoolgirls and singing merrily. Once home we all collapsed and went asleep until 6.00 p.m. and never got to the dance - life is like that ! Celia and I enjoyed our leave and our rare moments of 'togetherness'.

By April,1944 it was obvious that the invasion of Europe was imminent, and large convoys of shrouded tanks on trucks thundered through Blackheath bound for South Coast ports. Large houses were taken over and converted into hospitals, huge rocket batteries were already in place on the Heath itself and mass movements of troops were a daily occurence. A general air that something was about to happen prevailed, then in mi-April came the courteous telegram from Anglo-Saxon for me to appear at St. Helen's Court to discuss my next appointment. So off I went and was received by Jerry Walters in his usual friendly manner, he had the happy knack of making one feel you had made his day by appearing. A priceless gift and typical of his attitude. Jerry always had a sincere feeling for all his staff and was a major factor in keeping people in the company over the many years he was in the Staff department. After a cup of tea and a cigarette, he got down to brass tacks 'Mr. Allen, it is my pleasure to tell you that the management have decided to appoint you Chief Officer of the Macship *Adula*. A feather in your cap as only our best men go on these ships. Normally all Senior Officers like yourself have to go on a 'Philante' course but we have enough faith in your experience in North Africa and the 'Philante' will not be necessary (the 'Philante' course involved anti-submarine work with aircraft which all previous Senior Officers had undertaken).

'The Royal Navy holds you in very high regard, as we do' and he then took me out to lunch.

As I am very sarcastic, I thought that if the Royal Navy and Shell think that I'm that bloody good, how come I haven't got a medal. It was long afterwards that I discovered that Shell had indeed recommended me for a 'gong' but a spate of Russian convoys had used up the quota of medals as even they were rationed. So it was a case of bad luck, however I had always said that all I wanted out of the war was the Allied Victory Medal and be alive to receive it - at least I achieved that and am very thankful to be here. After this flow of soul and feast of reason assisted by a couple of Watney's ales, I returned home and shortly found myself in an L.M.S. train to Glasgow and *Adula*. It was hardly a fun trip as it was crowded with troops and I was glad to emerge early in the morning and present myself to the agents and thence on board *Adula*. I was to relieve Bob Birdsall, one of the most efficient deck officers I have ever met and a thorough gentleman. He took me through the take-over procedure at breakneck speed as he was to join my old ship *Cardium*. Capt. Jimmie Rumbellow greeted me with great enthusiasm which rather surprised me as Bob Birdsall was such a very good officer. I can only assume that Jerry Walters had given me a good C.V. and that Jimmie had found out that I had survived 15 months in the Mediterranean. Bob Birdsall and I perambulated around, over and across this 'flat-topped abortion' as they were called, all day and well into the evening until I felt I knew enough to take over. We were berthed at Glasgow for repairs of some sort but our normal home port was Greenock where we would anchor at the Tail of the Bank.

A word about these Macships would not come amiss at this point. Losses due to U-boat action in 1942 were very high especially in the area known as 'The Gap'. This was virtually in the middle of the North Atlantic and while Allied aircraft could patrol from the U. K., Iceland, U.S.A./Canada and the Azores, there was a large section which could not be covered. It was proposed to convert suitable merchant ships into 'baby flatops' and John Lamb, Senior Technical Superintendent of Anglo-Saxon, took up the idea with enthusiasm. Some nine of our tankers were converted and one was purpose-built with two of these under the Dutch flag. Starting with *Rapana* in February,1943 she was operational five months later, and in all 13 tankers were converted or built plus six grain carrying versions within 21 months. All of the Shell ships were of a similar class which helped to simplify and speed up the conversion. Initially the reception was lukewarm and a certain amount of 'tooth sucking' and 'tut-tutting' went on at the Admiralty and other bastions of power, but John Lamb and his staff soon proved their point and 'The Gap' was covered. Admiral Doenitz and his U-boats started to suffer heavy losses from mid 1943 and no longer had much success on the North Atlantic convoys. The Allies still suffered grievous losses but so did the U-boats.

The Macships operated three Fairey Swordfish (Stringbags) aircraft in the tanker versions and four in the grain-carrying versions, and were an outstanding success from the moment they became operational. The Stringbags were so-called because of the variety of armament they could carry - torpedoes, depth charges, bombs or rockets could be loaded, although in our case, torpedoes were not on the menu. They carried a crew of three - pilot, navigator and air gunner/radio operator.

Adula herself had the bridge on the starboard side as was normal in aircraft carriers. It was a small tower which also housed the radar, aircraft control platform and signalling platform (V/S). When flying aircraft on and off it became rather like the London tube during the rush hour. This imbalance of weights meant some neat and tricky footwork in the initial and final stages of loading and discharging, whether cargo or ballast but it became very simple when you got to know how.

I had complained bitterly about the spar deck on *Cardium* obstructing the view and complicating cargo operations but it had proved very good training for *Adula*. She was just a mass of heavy girders supporting the flight deck - vertical, horizontal and diagonal. Safety helmets were still on the drawing board and our service 'tin hats' were too cumbersome so we 'bore our scars' with dignity. Negotiating a Macship's maindeck, plus the narrow, torturous ladders leading up to the navigating bridge, required much concentration. The total complement was around 120 - roughly equal M. N. and R. N. plus eight Army gunners to man the two Bofors guns. There was a tremendous rapport from the very beginning between all personnel and it was especially so on *Adula*. The Services personnel were under Air Staff Officer (A.S.O.) Lt. Cmdr. Brian Walsh-Atkins R.N.V.R. and comprised five pilots - two of whom were 'batsmen' to guide the pilots on and off the flight deck, three navigators and the Doctor, David Moffat - all Lts. or Sub Lts. R.N.V.R. The rear gunners were Leading Seamen known as Telegraphist Air Gunners (T.A.G.) and there was a C.P.O. in charge of the maintenance gang of fitters, electricians, armourers etc plus radar operators and signalmen.

The original navigating bridge had been removed to make way for the flight deck but the original accomodation, at lower bridge deck level, remained. Forward of this accomodation a deckhouse on two levels had been constructed for the naval officers, plus air pilot wardroom, operating theatre and surgery. Abaft the bridge, a further accomodation block was built to house the service personnel and the radio room. The old engineer's accomodation under the poop had been converted to two-berth cabins for the crew and new quarters for the engineer officers had been constructed on the poop itself. The smokeroom, which ran across the forward end of the poop, was converted into a messroom for the engineer officers and some of the 'Branch' officers. Every nook and cranny was utilised as storage space for the vast amount of spares that we carried to keep the aircraft operational and there seemed to be dozens of doors everywhere, each with a cryptic message to inform the passerby of what lay inside. In no. 4 centre tank were two cylindrical tanks to hold the avgas for the Stringbags while the other twenty tanks were available for cargo or ballast - only about 10% of our original capacity was lost and we loaded around 10,000 tons of Admiralty fuel oil in Halifax on every voyage. We retained about 800 tons after discharge in the Clyde to refuel the escorts en route back to Halifax and this had a beneficial 'spin-off' effect. As we had no cargo on board we officially 'cleared' and were technically 'at sea' and thus entitled to a weekly issue of cigarettes, liquor, beer and chocolate at duty-free prices.

Macships had a distinct advantage over 'Woolworth' carriers which were of a similar hull design but carried more aircraft and were under the White Ensign. The 'Woolworth' carriers had a draft of around 17 feet and this could not be varied very much. They were very lively in any sort of bad weather conditions whereas in the

Macships we could pump in extra ballast and get them down to 24 feet draft or more, making them much more stable - without exception the pilots preferred Macships. The tanker Macships had no hangar and the Stringbags, wings folded back, were secured at the after end of the flight deck, surrounded by eight feet high steel plates which were hinged and lay flat on the deck when not in use. The whole set-up was called a 'zareba', a very apt term left over from the Boer War. All of the plates were perforated to baffle strong winds and the system worked extremely well. Despite some appalling weather from time to time we never had a plane blown away, contradicting the opinions of the pundits.

We moved from Glasgow to the Tail of the Bank and anchored off Gourock where various people who had been on leave rejoined. Next day out into the Irish Sea to take on our planes and conduct exercises. The 'Branch' boys and their planes were based at Maydown in Northern Ireland whilst their ship was in Glasgow or other Clyde port. Our Flight was 'P' Flight led by Lt. (A) John Godley R.N.V.R. and he was first on board followed by his other two pilots. John was actually the Hon. John Godley and is now Lord Kilbracken. There followed a busy day of landings and takeoffs and we were back at the anchorage at 1900 hours, when I was able to meet and talk to my new shipmates and a very cheerful and happy crowd they turned out to be. After my year with Force H I probably knew more about naval procedures than they did but they were really keen lads and we got on very well from the start. They were all in their early twenties except Brian Walsh-Atkins the ASO who was my age at 29 years with the 'Branch' boys probably regarding us as 'over the hill'.

We had several days doing 'working-up' exercises then we were off with a forty ship convoy to the Eastern seaboard of Canada and the U.S.A. The procedure in convoy was to give the Macship plenty of manoeuvring room to turn into the wind to fly off or recover aircraft as shown :-

```
                 ↑
                 |  LINE OF ADVANCE
                 |
     X   X   X   X   X   X   X
     X   X   X   X   X   X   X
     X   X   X   X   X   X   X
     X   X   X   X   X   X   X
     X   X   X   X   X   X   X
     X   X   X   X   X   X   X
     X   X   X   X   X   X   X
     X   X   X   X   X   X   X
     X   X                X   X
     X   X     MACSHIP    X   X
     X   X    OPERATING   X   X
     X   X      AREA      X   X
     X   X                X   X
     X   X                X   X
```

The voyage was normal with no U-boat attacks and the aircraft flying off on a variety of patrols as ordered by the Senior Officer Escort (S.O.E.) until 15th May, 1944 when we had a near tragedy. John Godley with his crew were on a patrol some 100 miles ahead of the convoy when their engine suddenly packed up and went dead. Charlie Simpson, John's air gunner/radio operator, tried to send out a 'mayday' distress call but the radio also packed up (the R.A.F. did not have a monopoly on gremlins). By a fortunate coincidence, their plight was seen by Ian Parkin and Stan Holness, pilot and navigator of another of our planes who directed the fishing schooner *Kasagra* from Lunenburg (NS) to where John and his crew had crashed. The *Kasagra* launched a boat and John, Jake and Charlie were rescued in the nick of time. They had been in the sea nearly an hour which is considered to be fatal in that part of the North Atlantic. However the crew of *Kasagra* were well versed in the treatment of limbs suffering from exposure and handled the aircrew with skill until they were transferred to a Canadian Navy corvette, then to the rescue/hospital ship which was part of every convoy by this time. Eventually they arrived in hospital in Halifax (NS) but were sufficiently recovered to rejoin and come back to the U.K. with us as passengers. In the meantime we went alongside the Imperoil jetty near Dartmouth (NS), our other two aircraft having flown off to the R.A.C.F station also at Dartmouth.

I got my first experience of deballasting and loading a ship with the navigating bridge on the starboard side. The trick was to take out all of the ballast except about 200 tons in no. 3 port wing. This balanced the weight of the bridge and kept the ship upright, and we then loaded a centre tank to capacity with fuel oil, so far so good. We then deballasted the port wing tank then gradually bled fuel oil from the centre tank to the port wing tank as the ballast was pumped out to the shore and the upright position was maintained. Simple really but it involved a great deal of whistle blowing as we couldn't see each other and there were no such things as 'walkie talkies'. Like everything else, we got used to it. After loading we went out several days for exercises with the aircraft but anchored every night in Bedford Basin and were able to get a couple of runs ashore for shopping.

We sailed for the U. K. again in another large convoy which was shepherded safely to its destination without incident. Our Stringbags were certainly effective in keeping the U-boats down. When not flying, we used the flight deck for rather lethal hockey matches and these and poker were popular pastimes. We organised quizzes and other indoor pursuits for the troops and generally kept up their morale. Maintenance was a permanent problem for my crew with plenty of overtime - always a welcome addition to any matelot's payslip. The aircrews flew off to Maydown as we approached the Clyde and we came to anchor at the Tail of the Bank on D Day when the Allies invaded Europe. All leave for service personnel was cancelled, except local leave, which caused a certain amount of disenchantment amongst the troops, especially as we went up to Finnart in Loch Long to discharge miles from civilisation. Three days later we were back at the Tail of the Bank and anchored off Gourock, awaiting our next convoy and more exercises. Shore leave was granted for most people and we had a regular service of drifters and similar craft to ferry personnel ashore and back. My shoregoing was pretty limited but as Celia had joined me and was living onboard, it was no hardship, especially as we now had a Fourth Officer to keep the anchor watch. Len Clark, an ex Humber apprentice pilot, was a very valuable addition and eventually was promoted to Third Officer and stayed with us to the end.

We had a couple of runs ashore to sample the delights of Glasgow then off to the Irish Sea for more exercises with our aircraft. John Godley had gone on sick leave and was replaced by Owen Johnson, a lanky New Zealander and one of many in the 'Branch'. He was a veteran flyer by the standards of the day and had over 1,000 flying hours in his log book. It was with Owen that I made my first ever flight in an aeroplane in an open cockpit Stringbag. We had often discussed over a pre-lunch gin in the wardroom, the reactions and feelings of aircrews, so we decided that some of us 'wingless wonders' should have a bash at the flying lark and see what it felt like. I must admit that I was the leader of this 'try anything once' brigade but chose Owen as my pilot as he seemed the least likely to try any stunts as he had such long experience. Just as well, as in the event, when we got back on deck and I was able to prise my fingers from the rim of the cockpit, it was found that my parachute had not been properly attached to the floor of the cockpit. The flight deck was some 460 feet long by 60 feet wide but looked awfully small when one was up in the air. Just the same, I found it most exhiliarating and did quite a number of flights including some from the R.C.A.F. aerodrome at Halifax (NS) where I was later a guest of the 'Branch' boys in January/February 1945 - each time making sure that I was firmly attached to the aeroplane.

So off we sailed from the Clyde in another 50 ship convoy, this time in company with another Macship, destined to become our 'chummy' ship. This was the Shell Dutch flag *Macoma*, manned by personnel of the Royal Netherlands Navy and Merchant Navy. She was owned by La Corona, the Dutch marine arm of Shell and had held this name since new, as had another Dutch-flag tanker conversion *Gadila*. During trials of *Gadila*, H. R. H. Prince Bernhard of the Netherlands inspected this vessel, and insisted upon landing on the deck himself. I hasten to add to those who may think this was another of those notorious cartels, that three other tanker Macships were manned by the British Tanker Co. Ltd (BP) personnel. In all there were nineteen Macships, ten Shell tankers, three BP tankers, four grain-carrying versions owned by the Hain Steamship Co. Ltd and two grain-carrying versions owned by Ben Line of Leith. There was no doubt that from the outset they made a very great contribution to winning the Battle of the Atlantic. We provided almost continual aircover all the way to Halifax (NS), and I seemed to be perpetually busy and time passed swiftly with my normal 4 to 8 watch morning and evening, and discussions with Capt. Jimmie Rumbellow, Brian Walsh-Atkins and Alec McGillivray, the Chief Engineer. I was always on deck for takeoffs and landings, being the ex-officio Damage Control Officer. Alec had the operation of the arrester wires and the barrier under his control.

The arrester wires ran from side to side across the flight deck and their purpose was to catch the hook projecting from the rear underside of the Stringbag and bring it to a halt. There was four of these wires, spaced some forty feet apart and most of our pilots were skilled enough to nominate a wire and catch it with the hook. The crash barrier was forward of the navigating bridge and a steel net, not unlike a ten foot-high wide-mesh tennis net, which stretched from side to side. This was to stop the aircraft falling into the sea if it failed to hook any of the arrester wires. A special arrester wire worked in conjunction with the crash barrier and was known as the 'Jesus Christ' wire, this being thought to be the expression used by the pilot and crew when they realised they had missed the proper arrester wires. The barrier was hinged and lay flat on the deck when aircraft were flying off. The arrester wires also lay flat during take-off but were elevated to one foot above the deck by vertical steel studs for landings. The whole system of arrester wires and barrier were steam-operated and controlled by Alec McGillivray from a position in the nets, close by the batsman on the port side near the stern. The 'batsman' was himself a 'Branch' pilot and was armed with what looked like 'ping-pong' bats and guided the planes on board by a variety of signals including the vital one of 'cut' to indicate that the aircraft engine had to be stopped as the hook was about to connect with the arrester wire.

Some five feet below flight deck level and along the whole length of the ship on each side were the 'Nets', and it was here that the aircraft handling parties were stationed during landings and takeoffs. Once landed, the barrier was dropped and the Stringbag motored up to the forward end where the handling parties folded back the wings and secured the aircraft to ringbolts in the deck. The barrier then went up and the next aircraft prepared to land on, with the three aircraft landing in as many minutes sometimes but usually it took a little longer. With such a small flight deck, it says a lot for the skill of our pilots in *Adula* as in the course of 17 months of operational flying they made some 300 deck landings, many in severe weather conditions without one case of damage.

Our only tragedy took place during the next voyage when Jack Harman and his crew were lost on the Grand Banks of Newfoundland. They had taken off on a dawn patrol when dense fog suddenly closed in. Ian Parkin, who was also on patrol, managed to get back by the skin of his teeth but Jack Harman ran out of fuel and crashed. We had a motor lifeboat slung out, ready to attempt a rescue, but a Canadian corvette recovered the bodies, steamed close to us and we took Dr. Moffatt over to see if anything could be done. I was in charge of the boat and returned to *Adula*, was hoisted inboard and we proceeded to catch up with the convoy. An hour or so later came a signal from Dr. Moffatt that all three were dead so once more I took the boat over to the corvette to pick up the 'Doc'. The fog was even thicker on leaving and in seconds we couldn't see a thing. Hiding my panic I headed in what I though was the right direction, and more by good luck than good management *Adula* suddenly appeared and I had to go full astern to avoid hitting her. We were soon back in the chocks and one very relieved Chief Officer hopped out of the boat. The corvette ranged alongside early that evening, and we reduced speed and Stan and his two crew were buried with full military honours. Almost to a man, our entire crew of R.N., M.N. and Army lined the flight deck to witness the ceremony and hear the customary three volleys fired as each man was committed to the deep - very sad and very moving.

We berthed again at the Imperoil jetty at Dartmouth (NS) to take on a cargo of Admiralty fuel oil, the two remaining planes having flown off to the local aerodrome. Brian Walsh-Atkins had a friend in the naval base, Lt. Paul Rowling who was aide-de-camp to the Admiral, and we had a brilliant idea of giving a party for the Wrens at the naval base. Paul was a terrific organiser and he hand-picked a number of delightful girls who were brought out in a naval launch, suitably escorted by two Wren officers and Paul. We had laid on lots of food, courtesy of the Chief Steward, and had a fair variety of drink. The beds in the hospital were dismantled and the space used for dancing to a portable gramophone. All of the ingredients were there and together with a guided tour of the ship the event was pronounced a huge success. There were lots of pre-war Shell uniform buttons on board with the Shell pecten embossed on them, so as a souvenir we presented each Wren with a button attached to a red ribbon and this went down very well. They had to be back at their barracks by midnight like Cinderella, but we had laid the foundation for many more parties in the future. More 'medals' were awarded at subsequent parties and previous gong holders had a blob of sealing wax attached to the red ribbon as a 'Bar' to the Shell gong - some even got four 'Bar's.

Our other social activity was the Saturday night dance at the one and only big hotel, the Nova Scotia, once more with Wren partners. These were very good affairs even though they ended by 11.45 p.m. as the last boat back to Bedford Basin was at midnight. We played *Macoma* at deck hockey several times when we were in harbour together but they were always too good for us. Just the same, it all made for a good party and we enjoyed it immensely. After two voyages, Owen Johnson was due for his rest period and John Godley returned with Jake and Charlie, plus two more very experienced aircrews.

We had been fitted by this time with gear for oiling at sea and used the new neoprene hoses with aluminium snap couplings. They were an absolute delight to use as we had some additional manpower, plus the space in the 'Nets' to stow the long sections of hose. We oiled escorts from then on both outward and homeward bound convoys, acquiring quite a reputation as a maritime service station. It was quite a simple operation, most of the skill involved being required by the 'customer'. We simply streamed out several hundred feet of hose over the rounded stern section of the flight deck on the port side. A 200 feet long rope was streamed from the extreme outer end of the hose with a small buoy on the end. The corvette then steamed up, keeping this rope on his starboard side, and when the rope and buoy were abeam of his oiling point he brought them on board with a small grappling iron. Once the rope was on board the corvette then steamed up, recovering the rope until the hose end was reached and hauled on board. The cap was removed, the hose 'snapped' on to the corvette's manifold and we were 'in business'. On the stern of *Adula* I had a signalman, complete with Aldis lamp, and he sent and received signals as required between us and the 'customer'. Sometimes we would oil six corvettes in a day during the long daylight hours of summer, and on two memorable occasions we actually flew off two aircraft while engaged in oiling. This had never been done before and was the subject of considerable discussion at the Admiralty. C.-in-C. Western Approaches sent a signal saying this was an excellent performance and congratulated Capt. Jimmie Rumbellow, the A.S.O. for that voyage - Lt. Cmdr. P. Elias D.S.C., and the pilots for their efforts.

However this signal never reached us and was discovered some 33 years later by John Godley, the leader of 'P' Flight, while researching naval records for his book 'Bring back my Stringbag' in naval archives. So *Adula* never got her 'pat on the back' nor did the escort or aircrews of 836 Squadron. This latter squadron had been formed to suply aircrews and ground personnel for the Macships. Each flight of three Stringbags had their own groundcrews and these always remained on the ship, although air crews were changed frequently for operational reasons. The 836 squadron 'party' song for nights in harbour went like this :-

'We sailed away from mother Clyde, we sailed across the sea,
to rid the North Atlantic of the horrid enemy.
Admiral Doenitz sent a signal to his submarines - beware !
836 are on the warpath, they're the terrors of the air'.

This and other verses ranked with such classics as 'The Ball of Kirriemoor' and 'The Harlot of Jerusalem'.

Our Stringbags were fitted with RATOG - Rocket Assisted Take Off Gear in late 1944. Two rockets were fitted to the underside of the plane, and as the name implies, were intended to be fired at the moment of takeoff and assist the plane to become airborne. Basically they were intended for use in calm weather when there was little or no wind over the flight deck but once installed, they were used all of the time. It was quite a sight to watch *Adula* turn into the wind and see the Stringbag trundling down the flight deck until just at the bow, the pilot would fire his rockets and two jets of smoke and flame would shoot down the deck as the plane literally leapt into the air and went into a climbing turn. By the time the system reached us the bugs had been eliminated, but earlier experiments had resulted in a Stirling bomber losing part of her undercarriage and three propellers, nobody was injured but the plane was a writeoff.

In September,1944 Hitler launched his buzz-bombs, doodlebugs and other forms of assorted missiles against London, and our flat in Blackheath had a near miss which rendered the whole building untenable. Celia and her sister were told to leave London if they had alternative accomodation. Fortunately their mother's house in South Shields was empty so they moved up north, leaving their furniture with friends. This proved to be a blessing in disguise as the local Labour Exchange, where Celia's transfer papers were held, was also bombed. As a result she was never called up again and was able to join me every six weeks when we returned to the Clyde.

Outward bound to Halifax (NS) our ocean escort left us a day or so before reaching our destination and a local escort group took over, with the ocean escort going to St. John's (NF). However on one occasion they carried on to Halifax so we invited them over for a drink and a chat. Unfortunately we forgot to specify a time and they started arriving at 11.00 a.m., and as the six ships had an average of five officers/ship they came over in relays which put considerable strain on our capacity to absorb alcohol. Fortunately we were able to whistle up our aircrews from the nearby R.C.A.F. base at Dartmouth to assist and I was able to claim pressure of work to avoid too much damage to my liver and stomach lining. It seemed we had half of the Canadian Navy on board but our cooks and stewards rallied round and dished out lots of food to act as blotting paper. It was a very good party anyway and the Canadians were impressed with the size of the ship - we were equally impressed with their ability to shift the old 'turps'.

We carried some 10,000 tons of fuel oil each voyage and always discharged at Finnart in Loch Long. Apart from a commando camp we seemed to be the only people around there, and it was 20 miles from civilisation with about two trains/day. Our fuel was pumped into holding tanks and then pumped across to Grangemouth to a refinery. Very beautiful country but subject to severe storms and we were always glad to get away and anchor off Gourock. Sometimes we got lucky and berthed at the deepwater quay in Greenock where we could come and go as we pleased. Otherwise we had to depend on a long and often wet trip in the liberty drifter, hazardous in the extreme during bad weather which the Tail of the Bank area specialises in. The Bay Hotel in Gourock was our favourite watering hole and we had some splendid parties there. The manageress was a very imposing lady who took no cheek from anyone so while one could say the parties were boisterous they never got out of hand. She took very good care of that and many a noisy serviceman, irrespective of size or rank, found himself thrown out on the cold, hard pavements of Gourock through trying to ignore her rules and code of behaviour.

We made some 17 crossings of the North Atlantic from April,1944 to V.E. Day on 7th May,1945, and no two were ever alike as routes were varied according to the U-boat situation. The Admiralty had this pretty well monitored and we did some high latitude sailing. On at least two occasions we were far enough north to be skirting pack ice and some humourist swore he saw a couple of metres of the North Pole sticking above the horizon. Our convoys were sometimes up to one hundred ships with two Macships in each convoy to give almost constant air cover. Morale was exceedingly high in every department and we were back in the Clyde every six weeks. Our Second Officer up to April,1945 was a genial Rhodesian called Bert Holman and was a splendid shipmate who one could always rely on and fifty years later we are still in touch. The same can be said for his successor, Len Park, who took over from Bert and stayed with the ship until she went back to be converted to a normal tanker. Len and I had been meeting often until we both retired and even now we correspond twice a year.

We carried extra stewards as we had 28 officers including five radio officers and there were some really 'wide' boys amongst them. It would be safe to say they had more 'fiddles' than the New York Symphony Orchestra but they were a good, hard-working crowd. Three in particular were from the East end of London and were doing a nice line in nylon stockings and other easily disposable goods. There were about 30 bags of laundry to go ashore each voyage and you can bet they didn't all contain dirty linen. Our three heroes always volunteered to pack and escort the laundry to shore. I never knew what they were bringing into Canada, if anything, but they certainly did their level best to rectify the shortage of nylons for ladies of the night in London. I think I was the only one who knew of their activities but I considered they were not doing any harm and were assisting the balance of trade figures between the U. K. and Canada. Jack, Maurie and Irving, if you read this - screw the hospital deadlights down properly when you are packing the linen.

We left the Clyde on our penultimate operational voyage around mid-April,1945 and were proceeding down the Irish Sea. We were just a few miles north west of the Liverpool Bar when a U-boat decided to have a last minute fling and from his position, less than two thousand metres off our port bow, prepared to attack. This was extremely unwise of him as there were several very alert escorts cruising around and two Coastal Command Sunderlands in the air so his chances of success were pretty remote, for which we were truly thankful. To cut a long story short all hell was let loose off our port bow with depth charges exploding, bombs dropping, guns banging away and tracer shells all converging on this one area which seemed right under our nose. One of our own Bofors and two Oerlikons added to the cacophony, and after less than a minute a rather battered-looking U-boat shot to the surface and surrendered to the cheers of the assembled multitude and was eventually taken into Liverpool. Our convoy carried on unharmed, picking up extra ships from the Channel and Continental ports and so across to Halifax (NS) for the eighth time.

Once more we loaded at Imperoil at Dartmouth (NS), had a couple of good parties both on board and at the Nova Scotia and were all ready to sail when we heard the news, which we had been expecting, that Germany had capitulated and the war in Europe was over. We had extra time in Halifax on that particular voyage and I was able to get a coat of paint on our very rusty and weather-stained hull. On V.E. Day of 7th May,1945 I had the dubious honour of getting my name in 836 Squadron 'Line Book'. This was filled with quotes that were considered to be different, stupid, funny, outrageous or just plain unbelievable. One of the more annoying expressions of the war was 'There's a war on, doncherknow ?' - usually to cover up for some inefficiency or shortage. I was nearly knocked over by a rating rushing along a dark alleyway and am alleged to have said 'What's the bloody hurry? - there isn't a bloody war on doncherknow !'. An old friend of Capt. Jimmie Rumbellow and mine in Capt. Tommy Franklin of the tanker *Athelprince* popped aboard just before we sailed and we drank a victory toast along with several Canadian Navy officers. There were all of the elements for a full scale party had we not been sailing and a certain amount of mayhem went on that day in Halifax (NS). Many crews were given leave and promptly showed their appreciation by raiding two liquor commission stores, then went on a rampage of looting and pillaging that would have made Attila the Hun envious. They were new recruits and most had never been to sea before but they did enough damage to warrant the Canadian Army being called out to restore order and Martial Law was imposed for a couple of days.

So off we went in the last convoy to leave Halifax (NS) and flew patrols and kept convoy formation all of the way to the U. K. No incidents occurred and it was strange to approach the British coastline and see lighthouses flashing with the Tail of the Bank lit up like a Christmas tree with ship's anchor lights and the whole shoreline illuminated - stirring stuff ! We discharged our fuel at Finnart and while we were there, Celia and I had a marvellous day, hiking up to the top of Loch Long, across the Pass of Arrochar to Loch Lomond then down to Luss, the legendary home of the Colquhouns. It was a perfect, sunny day and Luss was an absolute picture postcard village. All of the cottages wreathed in early roses and a general air of tranquility - a real tonic and balm to the soul. After lunch at the Colquhoun Arms we ambled back to the pass where we were joined by Bill Bailey, Chief Steward, and his wife Irene. Bill had brought a big bag of oranges and sweets which we distributed to the village children - they must have figured Santa Claus was a bit early that year.

We were 'de-Macked' at Gourock with almost indecent haste and within three days all of the army and naval personnel were off the ship, together with all the spares for the aircraft, radar and light armament including the ammunition - for which we were truly grateful. The magazine was in what had been the forehold and in the event of a collision, a potential Guy Fawkes night was in the offing. We sailed for Halifax (NS) for the last time to pick up the last of the Navy fuel at Imperoil and had a quick turnround with barely time to say farewell to our many friends before we were off to the U-boat free ocean. We discharged at Finnart on 26th June, cleaned tanks and then to Birkenhead for dry-dock and a welcome break from routine.

It was clear that the war in the Pacific was about to finish soon and during our docking our 4.7" anti-submarine gun was taken off the stern and as much protective armour as possible removed. But we were not yet finished with our involvement with the armed forces, even though we would not be playing an active role in the Pacific. Once the docking was finished we moved over to Liverpool and loaded a complete flight deck of P34 fighter planes still in their original crates. They were destined for the Pacific but probably never got there. We had enough spare accomodation to house some eighty men and most of this was filled with American G.I.s being repatriated. These were mostly senior NCOs from the U.S. 8th Air Force and had been in the U.K. and Europe for three years or more. A better-disciplined, better-behaved bunch of men it would be hard to find and the voyage to New York was an absolute pleasure. I was still on daywork as Nobby Clark, after his promotion to Third Officer, had been replaced by Ron Blackaby as Fourth Officer, so Capt. Jimmie Rumbellow appointed me as ex-officio liasion officer with the U. S. troops which suited me fine.   The Officer Commanding the troops was a Major in the Medical Corps but he delegated all contact to Capt. Doug Nieuman his second-in-command. Doug was a B17 bomber pilot who had completed two tours of duty and flown over 100 missions and he was a really splendid type but down to earth and very much in rapport with his troops.

The G.I.s looked after all of the lashings of our crated aircraft and we had a very smooth crossing, with programmes of entertainment for the troops. We also had the entire staff of Anglo-Saxon officers for one of the Lease/Lend tankers they were to pick up in the States. The Second Officer was Dougie Carr who was to join me in my next ship and with whom I am in contact to this day. Altogether a splendid and amusing crossing, in vast contrast to my previous ones.   Arriving at our appointed berth in Newark (NJ) we were met by all of the hype reserved for returning service personnel. A brass band (not the U. S. marines but very close), Red Cross, U.S.O. and a horde of relatives and friends. It was a heartwarming sight to see the reunions and the really fantastic welcome that was laid on for our shipmates, for this is how they were regarded, by this time. We were all invited ashore to participate in the dockside welcome and one could say the welcome home party was a huge success. This was around lunchtime and the serious business of discharging our aircraft began, with 'longshoremen' (stevedores) swarming all over the place. I was assured by the U. S. Army that they would take care of everything and as far as they were concerned I could go ashore. I put this to Capt. Rumbellow and he was reasonable as always and I left to sample the delights of New York.

We had a good night ashore and wound up at Jimmy Kelly's night club on 42nd Street where we had our pictures taken, leering over a collection of empty glasses and full ashtrays. Dougie Carr, Doug Nieuman and an oldshipmate from *Cardium* in George Robson were my companions and we had a great deal of difficulty in getting back to Newark (NJ) for breakfast. We moved over to a loading berth somewhere in the wilds of N. J. but even there I wasn't safe from the attentions of my friends. Several of them descended on me with suitcases full of groceries for their ever-loving familiies in the U. K., and I also enjoyed a visit from Lt. Palmer Long U.S.N.V.R. from my Mers-el-Kebir days. It was then that the first atomic bomb was dropped and the end of our war. However mankind subsequently made sure that there was always some sort of conflict going on somewhere in the world.

We were off again in three days with no waiting around for convoys, having loaded a cargo of commercial fuel which seemed no different from Admiralty fuel. This time we went to Southampton to discharge, weaving our way through long lines of M.L.s, L.S.T.s, L.C.M.s and various other sorts of landing craft which were awaiting disposal. This was now the cold, hard world of commerce and hauling oil was our business, but schnell ! to quote our recent opponents. This time we went to Curacao and loaded another cargo of fuel for Finnart where Capt. Rumbellow and I were told to go on leave. I had a week or so standing by with Capt. P.G.G. (Paddy) Dove, a character in his own right whose *Africa Shell* had been captured and sunk by the Graf Spee early in the war. Paddy had been a prisoner on *Graf Spee* until Capt. Langsdorf scuttled his ship in Montevideo, so Paddy was released to fight another day. Among the ships sunk by *Graf Spee* was my old Headlam tramp *Streonshalh*. I signed off after a succession of farewell parties around Clydeside on 13th October,1945.

During the leave period, which fortunately extended over Christmas and the New Year, Celia and I divided our time between South Shields, London and Celia's mother's place on the Scottish border. This latter area was very good for us as rationing was at an absolute minimum and mother-in-law dished up the food with a lavish hand. In the towns and cities, the rationing seemed more severe than ever but we managed to cope. I had a couple of interviews with Shell at St. Helen's Court and had a splendid reunion with Brian Walsh-Atkins and Dr. Moffatt and others from the air group.

IN COMMAND WITH SHELL

When my leave was up in January,1946 I was asked to to go down to Falmouth and join *Newcombia* as Chief Officer, being promoted to command of this ship in November of that year. When I joined her she was still in her grey wartime colours except that during her refit at Falmouth the hull had been painted Anglo-Saxon peacetime black and her funnel was buff with a black band around the top. The top strakes of her bow, 'midships and the poop were still grey but a small mountain of white, buff and black cans of paint on the deck indicated that the pre-war Shell colours were on the agenda. *Newcombia* had been launched at Belfast in November,1944 and then the hull was towed over to Glasgow where the Kincaid oil engine was installed and fitting-out completed at the Blythswood yard. She was well provided with armament having at least six anti-aircraft guns plus a 4 " gun at the stern. With the outbreak of peace, all of this warlike equipment and the gun platforms had been removed.

I presented myself to Capt. E.C.L. Jones (Eddy behind his back) and he seemed pleased to see me. Eddy hailed from Cardiff and had served in the minesweepers of the Dover Patrol during World War I as a Sub. Lt. RNR. He had been in command with Shell during World War II so it is not surprising that he was a pretty nervous citizen and preferred his Chief Officer to handle any unpleasantness - not that there was a great deal anyway. The Second Officer, John Renshaw, was good at his job as was 'Chunky' Griffin, Third Officer, and we also had the luxury of an extra Third Officer, Stan Duncan an ex-Tyne pilot apprentice. The Chief Engineer was Fred 'Tiny' Evans and like Capt. Eddy Jones had nearly thirty years with Anglo-Saxon. Jimmie Gemmell was the very competent Scottish Second Engineer and the rest of the engineers were a very amiable crowd. The two apprentices were Pete Wallerstein and 'Rufus' Worboys and excellent young men they proved to be. 'Shell' started to replace 'Anglo-Saxon' from this time onwards in correspondence and will be used from now in this narrative.

Newcombia was one of 26 sister ships of the 'N' class of 12,000 dwt and with a bit of luck her 3,500 bhp oil engine would drive her at 12 knots. All the Deck and Engineer officers lived amidships and the crew lived aft in two-berth cabins on the main deck. The Bosun, Stan Rees, was an old shipmate and we had a very good crowd as I was to find out. Some of them were still there two years and eight months later when I finally left her. We sailed three days after I joined and as soon as we reached good weather out came the paint brushes to tart up the old girl in peacetime colours. Although only about nine months old, she was a real rust bucket, probably being partly built of scrap steel and I began the everlasting anti-corrosion battle. We were bound for Abadan and I passed my old stamping ground of Oran without a tear in my eye and revelled in the sunshine and the freedom, but we took good care to stick to the marked swept channels enroute to Suez as the Allies had been just as generous in sowing mines as the enemy.

On arrival in Port Said we tied up for a few hours, awaiting convoy and we embarked Jerry Walters, who was second-in-command to Capt. Henry Russell, head of Shell marine personnel. Jerry had been advised by the Shell doctors to go on a sea voyage as his health had been a bit shaky, so what better than one of our own tankers. In addition, he was to do a bit of liaison work in Abadan. Unfortunately, immediately after our departure from Port Said early in the evening the engine broke down. We carried a boat and boatmen to take care of emergency stoppages so this boat and crew was dropped into the Canal to run our mooring ropes ashore. The boat's motor also broke down and the boat got jammed across our stem and was unable to move away. The French pilot on the bridge was screaming at me to drop the anchor but the anchor would have sunk the boat, not to mention severely injure the Egyptian boatmen. I had no desire to spend time in the local bastille so didn't drop the anchor and there were some pretty sharp words between the bridge and myself before I got the message across - we still didn't have 'walkie-talkies' in the Merchant Navy. Eventually it all got sorted out and I reported back to Capt. Jones around 10.00 p.m. to find him having a nightcap with Jerry Walters, who had been listening with amazement to the earlier exchange of views. I was invited to have a drink and I was able to tell Jerry some of the harsh facts of life when dealing with foreign pilots. Although Jerry had been dealing with marine staff for 28 years, one got the feeling thast some new expressions had crept into his vocabulary in the course of the evening's discussions between the pilot and myself.

I took over the watch at 4.00 a.m. having cleared Suez during the early hours of the morning and Stan Duncan was an extra watch officer. Capt. Jones was rather reluctant to let Stan take over a watch on his own, despite the fact that he had a Second Mate's certificate, but once clear of the Red Sea we managed to alter that situation. Capt. Jones, Jerry Walters and Tiny Evans were keen contract bridge players, in fact Tiny was almost a genius. The question of a fourth player cropped up and having a rudimentary knowledge of the game I was asked to join. The first game went on until almost midnight and while the three senior players could get their heads down until breakfast time, I was up at 3.45 a.m. to go on watch. This situation held for three days and like Queen Victoria I was not amused. The fourth day before lunch Capt. Jones was kind enough to invite me up for a gin with himself, Jerry and Tiny, and as it was a Sunday we had reinstated the pre-war custom of 'Captain's rounds' or 'Inspection'. This also involved the Chief Steward and an apprentice, Rufus Worboys, to take notes plus Jerry Walters as an interested observer. We completed a one and a half hour tour of storerooms, engine room, officer's and crew accomodation and settled down to enjoy a sip of Gordon's juniper-flavoured liquor. The 'rounds' and the refreshment were very much a feature of Shell Tankers and probably still are. I felt this to be a golden opportunity to bring up the subject of my lack of sleep, and full of low animal cunning I conveyed the impression that bridge sessions were an endangered species if I didn't get a little more shuteye. Furthermore extra Third Officer Stan Duncan would suffer an impaired career structure if he wasn't allowed to take over a watch. The sleepless

Chief Officer ably supported by Tiny Evans won the day or at least a reprieve as I only went on the Bridge at 6.00 a.m.

Meanwhile, chipping hammers, scrapers and paint brushes were in full-swing, hammers only in the morning of course, and gradually *Newcombia* shook off her dowdy grey and emerged as a glistening white Shell tanker, much to the joy of Jerry Walters, a traditionalist from way back. Arriving at the entrance to the Shatt al Arab, known as the Abadan Bar, we discovered a couple of dozen other ships at anchor, waiting for a berth at the refinery and were told we would have a three day wait so down went the anchor. Capt. Joe Miller OBE, my father-in-law, was there in his ship and we had a brief chat over the Aldis lamp before he went upriver to Abadan. I was able to give him the good news that he was to be a grandfather in August. Next day Jerry Walters was able to get a lift upriver in one of Hoegh's Norwegian cargo ships as he had business to discuss with the Anglo-Iranian Oil Co. Ltd. He suggested I come with him and meet my father-in-law (whom I always called Dad) and we talked Capt. Jones into letting me go as *Newcombia* was not coming up until the following day. I would stay aboard Dad's ship and rejoin *Newcombia* when she berthed, the fact that I had no passport was of little consequence. I had my seaman's I.D. card, was in uniform and the British Army was in control of the berths so where was the problem ! We had a pleasant trip upriver and were well entertained by several passengers and the Captain of the Hoegh ship. I put it about that Jerry practically owned Shell Tankers and we got V.I.P. treatment, landing about 6.00 p.m. courtesy of the pilot boat under the bows of Dad's ship.

There was a car waiting for Jerry so our identity was established and I was free to board Dad's ship. It so happened that Dad was visiting his old friend Les Grainger, Anglo-Iranian's Engineer Supt., but a quick telephone call had a car pick me up and I was whisked off to 'Chez' Grainger and joined a very convivial party. Dad and I got back to his ship around 11.00 p.m. and we were just enjoying a cup of tea prior to retiring when the Third Officer stuck his head in the door and announced that *Newcombia* was mooring at the next berth and spoiled my good night's sleep. We were loaded after things got sorted out and ready for sea two days later. Jerry Walters was supposed to transfer to another Shell tanker but that scheme was abandoned and he rejoined us for the trip home, disembarking at Suez. We had several hilarious bridge sessions between Abadan and Suez but as Stan Duncan had transferred to another ship I placed a firm embargo on any play after 10.00 p.m. Dropping Jerry Walters off at Suez we proceeded to Shellhaven where we arrived with *Newcombia* resplendent in peacetime colours.   Suitable admiration was forthcoming from the assembled multitude and within an hour our cargo of motor spirit was surging up the pipeline to the shore tanks.

We changed Articles and John Renshaw, the Second Officer, was replaced by Dougie Carr, an old shipmate from *Adula* days. Chunky Griffin, our Third Officer, remained as did all the Engineer officers. Celia was able to join me for the two or three days we were there and we managed to get one night ashore to have a quiet dinner and discuss our future and that of our unborn child. It was then that I decided, whilst I loved ships and the general maritime scene, the separations were unacceptable. So off we sailed to Curacao, loaded there with motor spirit and returned to Stanlow in time for Easter. Again Celia was able to join me and we managed to wangle a day off and explore the delights of the ancient city of Chester. After three days we were off to Aruba where we loaded an assortment of light oils for West Africa, first call being Bassa Point with light diesel and gasoline for the rubber plantations owned by the Firestone Rubber Co. Inc. The ship moored to buoys about a mile offshore and, as was frequently the case in those days, the submarine telephone cable had broken down so communication between ship and shore became a problem. It was resolved by sending Pete Wallerstein the apprentice ashore with an Aldis lamp and we managed to get the cargo out without 'breaking' anything.

Then to Monrovia, capital of Liberia, where once more we lay offshore and discharged into about twenty small barges, none of which could carry more than fifty tons, and some as little as ten tons. There was a big surf running the whole time and these little craft had to steer through a narrow passage into a lagoon. Once inside they were discharged by portable pumps into road tankers, a very time-consuming operation as we had around 4,000 tons of light diesel. The port of Monrovia (an artificial harbour) was still under construction by the Raymond Concrete Pile Co. Inc. of the U.S.A. supervised by the U. S. Navy as Uncle Sam was paying the bill. The bar crossing looked an extremely hazardous business and so it proved. Capt. Jones was obviously allergic to surfing over sandbars in worn-out wartime landing craft, so he delegated the chore of going ashore with the ship's papers to me. The main trouble was that the onshore wind and surf built up during the day and by 3.00 p.m. it was impossible to cross the bar and operations ceased until the next morning at daybreak. The Americans assured me that this was normal and they expected to have 90% of their craft out of service by the end of the discharge - they were correct ! I got ashore about 2.00 p.m. and whilst it was pretty terrifying I still had vivid memories of the North Atlantic in wartime so it didn't seem too bad - lifejackets were very 'de rigeur' in Monrovia.

I duly reported to the British Consul who stamped all the necessary documents and I returned to the U. S. Navy. There was no question of returning to the ship that night so I enjoyed the splendid hospitality of the U. S. N. who fed and watered me, invited me to their nightly movie show and gave me a comfortable bed for the night. There was a Commander of the U.S.N. and a couple of junior officers in the Navy mess, and the rest of the Americans were hard-bitten construction workers, about seventy in all. My experiences with the U.S.N. in North Africa stood me in good stead and the Commander was extremely affable so we had a late night to good effect. Capt. Jones greeted me like the prodigal son when I boarded at 6.00 a.m. the next day as he felt sure I had been drowned or kidnapped. So the discharge went on with numerous crises and in three days the shoreline was littered with wrecks - 'Not to worry' - said our American friends, 'We'll have them all salvaged and repaired by the time the next tanker arrives in two month's time' - guess they were right as there is now a port of Monrovia with wharves protected by huge breakwaters.

The wind and swell increased in force by the end of the fourth day and Capt. Jones was getting into a state of flux. As they were down to only two tiny tankers by this time, the Raymond Concrete Pile Company reckoned they had enough diesel to cover their requirements so bade us a fond farewell and departed into the night.

The four or five who had been aboard the whole time were nice guys but they knocked a big hole in our stock of liquor. Next stop was Bathurst where we were in and out in twelve hours, then on to Freetown where we able to replenish our Bar supplies and give the locals a few hundred tons of gasoline, kerosene and diesel. It was quite a contrast to my previous visit some three and a half years previously when alcohol was almost nonexistent as there were literally thousands of service personnel stationed there. By 1946 all of the orders must have caught up as the place was awash with drink of all descriptions, with about four ship chandlers vying for business. A real buyer's market and we took full advantage of it.

On then to Dakar, our final port where I had a hilarious evening on an Elder,Dempster liner in the passenger lounge before sailing for Curacao, my favourite port as I had a good friend there in Jan Nederhorst Snr. 'Uncle Ned' as we christened him was a civil engineering contractor of some standing in both Curacao and Holland. He had been a passenger on *Adula* from Curacao to the U. K. on our last voyage after the war together with a senior Shell civil engineer, Mr. van Lockeren Campagne. Capt. Jimmie Rumbellow, Uncle Ned, Van L. Campagne and I used to play 'lying dice' every night of the voyage and we became very friendly. Subsequently every time we visited Curacao, Uncle Ne would pick me up and take me home to have dinner with his charming wife and daughter, Ellie. Dougie Carr and Chunky Griffin were more than capable of discharging ballast and although Capt. Jones had a tendency to get upset whenever I was off the ship we managed to calm him down.

This voyage early in 1946 we were to load a cargo of gasoline for Rotterdam so Uncle Ned asked me to take foodstuffs for his family in Holland, where severe rationing was still in force. 'No need to worry about Customs' he said as two large packing cases were hoisted aboard and stowed in a spare locker, 'My brother in Rotterdam will fix all that'. On arrival in Rotterdam, Ned's brother came down and saw all the 'goodies' loaded on to one of his trucks and stayed for a drink and a chat. We were to be there at least a week so I saw a golden opportunity to nip home and see my beloved Celia who was in the last month of her pregnancy. Capt. Jones was 'sweet-talked' into letting me go but it transpired the ferries from the Hook of Holland didn't quite fit in. 'No problem, K.L.M. fly all the time' said Ned's brother. I pointed out that I worked for Shell and didn't actually own it so airfares were a bit outside my pocket. 'Look, I'll arrange transport, tickets etc. and you can pay Ned over the next six months or so - any questions ?' said Ned's brother. There were none from me and the next morning at 6.00 a.m. a car drew up alongside and by 9.30 a.m. I was on the doorstep of Shell in London with all the logbooks, accounts etc. which had been loaded on me and presented them to Jerry Walters, who thought it all a very good scheme. I borrowed a couple of pounds from Jerry then quickly reached King's Cross and was ringing my ever-loving by 5.00 p.m. to tell her to expect me home later that evening.

We had a deliriously happy day together before I caught the train the following night to London, missing our fifth wedding anniversary by just two days. I found that all had gone well when I got back on board by lunchtime the following day and we had another two days before sailing and that all operations were on schedule. Whilst loading in Curacao for Rotterdam the Dutch told us to stock up on cigarettes and coffee as we would be able to realise a handsome profit in Europe. Always ready for a 'honest shilling', Dougie, Chunky and I had invested in a few thousand cigarettes and during my brief absence they had managed to sell the lot. Thus I was pleasantly surprised to discover my share of the transaction was sufficient to cover the entire cost of my airfare and general transportation with a bit left over. It was the 21st birthday the next day of senior apprentice Pete Wallerstein so I took him ashore to celebrate and we had a splendid dinner at the officer's NAAFI in Amsterdam after spending a couple of hours on the beach at Schveningen. There were still a number of British Army units stationed in Holland so several NAAFI clubs were scattered around the various locations and we took full advantage of them. They were all very cheap and extremely well run with dinner and a bottle of wine coming to about a pound for the two of us.

We sailed again for Curacao having settled all of our debts, this time to load for Santos and Rio de Janeiro, both new ports to me. On the way from Curacao, I was watching the calendar very closely as Celia was approaching her 'delivery' date of 6th August,1946 when our daughter, Elizabeth Lesley, duly appeared and has been a source of love, joy and pride to us ever since. Cables were received and sent, toasts were drunk and the 'baby's head' well and truly wetted. Chief Officer's shore leave is usually pretty restricted but I did manage to get ashore in Rio for a few hours and sample the local brew.

We loaded back at Curacao for Antwerp, which was beginning to feel the loss of patronage from the Allied troops, most of whom had just departed. It was here I got ashore to telephone Celia who was staying with my mother and first heard our daughter's tiny cry in the background as we spoke - telephoning from the Continent was considered rather daring in 1946. After two days we sailed from Antwerp, threaded our way through the minefields of the North Sea and headed for Houston in Texas. During the war, Houston had several shipyards building 'Liberty' ships for Henry Kaiser and had been a hive of activity but by October,1946 there were just the gaunt shipyard skeletons lining the slipways, idle cranes and huge empty factories all the way up the Houston Ship Canal. A rather desolate sight but one on which we didn't have much time to dwell as we were on our way 36 hours later. This time we were bound for Sheerness where Celia introduced me to the little scrap of humanity who was to be a source of so much joy to us. Jerry Walters and his wife came down to visit us and brought the good news that I was to take over command of *Newcombia* from Capt. Eddy Jones, who was due for leave.

After the discharge was complete at Sheerness we proceeded up to Hull with the balance, gas-freed the tanks, then sailed down to Falmouth for dry-dock. I took over command on 24th November,1946 sixteen years to the day after I had signed my indentures. Once the formalities were over, I gave myself a few days leave and Capt. Jones stayed on board to hold the fort. Dougie Carr and Chunky Griffin went on leave and a new Chief Officer joined in Derek Booker and a new Second Officer in Alan Barnsley. They had the required certificates but Derek Booker was newly promoted whereas Alan Barnsley had some previous experience of the job but both proved extremely capable. There were no Third Officers available but I was informed that I could promote the senior apprentice Rufus Worboys to the position. Pete Wallerstein had left three months previously and Rufus had been on watch with me since then. I knew him to be keen, capable and conscientious and he had served about 20 months of his apprenticeship but had shown considerable ability and was extremely intelligent.

'Tiny' Evans our Chief Engineer was also due for leave and was replaced by Fred Tabbitt, a very senior Chief Engineer who had held that position on the Macship Empire Macmahon so we started off with that as a common bond. It developed into a friendship of mutual respect and we remained friends until Fred passed on some years ago. The entire catering staff were new, led by Chief Steward Harry Rae, himelf an ex chief cook, which position was now held by Howard Abdullah, son of a Welsh mother and Arab father and a real gentleman. They were both brilliant cooks and for the next two years there was never a complaint about the food, usually a European crew's favourite moan. I came back from leave and for the next two weeks was up to my neck in work during the refit. Derek Booker was still learning and I remember thinking that one particular job was a bit hard and I should pass it on to the Old Man then realised that was me and got on with it. This type of situation keeps recurring but after a while you get used to it but it is stil a shock to the system when it happens for the first time.

Late December we sailed from Falmouth bound for Curacao where we were supposed to load for the U. K. / Continent but in fact it turned out that by 'Continent' they meant Asia. We spent Christmas at sea and Harry Rae and his staff put on a very good dinner with a tot of rum and a couple of free beers for all hands. Prior to midday dinner I had got Derek to organise a 'sports day' on the after deck with spoon and potato races (eggs too fragile), sack races, three-legged races, tugs of war etc. The idea was to tire out the crew so that they would all sleep soundly after dinner and not sit around talking about the shortcomings of the Old Man and the ship in general. By 11.30 a.m. all these activities were over and all hands, except the watchkeepers, gathered on the poop where prizes were given out, abrasions attended to, and cold beer gurgled down thirsty throats. Jock Nichol the carpenter dressed up as Santa Claus in red bunting and cotton wool, gave out the prizes and a flow of soul and feast of reason ensued. We had a splendid dinner after which the deck and engineer officers served dinner to the cooks and stewards and a good time was had by all.

Bad news in the form of a radiogram from our lords and masters in London arrived on Boxing Day, informing us that we were to load a full cargo of kerosene in Curacao and Aruba for Hong Kong. This I needed like a hole in the head, never having been further east than Abadan as an officer. We took on part-cargo at Curacao and I was able to have a lively evening with Uncle Ned Nederhorst and family, then on to Aruba where my old shipmate Sugar Wormald was one of the harbourmasters. We spent New Year's Eve off Aruba but there were no jollifications as it is a bit of a dodgy anchorage and I had no intention of damaging my career structure by wrapping my newly-acquired command around the rocks of the Netherlands Antilles. We berthed on 2nd January,1947 and for the first time I was able to spend some time in the Marine Club and not have to worry about going back to take over a watch. Sugar Wormald and his wife took good care of me and I really enjoyed Aruba for the first time. The next day we were on our way to the Panama

Canal where we were alongside all night at Balboa taking bunkers and managed a brief run ashore, the last for five weeks.

The Pacific as with any other large stretch of ocean can be extremely boring except when the weather turns bad and then it can frighten the daylights out of any sailor who encounters it. Fortunately we were spared the bad weather so our only enemy was the boredom. This we fought by the simple process of giving the crew lots of overtime for which they were paid, then organizing quizzes, darts, competitions and various other activities in the evenings. On the whole they were a pretty amiable crowd and reacted very well, both with the officers and each other. It was perfect weather for 33 days with blue sea and sky until we approached the Bashi Channel to enter the South China Sea through the chain of islands stretching from Japan to the Philippines. Just when I wanted the sun, it disappeared behind overcast skies so we were not able to get a good 'position fix' for two days prior to negotiating the Bashi Channel. As luck would have it we would have to arrive in the middle of the night and although overcast, the visibility was reasonably good so we managed to get through without hitting anything but I spent an anxious few hours with Rufus and Alan Barnsley until I was sure there was no danger.

As we approached the entrance to Hong Kong, not only was the sun being coy and palely loitering behind the clouds, but a nasty damp sea fret had set in, reducing visibility to about a couple of ships' lengths. I was anxious not to wrap my ship around the Chinese mainland or even an offshore island for that matter, and reduced speed and was proceeding very slowly when out of the mist we heard a Royal Navy destroyer hooting mournfully on his siren as we were ourselves - much more exciting than the arrival of the U. S. cavalry in a cowboy movie and a great deal more useful. We hooted at each other until we were in sight, having radar he knew all about our prescence so he wasn't surprised to see us. Signalling by Aldis lamp he was able to give us a course and distance to Lie Mun Pass, the entrance to Hong Kong harbour. We had no radar as London was still 'evaluating' this electronic marvel and it was to be several more years before we got it - we were never ones to rush madly into anything new in those days !

A few hours later the weather cleared and there we were, facing the dark, brooding outline of China. Alan Barnsley had been to Hong Kong before and pointed out various salient features so I girded my loins and prepared to do my first bit of piloting for years. Lie Mun Pass seemed awfully narrow to me but the Admiralty chart assured me there was more than adequate room to allow my ship to enter Hong Kong harbour. So I crept carefully towards the entrance which seemed to be wall to wall full of junks, this feeling of uneasiness was repeated later in Shanghai. Alan assured me that despite 'rules of the road' the junks would keep out of my way so, saying prayers under my breath, I pressed on regardless. I am not sure the junk crews were pleased at my persistent blowing of the siren but at least they kept out of my way and we got into the broad inner harbour where the Chinese pilot boarded and took me to anchor in what must be the busiest harbour in the world. When the anchor was down I felt quite relieved that we had come over 9,000 nautical miles with 11,000 tons of kerosene and never spilt a drop - the longest sea voyage I was ever to make.

The agent came aboard, together with port health, immigration, customs and the usual horde, so a busy couple of hours ensued before I was able to relax and pour myself a small libation of Gordon's juniper-flavoured rectified spirit. Lots of small boats or sampans as they are called in Chinese waters were hovering around until the quarantine flag came down, whereupon they came alongside like bees to a jampot. They each carried a selection of 'filles de joie' and were known as 'meat boats' who were anxious to assist a bunch of sex-starved matelots get rid of their inhibitions. I was extremely apprehensive and had visions of safety rules being broken etc, but the agent assured me it was quite normal and that the visitors were well versed in tanker safety precautions. It was an unequal contest anyway, as there were more than a dozen 'meat boats' and the hearts of the crew were not attuned to 'repelling boarders' so I emulated Lord Nelson at Copenhagen, said a couple of 'Aves' that nothing serious would occur. I'm happy to relate that nothing did so I guess, like Lord Nelson, my judgement was vindicated. As we were not going to berth for a couple of days, the agent suggested that I might like a run ashore and sample the delights of Hong Kong. This seemed a splendid idea so off I went, leaving Derek Booker and Fred Tabbitt to cope with the problems.

This was my first time in the mystic East and I got a few 'sailing directions' from the agent, and by the time the first pre-prandial gin and tonic was due I was propping up the bar at a well-known watering hole of those days called the Gripps, a couple of floors up in the Gloucester Hotel and much favoured by the Royal Navy. Hong Kong was still a large naval base and all the armed forces were present in large numbers. This meant very good NAAFIs and fleet canteens, all very moderately priced and available to M. N. personnel on the production of an I.D. card. It was nowhere near the huge commercial centre it was to become and there wasn't much to be had in the way of shopping, but I hadn't come ashore to shop, just for a change of company. My luck was holding out as within half an hour I met three R. N. officers I had known well in North Africa. Mac and Pewsey had served in the same ship but were now on different ships and the third was a stranger, but I seemed to act as a sort of catalyst and a really enjoyable evening ensued. By midnight about a dozen of us were having a flow of soul and a feast of reason when, Cinderella-like, I realised it was indeed midnight and I was in a strange, oriental city with no knowledge of how to get back to my ship. 'Not to worry, my ship has dozens of spare cabins as half of the aircrews are at the R.A.F. base doing exercises' said Mac, so around 2.30 a.m. we boarded his aircraft carrier and I was duly shown to a very comfortable cabin and had my first unworried sleep for five days.

After a hearty breakfast Mac arranged a boat and came back with me to see how the other half lived. He was most impressed with my spacious dayroom, bedroom with ensuite bathroom and most of all with my 'brass hat' when I changed into uniform. All seemed well on board and I did a not too thorough inspection as it wasn't Sunday but I had got into the habit of doing an 'off the cuff' inspection, in addition to the normal Sunday one, from time to time to keep the crew on their toes. There were lots of industrious little girls washing clothes for the crew and busy about domestic tasks and all was peaceful for which I was truly thankful. Derek's boys were painting overside and Fred's lads were changing a piston so I felt quite superfluous. Mac and I departed after lunch, courtesy of a R. N. picket boat and later went to Pewsey's destroyer for drinks, dinner and a movie show. Once more an excellent evening and I returned at midnight, feeling being Captain was most agreeable.

We went alongside the next morning and two days later we were threading our way through Lei Mun Pass and out into the China Sea bound for Singapore for orders. The break did a lot for everyone's morale and we needed it for what was in store. Sparks came in with a brief message two days from Singapore 'Proceed Abadan for orders', so my desire to follow in the footsteps of Stamford Raffles was thwarted for the time being anway. Three weeks later we were anchored off Abadan bar and got orders to load about five different grades of mogas, avgas, kerosene and gasoil for five ports in Australia - Sydney, Brisbane, Gladstone, Townsville and Darwin. Now, loading five grades is easy, provided you know what is going where, but this latter information was not forthcoming nor was it on subsequent voyages. Our crystal ball was nearly in splinters during the following months, but I must say that this type of thing has since been eliminated. To complicate things we had to be on an exactly even keel on leaving the berth, in order to cross the Abadan bar so a certain amount of mathematical activity followed. Derek had never carried more than one grade and was still learning, and I had to do some work myself. We got it all sorted out and I left Derek to do the 'fine tuning' as he was a clever mathematician. The shore staff at Abadan were a good crowd, mostly ex-servicemen and I was well looked after by Les Grainger, BP's Engineer Superintendent, who was an old pal of my father-in-law. In addition, other old shipmates were the Rev. Derek Tyrie (BP's Chaplain in Abadan) and Capt. John Nettleship in the Shell tanker *Dolabella* at the next berth so three most enjoyable days followed.

I also met Neil Ashford at Abadan and his wife Liz who asked me to deliver a trunk full of clothes to her mother in Brisbane. This was most fortunate for me as during my subsequent visits to Abadan in the summer of 1947 and 1948 I was invited to be their guest in their air-conditioned house whenever I was in Abadan. Air-conditioning for ships was still on the drawing board and fiercely resisted by most shipowners. Being wartime built, the deck above the navigating bridge, chartroom and Captain's cabins was two-inch thick armour plating and very heat retaining. I had a maximum/minimum thermometer left over from the ammunition magazines and on subsequent voyages my cabin got up to 126 degrees on several occasions. This despite awnings and frequent hosing down, in this regard it was the worst accomodation in the ship. However, in March,1947 the weather was still bearable as we sailed off to Australia.

Taking into account various factors I decided to go to Sydney via the Torres Straits as we could carry more cargo, although the distance was some 600 miles greater. Our lords and masters were informed but they raised no objections so my economic reasoning was sound. We duly arrived at Thursday Island, about ten miles off Cape York, picked up the pilot Capt. Perry Hildebrand, who took us down the Great Barrier Reef, dropped off at Brisbane and we crept gently alongside the Shell installation at Gore Bay in Sydney and got our first indication of which products went where. Sydney was easy and we were out the next day but Brisbane presented a few problems. We had to go to four different berths but as this gave us four nights in harbour, everyone was very happy. Doubtless the 'freight department' in London were tearing out their hair and gnashing their dentures at our loitering but they should have thought of that in the first place.

The first day in Brisbane was very pleasant and Les Hardcastle, the Shell agent, took good care of Fred and myself. In those days Shell did their own agency work except for Townsville where Burns, Philp & Co. were the agents. Shell Australia shipping agents were the best we ever met, with second place going to Brinings of Liverpool. We had a very convivial evening with several Shell characters including a couple of guys from Public Relations, who asked me to talk to the press the next day, I promised to think of something and went off to bed.

Around 4.00 a.m. there was a loud explosion ashore and looking out of a porthole, the installation seemed to be on fire. As I scrambled into my clothes, Derek appeared at the door and informed me that we had just cleared the shore pipelines with water so the fire was nothing to do with us. However we were in a very dangerous position as the shore operators had gone to fight the fire. All hands were on deck by this time so we disconnected the hoses and dropped them ashore and had all of the fire hoses spouting at maximum capacity. Fred came with the bad news - two of his engineers and some of the firemen had just spent all night dismantling a piston, ready to change it in the morning and it would be at least two hours before we could move. By this time, fire engines were all over the place, pouring foam and spray over the offending shore tank. We didn't know it at the time but the bund walls surrounding the tank had some barrels of avgas stowed there, and the heat from the fire was causing these to explode and shoot into the air like Haley's comet - Guy Fawkes would have loved it ! However we, like Queen Victoria, were not amused as we were standing on 8,000 tons of very lethal, assorted gasolines.

I knew that even if we could get the engines going, we could never negotiate the bend at Breakfast Creek without tugs as the tide was ebbing, so I had visions if the worst came to the worst, of navigating stern-first upriver until we reached the bridge when we would have to anchor. This and other options, equally fatuous, raced through my mind but soon the fire was under control and things settled down. It appears they were gas-freeing a shore tank and a very gentle breeze was wafting the gas to an area where there was a hot water urn with a pilot light, and the flame had flashed back to the tank. After the sound and fury died down we resumed discharge and all hands went to breakfast, having had enough excitement for one day. However, fate was waiting in the wings for our next little episode, as I was conned by the shore people into loading some 300 tons of kerosene for discharge at Gladstone but the only available tank was one from which we had discharged mogas at Sydney. It was dry and gas-free but hadn't been washed, a requirement in those days. We loaded the kerosene then moved to the next berth to discharge more products - to my horror some guy in a white coat galloped on board and informed me the laboratory tests showed the kerosene was contaminated with 6% gasoline. Furthermore he suggested the gasoline had come from us, I pointed out that I had been against the deal from the beginning, that we had at least three valve separation, and the shore must have done it themselves.

It was years later that I found out the latter was the answer although in all fairness it was not known at the time and many months elapsed before the fault was discovered. Even now I remain convinced that their testing procedures were 'up the pole' and there was no real contamination. The reader may calculate that 6% of 300 tons is 18 tons, but when we eventually discharged the kerosene in Gladstone they received exactly 300 tons - what had happened to the 18 tons of gasoline ? - it was never there ! I will not divulge the many steps taken to remove the alleged contamination. They were unortodox to say the least of it and events during the following year indicated they could have been lethal but al least Gladstone got its 300 tons of kerosene.

I suggested to the Operations Manager in Brisbane that the episode would best be forgotten in view of the happy ending, but he insisted on informing London. Such being the case I reported the whole event and got a letter back eventually from John Lamb, the Head of Marine Technical, telling me in effect that I was a naughty boy and if I ever did it again he would hang me from the nearest yardarm. He added that in view of my relatively short experience as Master, plus the fact that I had been ill-advised by the shore staff, he would forgive me this time. I don't know what he wrote to Shell in Brisbane but on my return I was treated like Royalty.

We thought our troubles were over when the kerosene was got safely ashore in Gladstone, but more was to come. The cargo ship *Port Jackson* of Port Line was moored astern of us at the wharf and about 8 p.m. the tide began to ebb. The buoy, to which her stern was moored broke its anchor chains and slowly she swung round, eventually to snuggle cosily along our port side. As luck would have it, all my key men were standing chatting at the after end of the bridge deck - Fred Tabbitt, Derek Booker, Stan Reece the Bosun, Jock Nichol the carpenter and John Duggan the pumpman to gether with two able seamen. They saw and reacted promptly to the emergency and in the few minutes it took *Port Jackson* to actually make contact, we had stopped pumping, all sighting ports and ullage plugs were closed. Fire hoses were out and spraying and fenders ranged along our port side so the damage was almost non-existent - a really splendid team effort proving training pays off. And where was the bold Captain of *Newcombia* when all this was going on ? - Gallantly leading his men ? - Certainly not ! He was in a local pub with several officers of both ships, having a sing-song around the piano, played by Peter Guest, Chief Officer of *Port Jackson*. However, we heard the siren of the fire engines as they passed the pub, and a minute or so later I was wanted on the telephone, it was Alan Barnsley who announced this new crisis and suggested I might like to be in on the action.

I knew most of the crew were in the bar, next to where we were having our musical soiree, so I popped in and asked for volunteers. They all streamed out to a man, we commandeered a couple of taxis and charged back to the wharf to find the situation under control - who needs the Captain anyway ? Our next task was to secure *Port Jackson* until the tide turned and she could move out to anchor, her berth being untenable. Her winches were all electric, powered by a Kromhaut generator, the exhaust of which was badly in need of a chimney sweep. Great balls of red hot soot were drifting across our decks so the Kromhaut was stopped and we used our own steam winches to tie up the unwanted visitor. The pilot, Capt. Smith, arrived and around 2 a.m. *Port Jackson* departed and we continued our discharge. All hands were given a tot of rum and promised a few hours overtime so everyone was happy and those not on watch retired.

On to Townsville where no unfortunate incidents occurred, and where I bought a second-hand set of golf clubs as I decided to resume that pastime now that I had some leisure time in port. Darwin was our next port, which I approached with some trepidation, a completely strange harbour littered with wartime wrecks, no tugs and no pilot. We dropped off Perry Hildebrand at Thursday Island, he had been with us since Gladstone and was almost one of the family. I managed to put my ship alongside at Darwin without breaking anything, for which I was truly thankful and spent two days there. It was pretty primitive in those days with lots of people living in wartime Nissen huts and we were inundated with vistors including two London office trainees - very cheery, recently demobbed characters who were getting lots of 'outback' experience.

We sailed back to Abadan for a similar voyage to Sydney, Brisbane and Gladstone with lots of toys from Liz Ashford's mother for the three Ashford children in Abadan plus various goodies for Les Grainger. They were put on board the tugs for onward dispatch, and my old shipmate Mac Mackenzie was still in the tugs so Fred and I had a couple of excellent curry tiffins with him. It was getting very hot, being May, but I was able to get in a few short rounds of golf in the early evening and assured of a good night's rest in the Ashford's air-conditioned house. Three days later we were off on another 30 day voyage to Australia, fighting corrosion and boredom with equal ferocity. After passing Cape Leeuwin in Western Australia the sun decided to take a holiday so we pressed on, under autumnal Antipodean skies, in poor visibility. We managed to avoid hitting Tasmania as Sparks was able to get some bearings and position via the radio direction finder. Our first sight of land was the tip of Wilson's Promontory as the mist suddenly lifted, and on to Sydney where we arrived on a Saturday morning.

One of our sisterships was in dry-dock there, so I headed off with Capt. Dudley Speakman, a friend from Macship days, for the Sydney cricket ground after a brief visit to a deserted Shell office. We were lucky in that a really good game of Rugby was on - N. Z. All Blacks vs. N. S. Wales - we had a traditional pie lunch and thoroughly enjoyed our afternoon. Returning to the city we treated ourselves to a slap-up dinner and a touch of the local vintage, then our evening's entertainment was arranged. We were joined by Jimmie Gill, Capt. Speakman's Chief Officer, who had the foresight to book a table at the old Wentworth supper room. The barbaric 6 p.m. closing time of all watering holes was still in force but providing you booked and ordered in advance, you could wassail on to midnight. This we did, with several kindred spirits and their girlfriends, from both ships. Fred and I negotiated the torturous paths and stairs of Gore Bay around 1 a.m. feeling much uplifted in spirit. Off on Sunday afternoon, we threaded our way through what seemed a miniature Cowes Regatta as the nautically-minded Sydneysiders revelled in their aquatic pursuits.

At Brisbane we had four nights once more as we had to service four installations but managed it without incident this time. It was a very good port for us as there was something for everyone and there was time to enjoy whatever turned you on. Another sistership of ours was in dry-dock there so Fred and I were able to meet with 'our opposite numbers', chat up the locals and get some of the salt water out of our systems. Norman Moore, our Sparks, developed acute appendicitis and had to go into hospital and was replaced by a very pleasant young Australian, Geoff Pigott. Geoff was employed by Amalgamated Wireless Australasia (AWA) and was appointed on a temporary (sic) basis. Wireless companies, like oil companies, have a very elastic interpretation of the word 'temporary' and it was nine months before Geoff was relieved.

In the meantime as we wandered the sealanes East of Suez we kept losing bodies and acquiring new ones for a variety of reasons, mostly sickness, but one or two desertions. Some of the latter were due to drunkeness and missing an early morning sailing - now and again they would catch up at the next port. Capt. Tommy Thompson was our coast pilot from Gladstone, our final port after Brisbane, and Tommy took us to Thursday Island, but just before we got there the main engine started coughing and spluttering like an asthmatic hen. Fred Tabbitt diagnosed 'piston fever' which would necessitate a 48 hour stoppage. This would mean anchoring if we could find a reasonably safe place, but safe anchorages are in short supply around Cape York. Cureents are extremely strong but Tommy indicated a spot, west of Thursday Island, where he reckoned a lot of American supply ships had anchored for long periods during the war. The Admiralty chart indicated that the tidal currents ran at least six knots but Tommy reckoned that they were constant in their directions, with a regular west/east flow at ebb or east/west at flood (or vice-versa). Such being the case I gingerly took *Newcombia* to the point indicated and dropped anchor. She held very securely with plenty of chain out and when the tide changed she held equally securely, pointing in the opposite direction.

Fred and his gang started ripping the main engine apart so there was nothing much anyone could do in the deck department except paint the ship's side and fish. Tommy Thompson invited me to come ashore with him and spend the night at the pilot's mess, as Perry Hildebrand and one or two other pilots I knew were in residence. I packed my overnight bag and went off with Tommy for a little rest and relaxation, however Thursday Island is not exactly the fun capital of the Antipodes but they had a dance once a month and this was the night. After a couple of drinks, a good dinner and lots of chatter with the pilots, we headed off to the dance. It seemed everyone on Thursday Island was there and an amazing cross-section of humanity it was too. I harbour a feeling that multi-culturism started on Thursday Island from babes in arms to grandmothers and every shade of colour, everyone determined to live it up - and live it up they did until midnight when the missionary spirit prevailed and the band packed up. A fun night was had by all and we finished up for drinks at the pilot's mess. I had arranged with Harry Rae to have a curry tiffin laid on as I expected to bring some gests back. Just as well as the Chief Magistrate, Collector of Customs, the local bank manager, a couple of Shell merchants plus two pilots came back with me so we had a real 'hooley'.

Fred's boys had done a splendid job so we poured our guests into the pilot boat at 4 p.m. and were heading west two hours later with the diesel purring like a well-fed cat. We arrived at Abadan in early July in terrific heat and were glad in a way to get back to sea again. Our lords and masters couldn't have picked a worse trip as we were bound for Suez, and at this time of the year the Persian Gulf, Indian Ocean and Red Sea are baking hot and not my idea of a health holiday, but we all hoped for orders to go west from Suez. However, Suez after the Gulf, seemed realtively pleasant, I had a couple of rounds of golf with my old friends Alan Nelson and Reginald Saunders, and our Engineer Superintendent in Suez took me to Cairo to see the Pyramids and the Sphinx. The latter were done on foot and I must have lost a gallon of sweat but I wasn't game to try a camel ride. I replaced the sweat with Stella beer at the refinery club when we returned in the evening. The locals reckon that Stella was made from onion skins and camel dung, but it tasted all right to me - nothing like galloping around a couple of pyramids to work up a thirst. Our westbound hopes were dashed as we returned to Abadan.

Once more Australia was to be favoured by our prescence as a 'conveyor of fine oils in bulk'. At the end of August we were back in Abadan and that summer was a real scorcher with so many Europeans from ships dying of heat exhaustion, the agent had a nervous breakdown attending funerals. I had to hospitalise a couple of my lads but they recovered. Luckily I was able to pick up a couple of replacements so we were never really shorthanded. We were only able to stand about two hours on watch as the heat was so intense. I did a few two hour watches but was able to sleep in comfort at the Ashfords - my own cabins were completely untenable. Thankfully we departed and a month later sailed into Gore Bay, Sydney. We managed two days this time which was very good for everyone and later had four days in Brisbane which further improved our morale, even though our cash reserves got a bit depleted. It's amazing how a couple of months not spending anything causes a lot of folks to go berserk when let loose in shops. The previous voyage I had bought a lot of clothes (still rationed in U. K.) for Celia and in Abadan was lucky enough to meet a homeward-bound BP skipper who took them all to the U. K. for me.

On to Townsville where we got sailing orders to load at Balikpapan in what was then Dutch Borneo. We gave thanks that Abadan was off the menu and then entered unknown territory for us all. We spent the next two months threading our way through various islands which were extremely short of lights, beacons or any navigation aids whatsoever, visiting glamour spots such as Balikpapan, Pladju in Sumatra and Samboe near Singapore - made a change though and kept us on our toes as opposed to long, boring 30 day sea passages. Officially the Dutch were still in control but the revolution led by Soeharno was not far off and he was causing a certain amount of trouble although we were able to avoid the shooting. I have happy memories of Pladju and Samboe Clubs and managed to get to Singapore a couple of times.

At Pladju the Bar was very shallow and we could only lift around 9,000 tons each trip. On my third trip there I got stuck on the Bar when outward bound but after a rather torrid night I got off and then the pilot immediately hit it again then vanished. More frenzied activity and I was afloat again when the pilot reappeared. This time I told him I could wreck my ship just as effectively as he could, and I pointed *Newcombia* in what I hoped was the right direction. Lady Luck must have been tired of playing silly buggers because we emerged into the open sea without further trouble. It is not the function of the Captain to hit sandbars but rather to avoid them. I immediately wrote a lengthy report, explaining that it wasn't really my fault really, because the river level had fallen more rapidly than predicted. On arrival at Samboe I rushed across to our Head Office in Singapore and with fear and trembling laid the report on the desk of Capt. Jim Davidson, the Chief Marine Superintendent. Jim gave it a cursory look and with a bit of a grin said 'What took you so long to hit the Bar ? - If you don't hit it every other voyage, you're not loading enough cargo !'.

I went off to Ikey's bar in the arcade feeling very relieved to join some of my fellow rovers and ruffians who were the backbone of Shell's Far East maritime activities. At that time Shell were approaching the peak of their Far East fleet, with lots of coastal tankers taken over from the M. O. W. T. after the war, with both deck and engineer officers a mixed bag of Shell regulars and M. O. W. T. 'ring-ins'. These recruits were a mixed bag, some were just plain horrible but gradually they got sorted out. Lots of my old pals were around and we could usually gather a reasonable crowd together for a few drinks, lots of laughs and exchange of ideas. Later the Shell (Eastern) Fleet was formed but at that time London Office was the focal centre of our nomadic existence. Singapore, Bukom and Samboe were crowded with Shell tankers ranging from a few hundred tons up to the 12,000 dwt 'N' class and it would be a rare event, in the Far East, not to encounter a kindred spirit in any port. We shuttled around the general East Indies area until early December when we were told to load for Shanghai then proceed to Hong Kong for dry-dock.

Arriving at Shanghai we were greeted with the good news that the pilots, mostly European, had gone on strike. Mao Tse Tung and his red hordes were gradually pushing Chiang Kai-Shek and his forces further eastwards, confusion reigned supreme in December,1947 and we were in the middle of it. After a day or so at anchor in the Yangtze Kiang river, our agents Swires procured the services of a Russian pilot who had been a Captain in the Chinese Customs Service. He boarded to take us up the river to Shanghai and a few terrifying hours ensued. As we turned out of the Yangtze into the Huangpu river on which Shanghai stands, we were confronted with lots of junks which made the Lie Mun Pass at Hong Kong look like the Sahara desert. We were moving along at about seven knots and I drew the attention of the pilot to the potential dangers of the situation. We blew the whistle constantly and I dropped our speed to slow so by sheer good luck we barely touched them. A few mainsail yards, perhaps, as we scraped under their sterns, but nothing serious. There were dozens of them but I did notice that although their sails were up, they all had engines which they used when it became obvious that I was not going to stop.

The four or so hours it took us to reach Shanghai saw me a nervous wreck but the pilot seemed cool and unfussed. I figured that since he had been there since World War I it was all quite normal for him. The truth came out when we finally tied up and he started to fill out his pilotage chit. I had to do it for him as he was as blind as a bat, no wonder he wasn't worried - he couldn't see any danger ! Then the agent and the usual horde of officials came on board, who took up all of my time, booze and cigaretes for the next two hours. Before leaving I got the pilot to sign my visitor's book and I quote 'Wonderful job with you, Captain' - the signature was illegible but it was 2nd December, 1947 and in writing, his eyeballs were almost touching the paper.

The general situation in Shanghai was quite amazing. As I mentioned earlier Mao Tse Tung's hordes were pushing steadily eastwards and yet, apart from almost hourly fluctuations in prices, things seemed to be 'business as usual'. In Europe the Marshall Plan for the United Nations Relief & Rehabilitation Association was in full swing, and in the Far East a similar organisation CINRRA was endeavouring to do the same relief work but the end results differed vastly. So thousands of tons of cargo were landed daily from American 'Liberty' ships. Brand new fishing trawlers and tugs were arriving from the U.S.A. and Europe and practical help was pouring in. Unfortunately most of the cargo seemed to disappear onto the black market within hours of being landed and despite many police and soldiers, nobody seemed to be able to do anything about it. The Shanghai dollar pre-war was about on a par with the Singapore dollar i.e. twelve Shanghai dollars = £1 sterling. In December, 1947 the rate was 750,000 Shanghai dollars to the pound, however for some obscure reason we were given a rate of 414 Shanghai dollars to the pound. Thus very few of us went ashore and most of the trading was done in cigarettes and Singapore dollars.

Shell's Shipping Manager, Murray-Smith, had me ashore for dinner one night and Swire's were most hospitable, giving me lunch in the Shanghai Club and in the Long Bar where prices of drinks changed two or three times a day as the Shanghai dollar tumbled. Murray-Smith took me out another day for a round of golf and while Cathay was shivering in the 'winds of change' I was happily hacking my way round the golf course. We filled up the shore tanks, then moved alongside *San Melito* an old Eagle Oil tanker being used as floating storage - Shell could read the writing on the wall and figured there was no point in building new tanks for Mao Tse Tung to nationalise. Capt. Willie Young of *San Melito* and I had pleasant couple of days, swapping stories and putting the world to rights. We lost Rufus Worboys to *San Melito* and her Third Officer, Bill Evans, took his place as he had seatime in for his First Mate's certificate. The 'galley wireless' had us heading west after dry-dock, however we only got as far as Abadan.

We dry-docked at Hong Kong in Taikoo Dockyard ruining our finances but we all had a good time and got some of the salt water out of our systems. The Flying Angel Missions to Seamen had a very good club in Hong Kong run by Padre and Mrs. Weaver, who had run the Mission in Halifax (NS) during the war and were old friends of Fred and I. Christmas was a splendid effort then Fred had a week's leave, staying at the Mission with the Weavers. I had got myself a temporary membership of the Hong Kong Cricket Club, a very economical watering hole with lots of pleasant members. The NAAFIs were still in full swing so life took on a new meaning. I changed places with Fred at the Weavers during the first week of January and was able to do my accounts in peace. Derek came up most evenings to bring me up to date on progress, a lot of noise and hammering was going on aboard and we got a lot of rust removed and generally 'tarted' up the old girl. I got in several rounds of golf, then who should arrive also to dry-dock but Capt. John Nettleship and his gallant crew in *Dolabella*. The social scene became even more lively and most of us were secretly glad when we sailed in early January, allegedly for Singapore.

We signed on a young Dutch seaman from one of Shell's Dutch tankers for transhipment to Singapore. He had just been discharged from hospital as cured, but just two days out from Hong Kong he developed a lump on his forehead the size of a pigeon's egg. His temperature went up to 103 degrees and he became quite delirious. We sent frantic radio messages and were instructed to get him to a doctor as soon as possible. The nearest port was Saigon but we didn't have a large scale chart of the approaches as Saigon was normally supplied by coastal tankers. However, approaching near as I dare, we got in touch via the Aldis lamp with the pilot station at Cape Saint Jacques. Fortunately my fractured French from North African days was able to cope with the instructions in French of how to get to the pilot boat. At this period the Viet Cong were busily engaged in making life unpleasant for the French and this applied to anyone with a white skin. However the French pilots were most co-operative, which was just as well as our young Dutchman was in a pretty parlous state. We had to wait for a suitable tide and adjust our draft by deballasting so during this waiting period the pilot took Fred and I ashore for an excellent dinner in the pilot's mess. My experiences in Algeria lost nothing in the telling and the 'entente cordiale' was well and truly cemented. At 3 a.m. we set out taking good care not to show our noses on deck and by 10 a.m. were gingerly edging alongside the Shell wharf. It had not been built for ships of our size and it looked rather fragile to me but we didn't break anything. We had to use a couple of palm trees for our head and stern ropes but they seemed robust enough. An ambulance with jeep loads of soldiers as escort was waiting for us and we loaded the young man on a stretcher and Harry Rae and a medical orderly sat with him as Harry had been looking after him. I sat in front with the French driver, clutching a tommy gun, for about an hour and a half until we reached the hospital in Saigon at break-neck speed. I was very apprehensive of the Viet Cong shooting at me at first but the fear subsided as the journey progressed and we arrived safely. Our young patient was rushed into the operating theatre unconscious and I'm pleased to say he recovered.

We had to wait a couple of hours for return transport and the French surgeon told us the young man would have been dead in another six hours if they hadn't operated when they did. After a couple of cognacs we felt well enough to return in the jeep with two burly French Foreign Legion soldiers as escorts and by mid-afternoon *Newcombia* was chugging down the Mekong. There were one or two bursts of gunfire as we went downriver but nothing hit us so we presumed it was a local action ashore. After Singapore we did a couple of Pladju to Samboe runs then had four days in Singapore Roads for engine repairs. Anxious to keep up our morale, Shell arranged to take us to a nearby island for a picnic/barbecue/swimming party on the Sunday, so off went everyone except the watchkeepers. Fred and I nobly let all of our officers go and looked after the ship ourselves, not that anything could be done as half of the main engine was in a machine shop on shore. As a reward for our virtue, Fred and I had several of our fellow senior officers out to lunch. Neither Harry Rae or Howard Abdullah were keen on this picnic lark so they served us a magnificent curry tiffin. Our guests departed about 4 p.m. so peace reigned until the crew returned, full of beer and good cheer around 6 p.m. - they didn't need rocking to sleep that night !

The orders from London were to proceed to Abadan to load various grades for Sydney, Brisbane and Gladstone. Abadan was quite pleasant in February then off to Sydney, where on arrival our East coast of Australia tour was cancelled due to industrial strife up north so we spent three days wandering around Sydney harbour, dropping off parcels of premium, regular, aviation gasolines and kerosene at various installations - 'You can be sure of Shell' took on a new meaning. We sailed back to Abadan where we were beginning to be regarded as locals, hoping for a cargo for the U. K. we loaded instead for South Africa - made a change anyway ! East London was supposed to be our destination but at the last moment someone discovered the shore tanks were full so we diverted to Port Elizabeth, a very lively city where we had a ball.

Our visit coincided with that of Mr. Rowbottom, the recently-retired Managing Director of Shell Tankers Ltd, who was doing the mandatory world tour of retiring Managing Directors. The local Shell manager put on a cocktail party for Mr. & Mrs. Rowbottom to which the Mayor and other local luminaries were invited, and Fred and I just scraped in. Fred being a very Senior Chief had met him several times during and after the war but this was my first meeting, so while Fred got a very warm welcome a similar one to me was worded 'Ah ! Capt. Allen, I've heard quite a lot about you !'. My initial fears were allayed when he took us aside for a little chat and asked us about morale in the fleet. We had been wandering around like the legendary 'Flying Dutchman' for fifteen months, so Fred, never one to mince words and secure in the knowledge of seniority then spent half an hour, assisted by myself in telling Mr. Rowbottom the facts of life.

In all fairness we got a good hearing even though we were both extremely critical and parted the best of friends - the fact that both Fred and I became Shell Marine Superintendents eventually must prove something. Our piece of good advice was 'If you really want an answer, cable your query. All cables go to management but letters can go astray '. I had two good rounds of golf with an American Captain, a couple of lively evenings in the local nightclubs, stocked up with lots of Lion lager, the excellent local brew, then set off to sea. Once clear of harbour I got Sparks to send off a cable to our lords and masters in London requesting our future programme as a matter of some urgency. It was always a joke on ships about the so-called 'galley wireless' as we reckoned the cook was always the first to know where we were going - but this time it was true ! Sparks was busy transmitting the message when Harry Rae came in and said 'The galley boy has had a letter from his mother who says we are bound for Abadan, loading for Rangoon and Calcutta, then back to the Gulf to load for U.K./Continent and should arrive at the end of July'. Next day came the reply to the cable exactly as the galley boy's mummy had said so at least we knew where we were going.

So back to what was to be the last trip to Abadan, a round of farewell parties and off to Rangoon. Burma was in the throes of self-government and was a bit of a shambles which doesn't seem to have improved with time. At Calcutta I had to make a couple of crew changes, swapping with our sistership *Nassarius* captained by

'Kulit' Mackenzie. He had acquired the nickname just pre-war when he spent two years in the little 200 tonner *Kulit* and did some quite impossible things with her. I left the ship early and was in the Shipping Office as advised by 7 a.m. but in the time it took to sign off and on two men we could have changed the entire crew of the *Queen Elizabeth*. By noon I was hot, sweaty and frustrated but Kulit had been there three weeks and had got used to it. India was completely dry at the time but Kulit cheered me up by taking me to the Calcutta Swimming Club where he was a member and we were able to have a cold, foaming ale. It barely touched the sides of my throat as it went down, and after a few more and a good curry and a shower I took my two new crew members back to the ship. The Shell installation staff came aboard and were treated to my stock of South African beer. We sailed down the muddy Ganges and across to the Gulf in late June, all hands happy at the prospect of being homeward bound. Everyone had purchased green/khaki ex-American Army 'fatigues' so that we looked like a U. S. Army transport when we sailed, complete with long-peaked baseball caps. We also bought seventy metres of cheap cotton to make a 'paying off' pennant for the homeward voyage.

We had two domestic fridges but early in our Far East sojourn, Jock Nichol the carpenter, had made me an excellent insulated ice box which stood outside my dayroom door. At each port we topped up our supply of ice and a good solid block was put into my icebox every morning by Brian Holloway, the Second Steward who was the Captain's 'tiger'. The Engineer Officers, who lived on the saloon deck were able to use the domestic fridge in the pantry but Sparks, Harry Rae, the deck officers and apprentices on the lower bridge deck used my ice box. Thus everyone had a cold drink available in the hot weather, and the crew were able to use a special tap and water tank off the big cool room adjacent to the big main refrigerator. I always considered cool drinks in the tropics to be a vital necessity.

Once more into the Persian Gulf but with a slight change of scene as we went first to Bahrain for bunkers and then on to our loading port of Mina al Ahmadi, which had no bunkers and was just opening up. It was a buoy mooring about half a mile offshore with a submarine pipeline and that was the only facility there was. The loading rate was 1500 tonnes/hour, an unheard of rate then but at least it was over quickly. Twelve hours after loading started we were on our way and glad to be on the move. On the way to Suez we cleaned up the ship and sewed the 'paying off' pennant, all 126 feet of it (six feet for every month in commission) and flew it happily all the way through the Canal and close to Gibraltar as we left the Mediterranean. We were a new breed of men by this time and the crew really had the ship shining and after leaving Gibraltar I started on finalising my accounts.

The England / Australia cricket tests were on and we were down by the head with cricket fans, led by Bill Evans the Third Officer. He was nearly having a heart attack six times a day as our fortunes rose and fell. John Arlott was at his peak and we were so impressed with the general commentary that we sent a telegram (radiogram) to the BBC congratulating them on the quality. This was featured in the U.K. Radio Times giving favourable publicity to Shell Tankers. But back to my accounts - we still didn't know which port was our discharge so I took Rotterdam, the farthest, and worked on arriving end July,1948. However halfway across the Bay of Biscay we got orders to proceed to Heysham north of Liverpool and would arrive on

29th July. Some liar in an Eagle Oil tanker gave his E.T.A. six hours ahead of mine, as his Sparks had picked up my message and I'm sure he adjusted his time accordingly.

I got orders to anchor and wait until he had finished discharge but when I anchored there was no sign of the Eagle OIl tanker and it was a further ten hours before she arrived and went straight alongside. Flexibility was never a strongpoint at Heysham, which was a wartime mixture of Trinidad Leaseholds, Imperial Chemicals and Shell. The operating company was called Trimpol but that wasn't the name we used !

I had to do a fresh set of accounts which brought me into a new month and it wasn't just a question of adding another couple of days pay - being a new month income tax, national insurance, provident fund and various other items had to be worked out and this messed up my painstaking calculations. However Derek Booker had a very mathematical mind and he was a big help in sorting out this little collection of nonsense. We were cleared by Port Health and Customs on 30th July which was a Friday and the agent came out with a couple of London office guys and several wives, including my own beloved Celia. Our small daughter, now almost two years old, was being looked after by a sister as she knew it would be several days before I could get away. The weather was glorious and England never looked better as we lay at the calm anchorage but the wretched accounts took up most of my time. It was all manually done as we had no calculators or adding machines but eventually it was sorted out and I wrote 'finis' across the bottom of the current account and portage bill.

We got alongside on 2nd August which was a Bank Holiday in the U.K. and another guy from the London Office staggered up with a huge adding machine, weighing at least ten kilos and said with a smile 'There you are, Captain, all your accounts will be much easier in future !' I could cheerfully have wrapped it around his neck, however I just smiled back and said politely 'Thank you, but we are already finished'. It had taken three days to do the accounts, but ready they were. All hands paid off except four and Capt. Stanley Thompson took over from me. Celia and I departed the next morning and I felt not a quiver of regret as we left the wharf with my accumulated loot of two years and eight months and got the train home.

Hundreds more ships were to pass through my life as a pilot at Miri and as a Marine Superintendent in Australia and a couple of dozen as a Marine Consultant but I was never officially attached to any of them - purely advisory !

But that is another story !

APPENDIX 1. SHIPS SERVED IN BY THE AUTHOR

1. **SNEATON**   3677 grt   Steam tramp
1925 - Completed by Robert Thompson & Sons Ltd, Sunderland for Rowland & Marwood's Steamship Co. Ltd (Headlam & Sons, mgrs), Whitby. 1930/33 - Served in by author. 14.10.1939 -Torpedoed and sunk by U48 in position 49 5' N - 13 W on a voyage from Cardiff to Rio de Janeiro with coal, 1 crew lost.

2. **GOATHLAND**   3895 grt   Steam tramp
1924 - Completed by Robert Thompson & Sons Ltd, Sunderland for Rowland & Marwood's Steamship Co. Ltd (Headlam & Sons, mgrs), Whitby. 1933/35 - Served in by author. 25.8.1940 - Bombed and sunk in position 50 21' N - 15 8' W on a voyage from Pepel to Belfast with iron ore.

3. **STREONSHALH**   3895 grt   Steam tramp
1928 - Completed by William Pickersgill & Sons Ltd, Sunderland for Rowland & Marwood's Steamship Co. Ltd (Headlam & Sons, mgrs), Whitby. 1935 - Served in by author. 7.12.1939 Captured and sunk by GRAF SPEE in South Atlantic in position 25 S - 27 50' W on a voyage Rosario & Montevideo to the U.K. with wheat, crew taken prisoner.

4. **SANDSEND**   3612 grt   Steam tramp
1925 - Completed by William Pickersgill & Sons Ltd, Sunderland for Rowland & Marwood's Steamship Co. Ltd (Headlam & Sons,mgrs), Whitby. 1935/36 - Served in by author. 18.10.1940 Torpedoed and sunk by U48 in position 58 15' N - 21 29' W on a voyage from Port Talbot to Quebec with anthracite, 5 crew lost.

5. **GLAISDALE**   3777 grt   Steam tramp
1929 - Completed by Sir James Laing & Sons Ltd, Sunderland for Headlam & Sons Steamship Co. Ltd, Whitby. 1936/37 - Served in by author. 1957 - Sold to Liberia Maritima Corp., Monrovia renamed SONDICA.   12.7.1960 - Arrived Vigo for breaking up.

6. **THISTLEBRAE**   4747 grt   Steam tramp
11.1928 - Completed by J. L. Thompson & Sons Ltd, Sunderland for Albyn Line (Allan,Black & Co. Ltd), Sunderland. 1937/38 - Served in by author. 9.4.1940 - Captured by German tanks in dry-dock at Trondheim, having been damaged by aircraft on a voyage from the Tyne.   Renamed ALTKIRCH. 1944- Renamed INSTER. 3.5.1945 - Sunk by R.A.F. aircraft off Laboe in position 54 30' N - 10 23' E.

7. **KENNEBEC**   5548 grt   Steam tanker
1919 - Completed by Robert Duncan & Co. Ltd, Port Glasgow as WAR MOGUL for the Shipping Controller. 1919 - Sold to Anglo-American Oil Co. Ltd, London renamed KENNEBEC. 1939 - Served in by author. 8.9.1939 - Torpedoed & sunk by U34 in position 49 18'N - 8 13'W on a voyage from Aruba to U.K. with fuel oil, crew saved.

8. **CYMBULA** 8082 grt Motor tanker
7.1938 - Completed by Netherland Shipbuilding Company, Amsterdam for 'La Corona' (Dutch Shell). 1939 - Taken over by Anglo-Saxon Petroleum Co. Ltd. 1939/40 - Served in by author. 1950 - To 'La Corona' renamed MYONIA. 20.9.1957 - Arrived Hong Kong for breaking up.

9. **OPALIA** 6195 grt Motor tanker
5.1938 - Completed by Netherland Shipbuilding Company, Amsterdam for Anglo-Saxon Petroleum Co. Ltd. 1940/41 - Served in by author. 6.11.1956 - Set on fire & scuttled at Port Said during Suez Canal crisis. 4.1959 - Refloated & repaired by Egyptians and returned to service during 1961 under Egyptian flag as 23 DECEMBER. 1977 - Sold to Mohamed Nawar, Egypt renamed NAWAR. 1987 - Deleted from register.

10. **CARDIUM** 8236 grt Motor tanker
12.1931 - Completed by Swan,Hunter & Wgham Richardson Ltd for Anglo-Saxon Petroleum Co. Ltd. 1942/44 - Served in by author. 1948 - Sold to Counties Ship Management Ltd, London renamed HAWTHORN HILL. 1951 - Sold to Cia. Nav. Puerto Madrin S.A. renamed DON MANUEL. 13.8.1961 - Disabled by engine room fire off Dakar, towed into Dakar. CTL. 12.11.1961 - Arrived Vigo for breaking up.

11. **ADULA** 8040 grt Motor tanker
3.1937 - Completed by Blythswood Shipbuilding Co. Ltd, Glasgow for Anglo-Saxon Petroleum Co. Ltd. 1.1944 - Completed conversion to M.A.C. 2. 1944/45 - Served in by author. 1946 - De-macked. 15.5.1953 - Arrived Barrow for breaking up.

12. **NEWCOMBIA** 8292 grt Motor tanker
11.1944 - Launched at Belfast and towed to Glasgow for completion in 3.1945 by Harland & Wolff Ltd for Anglo-Saxon Petroleum Co. Ltd. 1946/48 - Served in by author. 26.9.1959 - Arrived Antwerp for breaking up.

APPENDIX 2.   MERCHANT AIRCRAFT CARRIERS (M.A.C.)

1. **RAPANA**   8017 grt   Motor tanker
4.1935 - Completed by N.V. Wilton-Fijenoord, Schiedam for Anglo-Saxon Petroleum Co. Ltd. 7.1943 - Completed conversion to M.A.C. 9. 1946 - De-macked. 1950 - To 'La Corona' renamed ROTULA. 1.1958 - Broken up at Osaka.

2. **ACAVUS**   8010 grt   Motor tanker
1.1935 - Completed by Workman, Clark Ltd, Belfast for Anglo-Saxon Petroleum Co. Ltd. 10.1943 - Completed conversion to M.A.C. 1. 1946 - De-macked. 1952 - To Soc. Maritime Shell, France renamed IACRA. 18.4.1963 - Arrived La Seyne for breaking up.

3. **ADULA**   See Appendix 1.

4. **ALEXIA**   8016 grt   Motor tanker
4.1935 - Completed by Bremer Vulkan, Vegesack for Anglo-Saxon Petroleum Co. Ltd. 12.1943 - Completed conversion to M.A.C. 3. 1946 - De-macked. 1951 - To Soc. Maritime Shell, France renamed IANTHINA.   17.8.1954 - Arrived Blyth for breaking up.

5. **AMASTRA**   8031 grt   Motor tanker
1935 - Completed by Lithgows Ltd, Port Glasgow for Anglo-Saxon Petroleum Co. Ltd. 9.1943 - Completed conversion to M.A.C. 4. 1946 - De-macked. 1951 - To Soc. Maritime Shell, France renamed IDAS. 27.6.1955 - Arrived Spezia for breaking up.

6. **ANCYLUS**   8017 grt   Motor tanker
1.1935 - Completed by Swan,Hunter & Wigham Richardson Ltd, Wallsend for Anglo-Saxon Petroleum Co. Ltd. 10.1943 - Completed conversion to M.A.C. 5. 1946 - De-macked. 1952 - To Soc. Maritime Shell, France renamed IMBRICARIA. 4.12.1954 - Arrived Spezia for breaking up.

7. **MIRALDA**   8013 grt   Motor tanker
7.1936 - Completed by Netherland Shipbuilding Company, Amsterdam for Anglo-Saxon Petroleum Co. Ltd. 2.1944 - Completed conversion to M.A.C. 8. 1946 - De-macked. 1950 - To 'La Corona' renamed MARISA. 21.7.1960 - Arrived Hong Kong for breaking up.

8. **GADILA**   8050 grt   Motor tanker
4.1935 - Completed by Howaldtswerke A.G., Hamburg for 'La Corona' (Dutch Shell). 3.1944 - Completed conversion to M.A.C. 6.   5.1946 - De-macked by Wilton-Fijenoord, Schiedam. 6.6.1958 - Arrived Hong Kong for breaking up.

9. **MACOMA** 8069 grt Motor tanker
5.1936 - Completed by Netherland Shipbuilding Company, Amsterdam for 'La Corona' (Dutch Shell). 5.1944 - Completed conversion to M.A.C. 7. 5.1946 - De-macked by Wilton-Fijenoord, Schiedam. 14.12.1959 Arrived Hong Kong for scrap.

10. **EMPIRE MACMAHON** 8166 grt Motor tanker
2.7.1943 - Launched and 12.1943 completed by Swan,Hunter & Wigham Richardson Ltd for M.O.W.T. (Anglo-Saxon,mgr). 1946 - De-macked and purchased by Anglo-Saxon Petroleum Co. Ltd renamed NANINIA. 17.3.1960 - Arrived Hong Kong for scrapping.

11. **EMPIRE MACCOLL** 8452 grt Motor tanker
11.1943 - Completed by Cammell, Laird & Co. Ltd, Birkenhead for M.O.W.T. (British Tanker Co. Ltd,mgr). 8.9.1946 - Purchased and de-macked by British Tanker Co. Ltd renamed BRITISH PILOT. 21.8.1962 - Sold for demolition and arrived at Faslane same day.

12. **EMPIRE MACCABE** 8477 grt Motor tanker
12.1943 - Completed by Swan,Hunter & Wigham Richardson Ltd, Wallsend for M.O.W.T. (British Tanker Co. Ltd,mgr). 16.9.1946 - Purchased and de-macked by British Tanker Co. Ltd renamed BRITISH ESCORT. 13.2.1959 - Sold toEasthill Shipping Co. Ltd, London renamed EASTHILL ESCORT. 3.1962 - Broken up at Hong Kong.

13. **EMPIRE MACKAY** 8908 grt Motor tanker
17.6.1943 - Launched as BRITISH WISDOM for British Tanker Co. Ltd and 5.10.1943 completed as EMPIRE MACKAY for M.O.W.T. (British Tanker Co. Ltd,mgr). 16.9.1946 - Purchased and de-macked by British Tanker Co. Ltd renamed BRITISH SWORDFISH. 21.5.1959 - Sold for demolition and arrived at Rotterdam same day for breaking up at Hendrik Ido Ambacht.

14. **EMPIRE MACALPINE** 7954 grt Motor tramp
23.12.1942 - Launched and 4.1943 completed by Burntisland Shipbuilding Co. Ltd for M.O.W.T. (Ben LIne,mgr). 12.1946 - Sold to McCowen & Gross Ltd, London and de-macked and renamed DERRYNANE in 1947. 1951 - Transferred to Power S.S. Co. Ltd and renamed HUNTSBROOK. 1959 - Sold to South Breeze Nav. Co. Ltd (John Manners & Co. Ltd,mgr), Hong Kong and renamed SUVA BREEZE. 1965 - Renamed DJATINGALEH by Manners. 1966 - Renamed SAN ERNESTO by Manners. 1968 - Sold to Cia Nueva del Oriente S.A.,Panama renamed PACIFIC ENDEAVOUR. 21.2.1970 - Arrived Hong Kong for scrapping.

15. **EMPIRE MACKENDRICK** 7933 grt Motor tramp
1.1944 - Completed by Burntisland Shipbuilding Co. Ltd for M.O.W.T. (Ben Line,mgr). 12.1946 - Sold to Mediterranean & Atlantic Lines Ltd (Goulandris Bros,mgr), London and renamed GRANPOND in 1947. 1950 - Sold to Cia Maritima del Este S.A., Panama renamed CONDOR. 1.1951 - De-macked at Hamburg. 1955 - Sold to Turnbull Scott Shipping Co. Ltd, London renamed SALTERSGATE. 1957 - Sold to Nav. Mar. Bulgare, Bulgaria renamed VASSIL LEVSKY. 5.6.1967 - Trapped

in Bitter Lake, Suez Canal and remained there for eight years until released in 5.1975. 22.7.1975 - Arrived Split for scrapping.

16. **EMPIRE MACANDREW** 7952 grt   Motor tramp
3.5.1943 - Launched and 7.7.1943 completed by William Denny & Bros Ltd, Dumbarton for M.O.W.T. (Hain Line,mgr). 23.10.1946 - Sold to McCowen & Gross Ltd, London and de-macked renamed DERRYHEEN. 1951 - Sold to Lyle Shipping Co. Ltd, Glasgow renamed CAPE GRAFTON. 1963 - Sold to Patricia Cia Nav. S.A., Liberia renamed PATRICIA. 4.10.1970 - Delivered for scrapping at Hsinkiang.

17. **EMPIRE MACRAE**   8252 grt   Motor tramp
21.6.1943 - Launched and 20.9.1943 completed by Lithgows Ltd, Port Glasgow for M.O.W.T. (Hain Line,mgr). 25.1.1947 - Sold to Moller Line Ltd,London and de-macked and renamed ALPHA ZAMBESI. 1954 - Sold to Vilhelm Torkildsen, Norway renamed TOBON. 1967 - Sold to Greek owners renamed DESPINA P. 2.5.1971 - Demolition commenced at Kaohsiung.

18. **EMPIRE MACCALLUM** 8252 grt   Motor tramp
12.10.1943 - Launched and 22.12.1943 completed by Lithgows Ltd, Port Glasgow for M.O.W.T. (Hain Line,mgr). 1.10.1947 - Sold to Clunies Shipping Co. Ltd, Greenock and de-macked and renamed DORIS CLUNIES. 1951 - Renamed SUNROVER. 1957 - Renamed EUDOXIA. 1959 - Sold to Greek owners renamed PHORKYSS. 10.11.1960 - Demolition began at Sakai, Japan.

19. **EMPIRE MACDERMOTT** 7952 grt Motor tramp
24.1.1944 - Launched and 31.3.1944 completed by William Denny & Bros. Ltd, Dumbarton for M.O.W.T. (Hain Line,mgr). 15.8.1947 - Sold to Buries Markes Ltd, London and de-macked and renamed LA CUMBRE. 1959 - Sold to Canero Cia. Nav. S.A., Greece renamed PARNON. 1969 - Sold to Somali owners and renamed STARLIGHT. 1976 - Sold to Cosco, China.